SPRINT

BY THE SAME AUTHOR

Adventurer's Road
The Trailblazers
Five Roads to Danger
European Cars 1886–1914
Automobile Treasures
The Motor Book
The Second Motor Book
The Vintage Car 1919–1930
A Toy for the Lion
Car Badges
The Wild Roads
Pocket Encyclopedia of Motor Cars
(various titles in series)

SPRINT

Speed Hillclimbs and Speed Trials
in Britain: 1899–1925

by

T. R. NICHOLSON

DAVID & CHARLES : NEWTON ABBOT

7153 4345 9

Set in 10 on 12 pt Times New Roman
and printed in Great Britain by
Latimer Trend & Company Limited Plymouth
for David & Charles (Publishers) Limited
South Devon House Newton Abbot Devon

Contents

List of Illustrations

Introduction

The classic cars, drivers and contests of long-distance motor racing have claimed far more authors' sweat and publishers' money than any other aspect of motoring history. This is proper, for as a sport for competitor and spectator and for its importance to the industry, this type of racing is unsurpassed.

However, in Britain between 1899 and 1925, another form of motor-car racing was considered by those who took part in it to be equal to, if not more important than the season at Brooklands or in Ireland or on the Isle of Man. This was sprinting; that is to say, speed hillclimbs and speed trials, in which all the most famous amateur and works drivers and all the most celebrated manufacturers participated.

They became important because they were the only form of speed competition possible on the public roads of the United Kingdom. France, Germany, Italy, America and other nations at various times permitted and encouraged long-distance road racing. Britain, outside Ireland and the Isle of Man, consistently forbade it. Nor did Britain have an artificial private track until 1907, and no other race track from then until 1933.

In their heyday, these short-distance competitions were extremely numerous. Almost seventy were recorded in 1907, and more than eighty in 1924. There were several reasons for their popularity. Being small-scale affairs, they were easily run by a provincial club of limited resources. There might be a suitable piece of road round the corner; a quarter of a mile might be enough, and seldom was more than a mile needed. The area they affected was limited, so they impinged little on the non-motoring world around when compared with long-distance races. Hence the fact that they were tolerated, even though the speed limit was broken from the earliest days. They were numerous, too, because they gave so many people what they wanted. The local speed merchant—the squire or businessman with his new Mercedes, anxious to show it off, or the boy with his much-tuned and lightened GN—was given a chance denied to him if he were faced with the expenditure of money and time involved in travelling to Brooklands or across the sea. Once established, they gave the manufacturer and his distributor the publicity they valued. Properly and imaginatively run, they could bring the organising club money, fame and prestige.

Owing to the immense interest taken by spectators, both lay and enthusiast, the classic events came to form an important part of local life in many areas. Although famous national figures in motor sport flocked to them, they retained their special regional flavour. Their settings helped in this. Nowadays, the surfaces of the courses are mostly the uniform, sombre black of tarmacadam. An examination of unsurfaced minor roads and tracks in the vicinity can sometimes show what the nearby courses were like in their heyday. They still reflected the regional geology. Hillclimb courses snaking up the Downs were white chalk scars. Yellow gravel might be seen in Surrey and Hampshire; in the West Country there were roads cut into old red sandstone. The colour of the clouds of dust or sprays of mud or slippery chalk 'soup' thrown up by spinning, sliding wheels and open exhausts varied accordingly. The dust-clouds and mud were no regional phenomenon—they characterised hillclimbs and speed trials everywhere, except on seafront promenades and the bleak beaches of the North.

Where courses were surfaced, which was generally the case only if they were on private land, they were most likely to be of gravel or the loose chippings of macadam. Tarmac was a luxury, particularly since organisers rarely could or would arrange an event on a road important enough, and therefore frequented enough, to justify such a surface. Courses were usually very narrow, and sometimes fenced and gated. Speed trial courses, in fact, might be lined with very solid trees, they might be twisty, and they might be switch-backs. Naturally, hillclimb courses were rarely straight, and generally had a nasty drop on one side and a bank on the other.

All in all, there was plenty of scope for excitement, some of it unsought, and organisers had to take what they could find. One of the most interesting of their finds must have been Syston Park in Lincolnshire (see p 103). It was on a private estate, and included a gated macadam farm road and an actual farmyard as well!

Sprints became a British institution. Other countries ran sprints as well, perhaps technically more important ones, but on nothing like the same scale. Further, if one sets out to recount the history of British sprints thoroughly, one finds oneself talking about almost every other aspect of motoring: social, sporting, legal, commercial and technical. As we shall see, they also played an important part in the development and encouragement of another typically British institution: the sports car based on a conventional chassis. After the Continental competitions of 1908–14, Britain's sprints, together with Brooklands, were the major forcing-grounds of the type.

They met their end, losing most of their importance, appeal and numbers, when the Royal Automobile Club, the governing body of British motor sport, stopped the holding of speed contests on public roads early in 1925.

The story of these years has not been told before, and this book is an attempt to fill the gap. It tries to combine facts, figures and information on cars and drivers with a leavening of lighter, if in the broad sense equally instructive, material. Much emphasis is placed on the wider social, commercial, legal and technical background; on the state of public opinion, the role of the motor clubs, and the reminiscences and impressions of drivers and laymen from their own mouths, from their own memoirs, or from newspaper reports.

The facts are given in quantity, so that comparisons of all kinds may be made wherever it is legitimate to do so, and so that fairly complete records of the successes of individual cars and drivers may be drawn up. However, technical details of the cars have not been stressed: space is not available. In any case, the main importance of sprints lay in the way in which they dominated the sportsman's attention, and became a national institution. Unlike road and circuit racing, sprints in Britain did not by themselves produce significant advances in mechanical design.

This book forms as complete a record as possible, within its scope. Ireland and the Isle of Man are outside its field. In those islands, long-distance racing on the public roads was both allowed and fostered, so that the state of affairs and atmosphere were similar to those obtaining in the rest of the motor-racing world: it has no relevance to the United Kingdom picture. At the same time, the speed trials and hillclimbs held in Ireland and the Isle of Man were regarded by British manufacturers as part of their province, so all the facts obtainable are given in the Appendix.

Only hillclimbs and speed trials proper receive attention. This book is not concerned with record attempts unless concurrent with a speed trial, with monstrosities like 'slow' hillclimbs, with the majority of 'stop-and-restart' events, or with untimed climbs held in the course of reliability trials. It ignores the very short sprints sometimes included with egg-and-spoon races in the frivolous 'gymkhanas'; the forerunners of today's very serious driving tests. Brooklands test hill was occasionally the scene of a club hillclimb, but it was too short and artificial to be counted as a sprint course in the general sense. The artificiality of the course also excludes the speed trials held now and then on the Brooklands track itself.

Events are only noted if it is known that they were held: not merely if they were announced and then forgotten. Cancellations to which attention was drawn at the time are noted, because they often reflected changing conditions in the sport. Nearly nine hundred sprints are dealt with. More undoubtedly took place. The sources do not mention every single one. They might be especially remiss when interest was so high that space was lacking, or when it was so low that to record all was not thought worth while. In the case of minor events, they always relied for reports on club officials, who might be lazy, busy, ill, no longer in office, or dead.

The date, the course, its character, the organisers, the winners of classes and their cars, any relevant, interesting, amusing or instructive points—all are given, with reservations. The sources, once again, may have left out many or most of the details, for the reasons already noted, or through simple carelessness. This sometimes leaves the picture confused and vague, and makes the interpretation of results and the forming of judgments a perilous business. The make of car may be given, but its type, model or cubic capacity omitted. This is extremely common, indeed usual, in reports of the nineteen-twenties. The rated horsepowers given may be inconsistent, and incorrect. The regulations, which might or might not demand a certain minimum of coachwork or number of passengers, may not be specified.

A car's time may be given, but no details of the course, or vice-versa. A course may be named, but we are not told where it is. We are not always told if this year's climb of the Clodmorden Cycling, Motor Cycling, Light Car and Dining Club up the slopes of Big Head is from a standing start, as last year, or if a flying or rolling start has been used; and if so, how long it was. We are not necessarily told if the course has been shortened or lengthened, or re-surfaced, or cut up by traffic, or whether it is wet or dry. Sometimes we do not even know what course is being used. We may not know if the meeting is open or closed. A word like 'restricted' might be used, which can mean 'closed' to the organising club in the usual sense, or limited to entrants of a certain status.

A winner on time, handicap or formula may be omitted altogether, if his success was not so important as some other. A driver's or entrant's initials may be left out, or given incorrectly, leading to confusion with others of the same name. It is not always possible to distinguish between a driver and an entrant; to say who is driving, in fact. 'Mr Charles Sangster's Ariel' may mean that he was driving it himself, or that he had only entered it. He may be doing both. Only occasionally it is clear that an entrant is indicated, not a driver. The Earl of Shrewsbury and Talbot did not conduct his sporting Talbots in person, though his son did. It is safe only to suppose that a trade name indicated a trade entry; such as in the case of Edge, Hancock, Instone, Rawlinson, Warwick Wright, B. S. Marshall, and a host of others.

A further word of warning is necessary. Because a car or a driver runs in a particular class, it does not mean that they fit only that class. Bold small cars were always allowed into larger car classes. Sports or touring cars could compete with the racers. Amateurs or novices could do battle in the 'all-comers' class as well as in their own. The sources do not often make it clear when these things occur. There are other factors we would not expect to have explained to us: whether a driver felt off-colour, how much he had tuned his car, whether it was on form or not, and so forth. Most confusing of all, information given by one highly-respected source will occasionally contradict that in another.

There are, therefore, some gaps and apparent peculiarities in accounts of a few of the sprints mentioned. Others have been filled in by deduction from circumstantial evidence, but only where the latter justifies this dangerous practice. Conclusions cannot often be arrived at in this manner. It may be that we are certain only of a car's time; the distance is unknown. Still, the time, and those of the entrant's rivals, are given, because there remains some basis for comparison, and because the reader might learn the distance from some other source and thus complete the picture.

Statistics are important, but considerations of space have led to the omission of certain details which are available, but which the author thought unimportant. Handicaps and formula results only become interesting and technically important from about 1906, when high-efficiency engines began to appear and make hay of old preconceptions. Before 1906, therefore, insignificant formula results are omitted. The best times are always given, even though the awards in an event may have been for formula successes alone. Two or three specimens of formulae are quoted, as examples.

Generally, only first, second and perhaps third place results are reported here. Except in rare cases, no attention is paid to classes won by 'walk-overs'. There is no contest when only one car makes the run, unless it is trying for absolute fastest time of the day. One-make classes are usually quite lacking in significance or interest, so are generally ignored. The results of preliminary heats are commonly overlooked, as well. The final heat is what counts, and anyway, the number and complexity of heats and cross-heats in many pre-1914 events were such that full accounts are impossible in the present compass. In the nineteen-twenties, a parallel fashion for minute sub-division of classes set in—closed and open, amateurs, novices and trade, light cars, cyclecars, touring cars, sports cars and racing cars, capacities up to 1,100 cc, 1,500 cc, two litres, three litres and 'unlimited'. These were the usual ones, leaving out of consideration more exotic fancies. All these, to the number of perhaps a hundred classes, many of them uncontested and many more containing only one or two cars, might be represented at one meeting.

A meeting which involves a very large number of classes cannot be fully reported in a book of this size, so in such cases a few of the least interesting and significant results may be omitted. The rest, for the sake of readability as well as space-saving, are not always defined. That is, George Bedford and his Hillman will be recorded as winning six classes at an event. His times and those of his opponents will be given. Unless he defeated opposition from cars that should have outclassed him completely, their classes will not necessarily be mentioned. In any case, these will often be obvious, from the details of the cars. On the same principle, the names of special trophies given for success in particular classes or events within events are not quoted, unless won at meetings of national clubs in open contests, or otherwise noteworthy or long-lived. They are of precious little general interest now, and would only confuse a reader already battered numb by a stream of proper names.

In the case of post-1900 events, this last consideration has led the author to relegate sprints that are unimportant, or more important but lacking in interest, to secondary appendices at the end of each Part. A humorous or spectacular incident will 'promote' an insignificant contest to the body of the test, while repetitive tedium—the mixture as before—will banish a middling-important event to one of these appendices. It would be misleading, too, to talk only of the latter in the text. The treatment here gives the 'flavour' of the sport without need to look at the appendices to the Parts. The provincial clubs held a great many quiet, cosy events, restricted, perhaps, to members who were amateurs, which never saw the headlines. However, in order to gain a true picture of the periodic spread and contraction of the sport, text and appendices should occasionally be looked at together.

Where it is said or implied that A's car beat that of B and C, it can always be taken that B and C occupied second and third place respectively.

All available information on the locations of courses has been given, so that anyone wishing to seek them out has some clues to start with. Complete page references for courses, clubs, cars and personalities may be found in the appropriate Index.

For the sake of conciseness, the names of clubs have been abbreviated after their first mention. For example, 'MC' after a region means Motor Club, 'AC' Automobile Club, and 'LCC' Light Car Club.

PART ONE

1896: False Start

Two weeks after the mismanaged, over-ambitious Emancipation Run had spread its noisome trail of recrimination and public ridicule over the sixty miles between the Metropole hotel in London and its namesake in Brighton, the instigator, Harry J. Lawson, bounded back unabashed with a new idea.

Late in November 1896, there appeared in *The Autocar* and *The Automotor and Horseless Vehicle Journal* an announcement over the name of Mr C. Harrington Moore. He was secretary of the Motor Car Club, an organisation founded by Lawson to further his efforts to bind and suck dry the newborn British motor industry. In the coming May, the paragraph said, a 'Two Thousand Guineas Contest' would be held, 'the principal point of which will be speed, which, we are of opinion, affords the most satisfactory test as to the excellence of construction of a mechanical vehicle'. 'Owners of race-courses and other large enclosures' were invited to contribute 'a full, level and straight mile', on which would be run the highlight of the contest, 'The Motor Derby'. A special prize was to be awarded to 'the first mechanically-propelled vehicle which accomplishes a mile in a minute'. For lack of any suggestion to the contrary, this was presumably to be achieved over the same mile course; that is, a standing mile in 60 seconds, or an average speed of 60 mph. This proposal should be compared with the actual world's land speed record set up two years later: 39·3 mph for a flying kilometre!

No events of pure speed had so far been promoted in Britain. The main reasons for this were the universal 4 mph speed limit, only just raised by the 'emancipation' of the Light Locomotives Act to 12 mph, and the relatively greater importance, and difficulty, which the inexperienced British motorist found in making his car go, keep on going, and climb hills at a time when it was still a rudimentary, experimental and primitive beast. Even if authority were to permit a race on Britain's public roads on the French model, a contingency then so remote as to be absurd, speed for its own sake was discouraged. On the other hand, unless human nature had changed, there might be some motorists among the few dozen in these islands to whom, once in a way, a legal, well-publicised comparison of speeds would appeal as strongly as it did to their brothers on the other side of the Channel. A private course, free from the attentions of the law, would be ideal. Naturally, illegal duels must have taken place on the public road ever since one car had met, and tried to pass, another.

But it was not to be. Although, like the Emancipation run, this idea could have been a sound one, it was ruined in the same way by ignorance, or disregard, of what was sensible and feasible, in the interests of sensational publicity. More accurately, it was aborted rather than ruined, for the 'Two Thousand Guineas Contest' never took place. In one sense alone Lawson was far-sighted: he must have noted the success of and publicity accorded to the first French road races—Paris–Bordeaux, Paris–Marseilles—and realised that speed was going to be the big public attraction. But, as always, the temptation of the over-grandiose gesture had been too much for him. He had laid himself wide open to attack. In a letter to *The Automotor Journal,* Sir David Salomons condemned the Motor Car Club's inflation of the importance of speed, because, he said, it was very far from being the sole criterion of a car's worth. *The Automotor Journal,* deriding the possibility of any high speeds being attained (a standing mile in a minute was a nonsensical proposition when the fastest French racing cars were good for only about 30 mph), commented caustically:

> If this is simply to be an experiment undertaken with the object of providing a new form of sport, we can only prophesy that the public will hardly be weaned from horse-racing by the spectacle of more or less cumbrous motor carriages making the best of their way over a length of ground.

It is to be presumed that the Motor Car Club so discredited itself with the wildness of its statements and its 'London–Brighton' record that, in spite of the size of the prizes offered, it was able to find neither a course nor support for the contest among motorists in general. The club, like Lawson's other projects, died in a few years, and the more responsible voices, such as that of the Automobile Club of Great Britain and Ireland, founded in 1897 by F. R. Simms, assumed the leadership of the motor movement. Nothing more was heard of speed in motor-car sport for two years.

Meanwhile, however, certain gentlemen who had grown up with cycles and cycle racing, such as J. W. Stocks, Selwyn Francis Edge and Charles Jarrott, had turned to and fostered the sport of racing powered machines—motor-tricyles—on private tracks. These 'motors' are not within the scope of this book; let it merely be mentioned that, being lighter, simpler and handier than cars, cheaper to run and possessed of a better power-to-weight ratio, needing less 'racing room', and being encompassed at birth by a company of sporting enthusiasts, they were raced at a time when a good day's sport in the eyes of the club motorist consisted of a run from Westminster to Sheen House, Richmond, at an average speed that was on no account to exceed 12 mph.

PART TWO

1899-1903: The Flag Falls

By 1899, the ACGBI had begun to take its responsibilities more seriously, realising that social runs for its members were no way of improving the breed; the most pressing problem of the age. It therefore promoted a series of general efficiency trials, to be held in the vicinity of London in June. This was to be the first sporting competition for motor-cars held in Britain. The club 'did not think that, as in France, speed should be the principal test of a car', but they knew that a trial was incomplete without it, so while such things as reliability, petrol consumption, braking, manageability and the ability to climb hills were to be considered, so also were speed in hill-climbing and speed on the level. These tests are what concern us; and they were to be the earliest instances of the only form of high-speed competition possible on the mainland of Britain until 1907.

The organiser, Claude Johnson, may have derived his inspiration from France, where in November 1898 the first speed hillclimb of all time had been held at Chanteloup, followed in December by the first level speed trial, at Achères. At all events, the hillclimb held on Petersham Hill near Richmond on 9 June 1899 was timed, even though the competing cars had to carry full loads. The forty or so entries had to face a severe ordeal. The 325-yd long timed section had an average gradient of worse than 1-in-12, with a good deal of 1-in-9 and 1-in-10, and the surface was poor even by contemporary standards. Incidentally, when discussing speeds put up in the early years of the sport, it is important to remember that gradients which would hold no terrors today could be rendered formidable by rough or slippery surfaces, and by lack of power and controllability in primitive self-propelled vehicles.

Fastest up Petersham, not surprisingly, was a Barrière tricycle, setting a speed of nearly 14 mph, but the vehicle making second-best time was an Electrical Undertakings Dog-Cart, which ascended at nearly 11 mph. While electric vehicles later gained a reputation for extreme sluggishness in comparison with motor and steam cars, electricity for speed over distances where a short-lived boost of 'juice' could be effective was momentarily fashionable. In 1898 it had been the Comte de Chasseloup-Laubat's Jeantaud electric which had established the first world's speed record at Achères, and his subsequent duel with Camille Jenatzy's electric *La Jamais Contente* had given this means of propulsion immense publicity.

Both tricycle and electric dog-cart were faster than the Hon C. S. Rolls' 6 hp Paris-Marseilles Panhard-Levassor, which could do no better than 8·75 mph up the hill. True, this machine was nearly three years old, but it was a racing car. The cars had also to descend the hill and stop within a given distance to test their brakes. Some drivers, including F. W. Lanchester on his new 'Lanchester Spirit Passenger Phaeton', now receiving its first public demonstration, asked too much of their cars' stopping capabilities. *The Autocar* described the startling performance of this and other cars:

> The unique Lanchester, the internals of which are as yet a secret . . . made a smart climb, but owing to its driver slashing downhill at about 18 to the hour he ran a considerable distance with his brakes asqueal after the signal to stop. The Tourist, a sociable cycle three-wheel car on Bollée lines . . . made the longest run of anything entered after the stopping signal, the car only being finally arrested by the driver putting his hand on the off leading wheel. . . . The brake was said to be out of order.

The speed trial was held on 14 June. No private road could be found, and in this, their first experiment in breaking the public-road speed limit in a big way, the ACGBI trod very gingerly. They dare not hold a race, naturally, but a sprint over a short, straight distance, one car at a time, might possibly be tolerated. As *The Autocar* charmingly put it, there was the double difficulty of finding a suitable road and '. . . authorities sufficiently alive to the requirements of the times to consent to overlook a literal infraction of the law'.

However, the pattern for the future was set at once. A Mr Stopes of Colchester, remotest ancestor of that priceless company of 'fixers' who were to make speed on the public highway possible, 'used considerable influence with the local authorities', with the result that there became available a straight stretch of 1½ miles of road 3 miles out of Colchester, near the Great Horkesley turn. Cars were to be timed over a measured mile, with a flying start. Unfortunately, by this stage in the preparations, time had run out, and competitors in the general efficiency trials could be given no notice of the speed event. It was a fiasco, only one official entry turning up. This was a Delahaye, which covered the mile at just under 27 mph. One other car followed it, but not being an official entry it could not compete, and anyway took more than twice as long to cover the distance.

Public interest was supposed to centre round the spectacle of the 'driving competitions' held over a number of days in the Old Deer Park at Richmond, but these, though they attracted such names as Théry (Decauville) that were soon to be famous indeed, were not tests of speed, but of driving skill and manœuvrability: the forerunner of the gymkhana and its successor, the driving test. This part of the trials, known as the Richmond Show, was designed to make propaganda for the capabilities of the motor-car by providing a sort of 'circus', but the show had, if anything, the reverse effect, for reasons which do not concern us here. The public stayed away.

On a more sober level, reliability and petrol consumption were tested in the course of runs between Southall and Stokenchurch on the London–Oxford road.

Already, the ACGBI had grown sufficiently in numbers and influence to feel its right to speak for the whole motor-car movement and assume powers of leadership and direction over it. Early in 1899, when the National Cyclists' Union had claimed the power to control all forms of automobile sport by virtue of its having been confined until then to motor cycling, the ACGBI had reacted vigorously. In June, the same month as the general efficiency trials, the ACGBI stated that it, 'being the only independent authority in this country recognised by public officials and the Continental automobile automobile clubs, constitutes itself as the recognised authority to regulate and control all automobile races, competitions and time trials in Great Britain and Ireland'. Now the Motor Cycling Club objected, but to no avail. There was to be no poaching, especially when the ACGBI was beginning to sponsor motor sport itself. The club was indeed the only independent motoring organisation in existence, since it had absorbed Sir David Salomons' Self-Propelled Traffic Association in 1898. The Motor Car Club was anything but independent. Most motorists, and all those of importance, belonged to the ACGBI, so its claim was not as unreasonable as it sounds.

The rest of 1899 was filled with further auguries of the future, for hillclimbs if not speed trials. The former had the advantage. At a time when a normal main road hill could stop a car, there was more practical excuse for them as improvers of the breed, and they did not necessarily involve a rude violation of the law: merely a gentle bending of it, over a short and unspectacular distance. The egregious E. J. Pennington, whose mechanical inspirations were almost as warped as Lawson's business morals, was engaged in a battle of words with the backers of the Mors car over the merits of their respective vehicles, and a hill-climbing match had been proposed to settle the argument. This idea, like so many in which Pennington was involved, came to naught, but it led S. F. Edge to propose, in a letter to the motoring press in July, the holding of an open hill-climbing contest independent of other trials. He suggested Westerham Hill between Westerham and Bromley in Kent, already known to racing cyclists, as a suitable course, being a very steep hill by the standards of the time. 'I feel sure that a test of this sort, which could be witnessed by a large number of people, held on a Saturday afternoon, would create wonderful amusement'. Edge stressed the need for attracting foreign drivers, so as to give the event importance and *éclat*. Edge, unlike the ACGBI, had in mind a purely sporting event in which speed, not general efficiency, was the prime factor, and which would also be a public spectacle.

This letter sowed its seed, but for the time being the ACGBI's more sober ideas held sway. On 9 October 1899, the club held the first of its long series of quarterly Hundred Mile Trials. These were again tests of reliability and hill-climbing combined, always over the same piece of the London–Oxford road between West London and Tetsworth, and always including timed climbs of the original (now Old) Dashwood Hill on the way out and Aston (not to be confused with the more famous Aston Clinton) Hill on the return journey. Often not more than two or three cars would participate, and these would generally be exceedingly stodgy vehicles. The events were of a uniform, deadly dullness, and of no real importance. They will not, therefore, be mentioned again.

In view of the fact that the provoncial clubs would in a few years come to overshadow the parent completely in the promotion of sprints, let it be recorded here that the first of their number, the Manchester Automobile Club, was founded as an off-shoot of the ACGBI at the end of November 1899, followed by the Scottish Automobile Club a few days later. True, the Liverpool Centre of the Self-Propelled Traffic Association dated before to October 1896, but it was not a social or sporting club. Its purpose was the 'scientific investigation of self-propelled vehicles and locomotive road traffic'.

Having described the first speed hillclimb and the first speed trial held on Britain's public roads, both events involving violation of the law, it is necessary before going further to stop and explain how such liberties could be taken, now and later. There were four reasons. Firstly, rural and even main roads at this time were deserted by present-day standards. Long-distance traffic went by rail, and local traffic, except on market day, consisted of the odd haywain, flock of sheep and cyclist. In any case, organisers always chose a remote location if they could, to avoid annoying the locals with their crowds and their noise, to avoid attracting too much attention, and to reduce the hold-ups involved in allowing normal traffic free passage. The road was everyone's right of way, and no public highway could legally be closed. The author has been able to find only one instance, quite unexplained, of the closure of a public road other than a seaside promenade for a speed event, in all the twenty-three seasons involved.

Secondly, the events were short, so as to avoid the appearance of sustained law-breaking. This activity did not normally take place over more than a mile of road; perhaps it would occupy only a quarter of a mile. In the early years at any rate, no very high speeds could be attained, and as the event encompassed only a limited area, its local repercussions were circumscribed. Thirdly, the 1896 Act, which had decreed the speed limit, was applied by the county councils and often enforced by local authority at a lower level still. This meant, as often as not, a person of humble station and elementary education such as the village bobby, or at best, the local JP. Now, private motorists, at least until the First World War, were by definition comfortably off; while a motor sportsman had to be rich, either from his own money or from that of his business if he were in the trade. Many of these men wielded considerable influence, and if they lived in the vicinity of the proposed event, they might own a good deal of property locally. In a word, they would be gentry, and the policeman, when subjected to pressure subtle, gentle and perhaps irresistible, would be at a heavy disadvantage. There were few things which could not be arranged in friendly fashion over a pint in the local, or over tea with the squire and the JP. In industrial areas or holiday resorts, where commercial interests were strong, there might be still less difficulty, for the local council would include a heavy proportion of men of less conservative ways, to whom the public appeal of a speed event meant money.

Incidentally, those motorists who were wealthy in land, with a suitable stretch of private drive, might be induced to offer it as a course. All these men at this early, enthusiastic time were probably members of the local motor club; usually the president, patron or at least secretary. Few clubs lacked some sources of influence or flying half-miles.

Lastly, the ACGBI itself, the ruling, co-ordinating body of the sport was, as we have already seen, in favour of a certain amount of speed in competitions. This was due, apart from common sense, to the influence of the sportsmen high in the club's councils, and that of the representatives of the trade, who might be one and the same. A large part of the trade came to realise that nothing attracted the public's attention so strongly as speed, even if it were sometimes adulterated by weight handicaps and complicated equations seeking the best criteria of general 'efficiency', merit, or such like. Speed brought sensational publicity, which could mean orders for the successful. Thus the controllers of motor sport always included a strong proportion of men who were willing to condone the breaking of the law, so long as the local authorities who applied it were willing to turn a blind eye.

* * *

The twentieth century opened with an event of little importance, but worthy of record because it seems to have been the first independent hillclimb, unattached to a reliability trial. It is also remarkable for being so unseasonable. In the last week of January, light cars and motor-cycles exhibiting at the fourth Birmingham Midland Cycle and Motor Show engaged in a timed climb of Mucklow Hill, Halesowen. The distance was rather over a mile of tortuous and very stiff going. It was 'miserably cold and snowing heavily', so that what with one thing and another, the fastest car, a Mors *Petit Duc*, could do no better than 9m 2·4s, followed by Herbert Austin in a Wolseley. Such fortitude foreshadows the exploits of the twenties of the Southport Motor Club, whose competition season opened on the gale-swept seashore before the fogs of New Year's Eve could fairly have dissipated.

Having asserted its hegemony, the ACGBI, foreseeing that the sport would grow and need to be controlled, issued its first set of competition rules in March. At this time the club had about six hundred members.

All competitions were to be held under ACGBI rules. An ACGBI permit was essential for every competition. Anyone taking part in an unauthorised contest (one without a permit) would be struck off the

ACGBI register—all competitors and their cars had to be registered with the club—and excluded from other contests. Competitors were classified in the register as private individuals, manufacturers or their agents, and 'paid drivers or artisans'. Their cars were divided into classes by weight. Those competitors or vehicles not registered could not take part in any event. All handicaps were to be framed by an officially-appointed handicapper. Competitions could be either 'open' or 'reserved'. 'Reserved' did not, of course, mean restricted to a particular automobile club—few others but the ACGBI existed as yet, none was important, and none had promoted competitions—but signified restriction to cars of a particular weight class. Standing starts were foreseen as the general rule, but flying starts were allowed. Significantly, a postscript added that 'speed competitions on the public highway with the consent of the authorities' were envisaged for the future, even though only one contest of speed unalloyed—if the Birmingham excursion can so be called—had yet taken place.

These rules were issued just in time to govern the Thousand Miles Trial, the ACGBI's second, and much more spectacular and successful public demonstration of the capabilities of the motor-car. Although primarily a reliability trial on an unprecedented scale, it included four timed hillclimbs and a speed trial. Not surprisingly, an Ariel tricycle was fastest up Taddington Hill near Buxton on 27 April, at 18·9 mph, but the Hon C. S. Rolls' 12 hp Panhard was second best with a speed of 17·7 mph for the timed 2½ miles. This hill averaged 1-in-12. The ascent of Shap Fell on the 30th was so severe in terms of length—nearly nine miles—that it was optional, but Rolls' Panhard was second to a tricycle and fastest car at 13·29 mph. On 1 May, Rolls was fastest again, on Dunmail Raise between Grasmere and Keswick, at 20·54 mph with four up; and repeated the performance on Birkhill the other side of Moffat on the following day, where his speed was 16 mph with the same load. His time up Dunmail Raise was especially creditable, this hill being as steep as 1-in-8·6 in places.

The speed trial section of the contest was held on 11 May at Welbeck Park, where a flying mile of private drive was contributed by the Duke of Portland. If one omits the Colchester fiasco, this was Britain's first speed trial. It was an exciting occasion with some of the attributes of a race. Cars were released at ½-minute intervals, which meant that at times there were three on the course together. A Panhard, a De Dion and a Gladiator finished within seconds of one another, the Gladiator taking to the grass verge while passing. C. S.

Rolls again made fastest time, at 37·63 mph; the mean of two runs in opposite directions along the slightly-climbing course. Mark Mayhew's 8 hp Panhard and Edward Kennard's 8 hp Napier (the firm's first car, driven by S. F. Edge) tied for second place with a speed of 29·6 mph. The Napier was fastest in its class on all hills, and at Welbeck.

The course in Welbeck Park was to become famous for its speed trials, but (to anticipate a little) such a prospect must have seemed extremely unlikely a year or so later, in the summer of 1901. In the words of *The Autocar*, 'The Duke . . . was on a bicycle [riding through his own parkland] when he met an autocar coming sharply in the opposite direction. It appears that the Duke was forced to take to the hedge-bottom, and came off his machine in so doing, while the driver of the car made matters worse by crying out in passing something about "learning to ride properly instead of wobbling".' The Duke was understandably displeased, and forthwith banned all motor-cars from his estate.

In June 1900, S. F. Edge's proposals of 1899 bore fruit. On the 30th, the Catford Cycle Club held a hillclimb at Westerham which included a class for cars. The timed mile had a good surface, but its gradient, including 208 yd of 1-in-6·25, was a good deal worse than any encountered in the Thousand Miles Trial or anywhere else. S. F. Edge had hoped to compete with his new 16 hp Paris-Toulouse Napier, easily the fastest English-built car at the time, but it suffered an unspecified derangement on a practice ascent and was unable to run. It had also been scratched from the Thousand Miles Trial. In the end only two cars competed, and H. Weguelin's 12 hp racing Panhard was the faster by a considerable margin. It ascended at an average speed of 15·72 mph, while its rival, a 6 hp Daimler wagonette, could do no better than 5·1 mph. Much quicker than either was Edge on his second mount, an Ariel tricycle, climbing at 22·22 mph.

This event was overshadowed at the time by the more important climb held the following weekend (7 July) by the English Motor Club on Tilburstowe Hill, near Godstone Green in Surrey. The English MC was the Motor Car Club in a new incarnation. The climb was not severe, covering only 972 yd with a maximum gradient of 1-in-11·5. There were twenty-two starters, including eight cars, out of twenty-eight entries, and they were divided into classes by price. (So much for the ACGBI's weight classification.) Results were calculated on a formula taking into account weight, price and speed, but fastest up the hill was Charles Jarrott's 6 hp De Dion tricycle (at 25·8 mph), which climbed quicker than two racing cars; Edges's 16 hp Napier (18·39 mph) and Weguelin's Panhard (17·86 mph). Edge won his class on time, while O. E. Lord's 12 hp Peugeot took it on formula. A 3 hp De Dion and a 6 hp Daimler won the other car classes on speed. *The Autocar* said of this event that it was 'eminently successful' and that:

> Such contests as the climbing of Tilburstowe Hill, Godstone, by motor vehicles of different classes, when promoted and properly handled by responsible parties under the rules of the ACGBI, perpetuate the work and foster the plant, the good seed of which was so well sown by the Thousand Miles test.

As the motor-car became a more widespread and familiar phenomenon, the motoring movement began to suffer from its own propaganda. In 1896, the car was regarded as a rather nasty joke whose appeal was limited to a tiny handful of fanatics. By 1900, when the fanatics and their cars were much more numerous, the nastiness of the latter was much more noticeable; hence the growth and vociferousness of the opposition matched the spread of automobilism rather than declining as it advanced. The less responsible propagandists for the motor-car liked to suggest that their opponents were either cranks or upholders of vested interests in the many industries appertaining to the horse, but this generalisation was as misleading as the counter-suggestion that all motorists were selfish, anti-social madmen. In fact, the main enemy of the motor-car was a strong conservatism, ill-defined and instinctive, roused to militancy by several pretty well unavoidable circumstances.

By their very nature, cars generally were more offensive to the conservative lover of the quiet life than horses, able to travel faster, raising more dust, producing disagreeable noises and equally unpleasant fumes from petrol and oil. Most motorists were inevitably tyros, and, just as inevitably, they included a certain proportion of irresponsible exhibitionists. The cars of the tyros, not easy to drive in the first place, were noisier, smokier and smellier than those of the experts, and more prone to breakdown and accident. The show-offs' contribution was the less excusable, being deliberate. Because the motor-car was news, some newspapers seized upon and inflated reports of accidents or incidents for the sake of sensation, thus exacerbating popular feeling. When speed meetings were held on the public road, dust, noise, fumes and speed were correspondingly magnified and multiplied. In addition, offence was caused to local residents by the presence of large crowds of spectators, who might be noisy or thoughtless, or both.

This opposition was leading some county councils to ask the local government board for lower speed limits, especially in the south where motor-cars were more numerous and the influential sections of public opinion more conservative. In 1901 these measures led to a counter-campaign by the ACGBI, aimed at persuading county councils that, in general, the motor was a safe, practical vehicle with a limitless future, and in particular that the speed limit, far from being cut, should be abolished.

Discrimination against motorists in courts of law led in the same year to the foundation of the Motor Union, 'a defensive association [of motor clubs] for the protection of the civil rights of members'. Protection and strength were sought in unity of voice and purpose. By the beginning of 1901 the Yorkshire, Nottingham, Lincolnshire, Reading, Mid-Kent, Midland, Wolverhampton and Irish automobile clubs, and perhaps others, had been born, as well as the Manchester and Scottish clubs. They were regarded, by the ACGBI anyway, as its offshoots and the Motor Union as a limb. The latter was certainly true; the Motor Union was almost a department of the parent club. The provincial clubs were affiliated to the Motor Union, while the latter was so closely tied to the ACGBI that the affiliation was in practice with the ACGBI. The growth of the Motor Union, which included all the most important clubs, is interesting in this context, because it shows how the provincial clubs, responsible for nearly seventy sprints a year by 1907, multiplied. In 1903, ten clubs with 3,088 members made up the strength. By 1906 the MU had swollen to sixty-four clubs with 11,250 members, and had become strong enough to achieve a degree of autonomy within the RAC.

The spread of regional and national clubs (the English MC being national) led to a change in the ACGBI's competition rules early in 1901. After protests by the English MC, organisers of the successful Tilburstowe climb, compulsory registration with the ACGBI of drivers and vehicles for competitions was dropped, except in cases where they were to compete in an event promoted by that club. Also, it was no longer essential to employ an ACGBI-approved handicapper. Further erosion of the club's self-delegated authority would be attempted as the other clubs grew in strength.

On 2 May the ACGBI held its first independent speed hillclimb, on Dashwood. This hill on the London–Oxford road, already mentioned, had a worst gradient of 1-in-9·8. Its timed 1,434 yd included 366 yd of 1-in-10·3. Each car was allowed no fewer than seven ascents. In view of the growing antagonism to motors, and the club's endeavours to win over the county councils, no times or speeds were published in cases where competitors ascended at an average of more than 12 mph. The Hon John Scott-Montagu's 24 hp and 12 hp Daimlers were fastest, in that order, and there were several smaller cars whose achievements were similarly glossed over by having no details of their performance published. The practice now began of referring to such performances on the public road as being 'up to the legal limit'. A variation on this theme, and even less convincing, was tried at another ACGBI climb at Dashwood on 6 July, when S. F. Edge's 50 hp Napier was quaintly credited with 12 mph dead. One wonders who was supposed to be deceived. . . .

These devices detracted from the interest, but avoided presenting the police and 'antis' with free ammunition. However, they were never adhered to consistently, and lost their usefulness somewhat when one journal virtuously refrained from publishing speeds while a rival splashed them across its pages.

A case in point occurred after the English MC's second Tilburstowe climb on June 15. *The Automotor Journal* published no times, but *The Autocar* had no hesitation in telling its readers that S. F. Edge's monster 50 hp Napier set up fastest time of the day with a speed of 37·72 mph (1m 7·8s), easily seeing off Mark Mayhew's 20 hp Panhard, which ascended at 29·48 mph and (in the class for cars up to 16 hp rated) Charles Jarrott's 10 hp racing De Dion 'Spider'. The De Dion achieved 26·38 mph. Mr St John Nixon described the vehicle he drove, an Empress made by the French Hurtu company, as a very badly-designed car. It had a 4½ hp De Dion engine.

There were no fewer than forty-eight entries and thirty-seven starters for this contest, which followed two minor events held by the same club at the Crystal Palace cycle racing track in the spring. It was held on a course about 200 yd longer than in 1900. The entrants, divided into horsepower classes, included one of the new 35 hp Mercedes, and Charles Jarrott's 16 hp Panhard, as well as the cars mentioned, though Edge's Napier was naturally the big attraction.

Although they were said to develop 75 bhp (two were built), these cars were not a success in the *milieu* for which they were designed: international road racing. Edge's machine had been intended in the first place for the 1901 Gordon Bennett Trophy, run concurrently with the Paris–Bordeaux race, but it was too heavy for the British tyres which had to be used in the former, so could not compete for the Trophy, and developed too much power for its clutch, a failing which put paid to its chances in the Paris–Bordeaux. The Napier was a great deal more successful in sprints, where endurance was not demanded of it.

This Tilburstowe climb was marked by the first of the countless phenomenal avoidances which were to bedevil public-road events. In *The Autocar*'s words, 'The difference in times of Mr Mayhew's 20 hp and Mr Jarrott's 16 hp Panhard is wider than would seem to be warranted by the difference of four horsepower, but the fact that Mr Jarrott was badly interfered with on the 1-in-11 section by an old lady who selected the very moment of his passing to rush across the road must be taken into consideration.' Such phraseology could have done little to soothe the increasingly savage public breast.

The distinction of being the first provincial club to run a speed event seems to lie with the Reading Automobile Club, whose members on 26 June climbed 267 timed yards of Peppard village hill, between Rotherfield Peppard and Newbury. The steepest gradient here was 1-in-6. Dr Major's 2¼ hp air-cooled Renault took 54s to do so, but an Ariel tricycle took little more than half that time.

By far the most important event held north of the Border to date was the Five Hundred Miles Reliability Trial of the Scottish Automobile Club, consisting of daily runs out of Glasgow. Three hill-climbs were held during the three days of the trial, 4, 5 and 6 September. Those at Fintry (Lennoxtown, near Glasgow) and Gleneagles, though long, were commonly agreed to be dull, but the same could not be said of Whistlefield. This hill, between Arrochar and Gairlochhead, was less than a mile long but boasted the fierce gradient of 1-in-7·8 at its worst point. Many cars failed altogether, even though the ascent was optional; its inclusion on any terms was the subject of bitter recriminations afterwards. Still, it was perfectly possible to put up a creditable time, even in a low-powered car, as proved by Mr Moffat Ford. He ascended at 12·4 mph in his Decauville.

The season closed with the first of that illustrious line of hill-climbs promoted by the Midland Automobile Club, held at Gorcot between Alcester and Birmingham on 5 October. Its timed furlong was not severe, but it included some sharp bends. Mr A. E. Crowdy's 8 hp Darracq was the fastest of the cars, and, once again, Ariel tricycles overshadowed them, but no times or speeds were published. The main interest of the event lies in the entry list, which, because of the proximity of the heart of Britain's growing motor industry, included such famous names as Lanchester and Herbert Austin with his Wolseley.

By this time, the increase in popularity of speed events had led to searches for suitable tracks both for sprints and for races, stretches of public, but disused, road being favoured. It was thought that if the surface was restored, a length of straight Roman road, such as Ermine Street between Lincoln and Ancaster, would be appropriate. Others suggested a circuit of eighteen miles through dry marshland near Oulton Broad; but the talk came to nothing.

* * *

In these stern times, it was hard to say when the old competition season ended and the new began. The icy wastes of Welbeck Park echoed to the boom of exhausts and the whir of transmission chains as early as 11 January 1902. This event consisted mainly of a series of braking demonstrations for the benefit of county councillors, but there was also a speed trial, in which the 20 hp touring Panhards of Rolls and Mayhew participated. The Duke of Portland, now reconciled to motors, had mellowed so far as to straighten-out the course to make a full, perfect flying mile.

The ACGBI's climbs of Petersham Hill and a gradient in Richmond Park on 8 February were minor contests notable for only two things. Mr Ginder's tiny 4½ hp Locomobile steamer which ascended at 16·5 mph made all the big petrol cars except a 20 hp Milnes-Daimler look rather foolish. Steam cars, like electrics, had a capacity for short bursts of speed which could seldom be matched in the early years. On this occasion S. F. Edge's 16 hp Napier and two Panhards of the same rating were among the sufferers.

It was remarked that most of the entries for these two events were from the trade; a foretaste of the future. The organisers hoped to hold another series of hillclimbs in the same places in June, but this was forbidden by the authorities. Speed events in such a crowded suburban district were no longer safe.

On 29 March, during the ACGBI Easter tour to Cromer, speed trials were held on Lord Cromer's estate, Gunton Park. Although Edge's 50 hp Napier was among the nineteen starters, times were disappointing. The course was soft and sticky, slightly uphill and full of bends, while an unfavourable wind added to the competitors' troubles. The Napier returned 44 mph for the flying kilometre, and R. Bird's 24 hp Mors 40·08 mph.

Attacks on Dashwood by the ACGBI this year were combined with petrol consumption trials. The first climb, on 10 May, promised to be an especially important occasion. After a fast run down in the

Page 33 (above) *The officials, who made sprints possible: Claude Johnson and his party man the control at the top of Fintry hill, during the Scottish Automobile Club's trials of 1901. The car is a New Orleans;* (below) *Mors* grande voiture *at speed: Baron de Forest's Paris–Madrid car at the Phoenix Park speed trials held during the Irish Fortnight, 1903*

Page 34 (above) *A 96 hp Wolseley* (*left*) *and 100 hp Darracq under starter's orders, Blackpool speed trials, 1904. As was customary, cars in the racing classes were run stripped to the bone;* (below) *R. S. Witchell in his racing Straker-Squire. This car, although used for sprints successfully, illustrates the Brooklands 'shape' very well*

cold from London in the Hon J. Scott-Montagu's 20 hp Daimler, Mr A. J. Balfour, the motorphile Prime Minister, was to be seen sitting in a ditch with a plate of cold beef balanced on his knees and a row of Bass bottles beside him, eagerly awaiting the excitement. His presence could be taken as approval in the highest quarters for properly-conducted speed events on the public road. It was all the more unfortunate that Montague Grahame-White on his 28 hp Mors should be disqualified and suspended from further competitions for speeding on his return down the hill. He was said to have descended Dashwood at something like 60 mph, scattering spectators at the roadside. On the same day, motorists were alleged to have insulted trap drivers for getting in their way. The day's work provoked considerable local ill-feeling and irate letters to the press; to the extent that it was suggested that Dashwood be abandoned in favour of Kingston Hill, running parallel with Aston Hill further along the Oxford road. Nothing came of this; for the time being, Dashwood was still thought usable. Campbell Muir's new 40 hp Mercedes, the first of its type to appear in England, provided another sensation on this occasion.

By far the outstanding event of the year was the Bexhill Speed Trials, held by the ACGBI at Whitsun (19 May). Speed trials had been held on the Promenade des Anglais at Nice in 1901, but this was the first occasion on which the long promenade of a British seaside town had been used for such an exhibition. This was the best kind of course available, being usually fairly straight, wide and well-surfaced. Starting at the top of Galley Hill and including the De La Warr Parade, it provided, in the case of Bexhill, a flying kilometre by courtesy of Earl de la Warr, 'to whom', *The Autocar* succinctly commented, 'Bexhill belongs'. Being a private road, the course was free of interference by the authorities. In any case, the corporations and chambers of commerce of the seaside resorts which were to welcome racing cars and close their promenades during the next twenty-odd years were influenced by the prospect of gain as much as by respect for birth and wealth. The spectacle would attract visitors who, if not always quite nice, would spend a lot of money.

This attraction was practically guaranteed. *The Autocar* might say reassuringly that 'a rate of seventy miles per hour without danger can be attained', but danger was precisely what the public wanted to experience—vicariously, of course:

> There is no doubt that the coming carnival of speed will be a most sensational spectacle. It will be far more interesting to lookers-on than

> any of the previous speed trials, owing to the fact that there is room for two cars to race, and the contests will be run in heats, and not solely against time.

The organisers promised exciting finishes, and in fact they were to be rather more exciting than anyone had bargained for. Just after the finish, and before cars could have time to slow down, there occurred a right-hand bend with a steep outward—seaward—camber. At this point, too, spectators were allowed on to the road, it being outside the timed distance. So, while a competitor was avoiding the wandering public, he was simultaneously trying to prevent his machine from taking off across the sea wall and into the English Channel.

In preparation, Earl de la Warr went so far as to construct a starting ramp on Galley Hill, to give the cars an extra boost. It was necessary, since even with this aid the descent was too short to allow cars to reach their maximum speeds before the beginning of the flying kilometre. Electrical timing was to be used. Special trains were to be run by the London, Brighton & South Coast Railway and the South Eastern Railway from London, Hastings, Eastbourne and Tunbridge Wells. It was expected that this event would be the first speed meeting of truly international importance to be held in Britain. As it happened, Bexhill attracted 20,000 spectators, and several of the Continental aces. Trophies were offered by the newspaper tycoons, C. A. Pearson and Alfred Harmsworth, showing that the Press appreciated the sensational publicity that motor racing attracted. Surprisingly, *The Country Gentleman* magazine also presented a cup. So, more predictably, did that dedicated enthusiast, the Hon John Scott-Montagu, and Earl de la Warr himself. Silver and bronze medals were to be awarded in each class. A flood of last-minute entries meant that the meeting was greatly over-subscribed.

Only the normal, quiet-loving visitors to Bexhill could complain, for, as the *Bexhill-on-Sea Observer* commented wonderingly:

> No matter where one might go, he was sure to encounter a car. . . . They swarmed in hundreds all the day long, making the place hum with rattling machinery, and causing a cyclonic disturbance of the air as they flew past. . . . The town reaped a good harvest of golden grain. . . . Although Bexhill has always prided itself on its peace and quietness, it apparently has no objection to having its Arcadian stillness disturbed for a time by millionaire motorists and other less wealthy people who drive a car . . . [the visitors] filled up every large hotel and overflowed into every boarding house.

Every available shed was commandeered to shelter cars; even, prophetically, the stables of the jobmasters. Motorists overflowed into Hastings and St Leonards.

Competitors were divided into classes by weight and by type: touring and racing. The definition of a touring car was very loose: it had simply to carry a full complement of passengers and full touring coachwork. Little was done to modify this vagueness and, as we shall see, it was to be a cause of much heart-burning in coming years. The most powerful racing cars were released one at a time and the smaller ones in pairs, so as to strengthen the illusion of a race. Some of the speeds may seem low for a flying kilometre, but the flying start was very short: hence the desirability of the ramp.

Fastest time of the day was set up by Serpollet in his racing steamer at 54·53 mph, or 41·8s. This car was said to develop 120 bhp. A. Georges-Richard won the under-400 kg *voiturette* class at 28·66 mph, while Baras and Gabriel on 20 hp Darracqs dominated the class for *voitures légères* of less than 650 kg. Baras led with a speed of 52 mph. The 'special' 800 kg class was ill-supported, and Mercier's Gladiator managed to win it with a speed of 39·93 mph. The under-1,000 kg class, the most popular in international racing, was correspondingly well filled. Charles Jarrott's 40 hp Panhard, the car in which he took second place in the Circuit du Nord, carried off the honours at the same speed as the winning light Darracq: an indication that the *voiture légère* was already a formidable force. C. S. Rolls' 40 hp Paris–Berlin Mors came second at 49·69 mph, in spite of a cracked cylinder-head joint which let water into a cylinder and thence into the carburettor. Herbert Austin's 35 hp racing Wolseley could do no better than fourth place. Réne de Knyff and Girardot, down to drive Panhard and CGV respectively, were nowhere at all.

The over-1,000 kg class, like the 800-kg category, was not one that was catered for in current Continental racing formulae, and was filled mostly with stripped tourers or obsolete racers. Times were slower. A 28 hp Mors, a 1901 racing type that developed more like 60 bhp, was fastest at 48·61 mph. Edge, with the 50 hp Napier, came second with 47·57 mph. Two other interesting cars present were the new 40 hp Mercedes of Baron Henri de Rothschild and Alfred Harmsworth, but neither figured in the results. The touring-car classes saw wins for Mark Mayhew's 20 hp Panhard, and Edge's 50 hp Napier respectably dressed. J. P. Petty's 6 hp Gardner-Serpollet (a more sophisticated contrivance than the Locomobile) was the best of the touring steamers.

There had been little to mar the success of the meeting. Times generally were slower than might have been expected even with the short flying start, owing to cross winds and to the fact that the course was neither entirely smooth nor straight. The crowd had another complaint, in that the sequence of events could not be followed easily owing to lack of programmes, and that there were delays between runs: there was no telephone between the starter and the operator of the telegraph board at the finish. The racing numbers on the cars were too small and blew off. It was commented that numbers stencilled on the cars themselves, as in the Circuit du Nord race, would have been more satisfactory. Some racing cars with touring bodies had found their way into the touring classes, and in June the ACGBI ruled that any car rated at over 30 hp, even with a touring body, would be transferred to the racing-car classes. The criterion of a racing car was still sheer size.

Still, as a first attempt at an international race meeting, the Bexhill affair was a triumph, and the experience taught the ACGBI a lot. The Bexhill event had also the distinction of being the only English speed trial ever to attract a representative force of Continental drivers. The town, generally speaking, was delighted. Its intoxication with the new locomotion was neatly epitomised when Earl de la Warr bore its Charter of Incorporation round Bexhill in an 8 hp Argyll; the first time such a ceremony had been performed by car. An 'appearance competition', or *concours d'élégance*, rounded off the occasion. This was not an innovation; the only remarkable thing about it was that no fewer than thirty Members of Parliament, supporters of the motor movement, had contributed towards the cost of the first prize: the House of Commons Cup. Prudently, the Hon Members refrained from associating themselves with speed events. As *The Autocar* put it, this was 'an amusing event for those not seriously inclined'. The winner was S. F. Edge's 16 hp Napier.

The success of the first Bexhill meeting led the ACGBI at once to plan a repetition, but they met with setbacks. A meeting scheduled for 9 July was postponed to 4 August, but it then became known that a Mr Mayner, a jobmaster and resident of Bexhill, had sought and secured an injunction against Earl de la Warr restraining him from blocking his (Mr Mayner's) right of way on the Marina for the purpose of holding speed trials. Mayner was within his rights so, notwithstanding blistering editorials in the motoring press, and possibly even more emotional reactions among Mayner's fellow tradesmen and hoteliers, the trials were removed to Welbeck.

Here on 7 July the mean time of two runs over a flying kilometre was taken. Once again, cars were divided into classes by type and weight. Among the racers, the best 400-kg *voiturette* was Vonlatum's

12 hp Clément, at 45·07 mph. Of the *voitures légères* (650 kg), Théry's 18 hp Decauville was fastest, at 50·08 mph. The 1,000 kg and unlimited classes were both carried off by Charles Jarrott in his 70 hp Panhard, at 61·41 and 63·87 mph respectively. Among the tourers, a fine time was set by C. S. Rolls' 20 hp Panhard, which covered the flying kilometre at 46·57 mph, but Rolls was disqualified for using a racing-type body. So was the 20 hp MMC of A. Burgess, for the same reason, so that the car making third best time in this class, E. M. C. Instone's 22 hp Daimler, won it in 58·8s. The steam car class was won by W. H. Dew's 6 hp Gardner-Serpollet in 51·6s. These times, given a ½-mile run-in to the kilometre, would have been better still had not the course been so wet and slippery. Several cars nearly left the road, and all threw up plumes of black mud fifteen or twenty feet high in their passing.

The defeat at Bexhill was followed very soon by another. From Welbeck, twenty cars wended their way to Dashwood for a hillclimb open to the speed trial competitors. Awaiting them at the hill were a sergeant and a dozen constables of the Buckinghamshire police. The sergeant informed the party that he had orders to take the names and addresses of drivers who exceeded 12 mph over a timed stretch of the ascent. Naturally, the climb had to be abandoned. Thus did contestants' behaviour at the May meeting come home to roost. Dashwood, that quietest of hills once genially ignored by the county police on 'race days', was lost so far as major meetings were concerned. One more was to be held, but it was clandestine.

At the Yorkshire Automobile Club's climb of Harewood Bank on 25 August, plain-clothes police almost outnumbered the competitors, but the two hillclimbs in the ACGBI's 650-Mile Reliability Trials in the following month did not suffer, perhaps because they were suitably overlaid by the emphasis of the trials on reliability. On 5 September the cars were timed up River Hill, between Tunbridge Wells and Sevenoaks, the fastest being a 6 hp Gardner-Serpollet steamer at 16·84 mph. The dreaded Westerham was climbed on the same day, a 20 hp Wolseley getting up at 12·34 mph. The organisers had announced piously that no marks would be given for speeds of over 12 mph, and that timed speeds of over 15 mph would entail disqualification, but nothing further seems to have been heard of this rule.

A season that had been pretty discouraging, apart from the success of the Bexhill meeting, closed with two hillclimbs run by the Midland

AC. The more important was held on 11 October, when Gorcot was attacked by a number of very exciting motor-cars. Harvey du Cros' 70 hp racing Panhard set a time of 1m 3·8s, which neither A. E. Crowdy's 45 hp nor Herbert Austin's 30 hp racing Wolseley could match. Wisely, neither the speeds nor the length of the course were published. We only know from the times that it must have been a great deal longer than the furlong of 1901. E. W. Lewis' 22 hp Daimler won its class from J. A. Holder's 16 hp Napier. Other class leaders were Herbert Austin's 20 hp Wolseley, George Lanchester's 10 hp Lanchester and E. M. Iliffe's 7½ hp Wolseley.

In spite of Mr Mayner's *coup* at Bexhill, other resorts envied the success of the town's speed trials. In October, it was announced that Blackpool wanted to follow suit, while Brighton planned a speed meeting and exhibition for June or July of the coming year. Run under the auspices of the ACGBI, the Brighton meeting was to be held on the Madeira Road, which was to be closed for the occasion. (It was not renamed Madeira Drive until 1909.) The *Brighton Gazette* was in favour of the idea, but at this time *The Autocar*, nervous of the repercussions of further displays of uninhibited speed, warned that 'it is a mistake to overdo these meetings'. In the event, Brighton held no speed trials for another three years.

The year 1903 was one in which Britain had to defend her possession of the Gordon Bennett Trophy, won by S. F. Edge and his Napier the previous year over the Paris–Innsbruck course. Two of the British Gordon Bennett team, Jarrott and Edge on their Napiers, were chosen by the ACGBI on the strength of the Napier's 1902 performance, but a third place remained to be filled. On 25 April eliminating speed trials were held on the Clipstone Drive at Welbeck between Napier and Star cars, a 50 hp Wolseley having turned up too late to participate. It was a windy day and the surface was loose, but otherwise conditions were ideal. Watched by 3,000 spectators, each car made three runs in each direction, first over a flying kilometre and then over a standing mile. C. S. Rolls' and J. W. Stocks' 45 hp Napiers each achieved 72·1 mph over the kilometre on the 'down' run, with a short run-in. Mayhew's 35 hp Napier could do no better than 60·4 mph, and Lisle's Star, credited with no less than 80 hp, only 58·8 mph, but this latter car was sadly overgeared. Stocks was best over the standing mile, with 55·4 mph.

Quietly the word was passed round that the cars should wend their way south to Dashwood for the second part of the eliminating test, assembling at the foot of the hill at 4 am on the 27th. C. S. Rolls put up the best average of three climbs in the course of these furtive proceedings, but Stocks had done better still at Welbeck, so he filled the third place in the Gordon Bennett team. No times, speeds or distances were given. Instead, we see the first use of the differential method, by which the fastest car was allocated zero or *x* time, only the difference between its time and that of slower cars being given. The Star showed up worse than ever on this steep, heavy surface; it was up to half a minute slower than the rest.

A crop of small club events intervened in the spring and summer. Very much more important was the first really ambitious hillclimb staged by the Midland AC, run on Sun Rising Hill between Banbury and Stratford-on-Avon on 25 July. This was counted as a very severe hill indeed, nastier even than Westerham, with 270 yd of worse than 1-in-8 and a stretch of 1-in-6·25, punctuated by acute corners which could baulk and stall an ascending car and overthrow one descending too fast. A course of 1,000 yd was marked off, with a standing start, and a stop-and-restart test on a piece of 1-in-6·75. Of twenty starters, all of them touring cars fully laden, three failed altogether. Numerous spectators watched Cecil Edge's 20 hp Napier put up the remarkable time of 1m 55·8s for the whole test. This car was 8 cwt heavier than that of the second man home, George Iden in his 20 hp MMC, who could do no better than 2m 21·8s. It was darkly hinted that the Napier, though entered as a touring car, was fitted with a racing engine; one, indeed, out of last year's Gordon Bennett team. Other contestants included J. W. Cross in the 20 hp Humber which had done so well in the 'Irish Fortnight' (see Appendix), but which now retired, C. S. Rolls in a 15 hp Panhard, Archie Millership and George Lanchester in Lanchesters, Herbert Austin in a Wolseley, and Captain H. H. P. Deasy in a Rochet-Schneider, the fast French machine he handled in this country.

The Lincolnshire Automobile Club held the first of its hillclimbs—perhaps more appropriately called speed trials, as the average gradient of the kilometre was only 1-in-18—on 8 August in the Red Deer Park of Grimsthorpe Castle, Earl Ancaster's estate near Bourne. Captain H. E. Newsum's 12 hp Richardson was fastest, with 1m 12s.

Sun Rising drew back the Midland AC on 12 September, but this time, to make things more interesting, only 400-odd yards of the stiffest section was used, with a standing start on a bit of 1-in-9. Eight out of twelve entries started, and of these J. A. Holder's 24 hp Panhard was fastest, returning 1m 9·8s against the same gentleman's

16 hp De Dietrich. Neither car won the contest, which was a handicap. The winner is not recorded. Another climb was planned for 10 October, then postponed to the 24th, and finally abandoned. This event, known as 'Mr Holder's Hill-Climbing Competition', was to have been decided by a formula which was to remain secret until the day, so that competitors could not prepare their cars in any special way.

On the same day the Nottingham AC again gathered to climb Kettleby Hill. S. F. Edge was there with a Gordon Bennett Napier; also a Mr Lloyd in the 45 hp machine driven by Stocks in the race. No results were given, and wisely, no times published. Awe overcoming grammar, *The Automotor Journal* commented: 'The sight of their cars ascending the hill afforded the most unique spectacle.'

Following the example of his fellow peers, Earl Fitzwilliam threw open the grounds of Wentworth Woodhouse to the Yorkshire AC on the 19th. Several hundred spectators gathered to watch runs over the flying ½-mile by racing cars, touring cars and motor cycles. Unfortunately, no racing cars turned up. In the touring classes, a 20 hp Brush was tactless enough to thrash a flock of 22 hp Daimlers belonging to the host, averaging 41·04 mph.

That year's ACGBI reliability trials were more ambitious, covering 1,000 miles, and including four hillclimbs and a speed trial, as in 1900. It was noticeable that the great majority of the entrants were from the trade. Both police and spectators were out in force, the former trapping and the latter getting in the way. Westerham was first ascended on 19 September, a 22 hp Daimler being fastest at 'over 14 mph', whatever that meant, but so many cars were baulked by the public on their lawful, if inconsiderate, occasions that the climb was repeated on the 28th, when a 10 hp Gardner-Serpollet rocketed up at 22·23 mph. It was followed a long way behind by a 16 hp Rochet-Schneider. Earlier, on the 21st, the Rochet-Schneider had been fastest up Bury Hill at 'over 17 mph'. On the 23rd the Gardner-Serpollet had vanquished Hindhead Hill at a contemptuous 33·86 mph. On the 24th, in the middle of the trials, came the speed test on the front at Bexhill. Only touring cars and a ½ mile of road were involved; one assumes that this was insufficient to arouse Mr Mayner from his lair. Fastest car was George Iden's MMC with 44·6 mph, rather surprisingly quicker over this short course than the Gardner-Serpollet. The timed ½ mile of Hand Cross Hill was climbed on the 26th, when the Gardner-Serpollet, with a speed of 26·7mph, came back into its own by defeating a 14 hp Martini. Here again spectators baulked the ascending cars.

Southport was the first resort to follow the example of Bexhill. Speed trials under the auspices of the ACGBI and the venerable, highly-respected Liverpool Self-Propelled Traffic Association, famous for its heavy vehicle trials, were held on the promenade on 2 and 3 October. They were originally to have constituted the ACGBI's spring event, but had to be postponed. The local authorities co-operated enthusiastically, and no one could have wished for a better home entry, which numbered no less than 188. The touring cars, all to run fully laden, were divided into price classes, and the racers were classified by weight. The cars ran two at a time but, though the surface was pronounced excellent, there was half a gale blowing when the fastest machines were due to run, so speeds were not so high as they might have been. A. Rawlinson's Darracq *voiture légère* won the 650 kg race at 60·74 mph (36·8s). In the heats for the 1,000 kg class, S. F. Edge's 45 hp Napier beat the new 36 hp Wolseley, but the latter's slow time was due to the refusal of its clutch to engage properly. G. Higginbotham's 60 hp Mercedes defeated Rolls' 70 hp Mors, and J. E. Hutton's 70 hp Panhard disposed of a 35 hp Napier in the excellent time of 33·4s. More surprising was the defeat of another 60 hp Mercedes by Edward Lisle's Star racer. Perhaps it was now more suitably geared. In the final, Edge beat Hutton in 33·2s (67·33 mph; the fastest official speed of the meeting). Rolls was to have used a bigger, 80 hp Mors at Southport, but this car was unfortunately a non-starter.

Hutton had his revenge in a scratch race, his 33·6s bettering Edge's 35s, and these two thrilled the spectators with their neck-and-neck duelling. Hutton's Panhard later went sick in an open race with A. Fletcher's 60 hp Mercedes, which itself could do no better than 57·3 mph. During some unofficial runs after the main events, however, Hutton achieved a rousing 69·43 mph, with the benefit of wind and gradient. A 60 hp Mercedes was only fractionally slower, while the Wolseley, apparently also cured, was persuaded to attain 62·4 mph. The touring classes were enlivened by the spectacle of Charles Jarrott, passed by Iden's 25 hp MMC in one heat, slipstreaming him in his 24 hp De Dietrich and dead-heating with him on the post. Jarrot went on to beat Iden, but in the final of this class he was beaten by E. A. Nesbitt's 24 hp FIAT. S. F. Edge's 20 hp Napier defeated T. T. Vernon's 18 hp Mercedes in another touring event. Amazing to relate, A. Rosenheim's 24 hp Georges-Richard was led home by the very touring 16 hp Lanchester of L. Williamson. The Lanchester's time was 59·2s, the Georges-Richard's 68s.

From this rush along the Southport promenade, the sprinters returned to the hills when the Wolverhampton and District Automobile Club stormed Hermitage Hill, Bridgnorth on 24 October. W. Clarke's 25 hp MMC was fastest, with such famous names as J. Lisle and Star, and T. Cureton and Sunbeam, among the entrants.

This year there was a proposal to build an artificial racing circuit for the ACGBI at Purley in Surrey; a banked 6¾-mile course with a track 60 to 70 ft wide being envisaged. Four years later and a few miles away at Weybridge, a less ambitious project was to be realised, but its time was not yet. A plan to use a road circuit in Lincolnshire for the 1903 Gordon Bennett race had met the same fate.

At the same time, *The Autocar* was already commenting on the fact that, as the motor clubs multiplied, their first action on birth seemed to be to organise a speed event, usually a hillclimb. From 1904 onwards, the number of sprints held each year never fell below thirty, except in 1919, the year of recovery. It approached seventy in 1907, and exceeded that total in 1923 and 1924. The flag had, indeed, fallen.

APPENDIX OF OTHER EVENTS

(ST = speed trial; all others hillclimbs; FTD = fastest time of the day)

1901

8 April — English MC, Crystal Palace, London. ST. 1 mile. FTD: Charles Jarrott, 8 hp Panhard, 2m 16·6s.

27 April — English MC, Crystal Palace, London. ST. 350 yd. FTD: C. S. Rolls, 24 hp Mors.

20 July — Nottingham AC, Broughton Hill (Kettleby Hill), Nottingham-Melton Mowbray. 1 mile, max gradient 1-in-7. FTD: Percy Richardson, 18 hp Daimler, 5m 0·6s.

1902

May — Provincial clubs, Taddington Hill. FTD: 24 hp Daimler, 15·9 mph.

14 June — Scottish AC, Glenlude Hill (Paddy Slacks), near Innerleithen. 1 mile. FTD: Alex Govan, 9 hp Argyll, 22·6 mph.

8 Nov — Midland AC, Weatheroak Hill.

1903

16 May — Sheffield AC, Padley Wood, Grindleford Bridge. FTD: Locomobile.

23 May — Scottish AC, Kirkfield Bank, Lanark-Hamilton. 701 yd, max gradient 1-in-5. FTD: C. G. Sinclair, 20 hp Gardner-Serpollet, 17·17 mph. 2nd, W. Holmes-Kerr, 20 hp Wolseley.

13 June — Reading AC, Peppard Hill. 300 yd. FTD: 6 hp Gardner-Serpollet, 39s. 2nd, E. J. Wickens, 15 hp Fiat.

8 Aug — Derby & District AC, Hill Cliff Lane, near Turnditch. 1 mile, max gradient 1-in-7. FTD: M. J. Astle, 12 hp De Dion, 3m 30s. 2nd, Gardner-Serpollet.

August — West Surrey AC, Hindhead Hill. 2 miles, 1,458 yd, max gradient 1-in-13. FTD: Buttemer, 10 hp Decauville, 11m. 1st on handicap: Major C. G. Matson, 6½ hp Benz.

29 Aug	Kent AC, Vigo Hill, Wrotham-Gravesend. ½ mile, max gradient 1-in-9. FTD: H. O. Hall, 24 hp Darracq, 25·3 mph.
29 Aug	Kent AC, Trottiscliffe Hill. 570 yd, max gradient 1-in-5·2. FTD: Lucas, 12 hp Lucas (two-stroke), 11·4 mph. 2nd, H. O. Hall, 24 hp Darracq.
Nov	Cambridge University AC, Offley Hill, near Hitchin. Max gradient 1-in-8. FTD: 20 hp MMC and 12 hp Lucas tied 1m 24s.

PART THREE

1904-1907: The Heyday of the Monsters

The Nottingham AC were first in the field in 1904, assembling on 12 March to climb Kettleby on the Nottingham–Melton Mowbray road. W. S. Foster's 24 hp Georges-Richard was fastest, with 2m 12·6s for the measured mile, the runner-up on speed being H. Belcher's 25 hp Humber. Another Georges-Richard, a 10 hp model, was best on formula, or, as the results put it, 'made the most meritorious performance'. The bigger Georges-Richard, which had been successful in the Castlewellan hillclimb during the 'Irish Fortnight' of 1903, was helped by the fact that it carried the sketchiest possible body: a seat and little else. By 1904 the practice of running stripped touring chassis, or even racing chassis carrying rudimentary touring bodies, in touring classes had grown sufficiently to cause widespread dissatisfaction among less unscrupulous or ingenious competitors. We have already seen this happen at Bexhill and Sun Rising, and now the practice was spreading.

The second day of the Scottish AC's Glasgow–London trial—20 May—involved a timed climb of Woodcock Hill, between Elstree and Barnet in Hertfordshire. This had a worst gradient of 1-in-7·3 in its 237 yd. Fastest up was a 16/20 hp Martini, at 15·03 mph, but the most meritorious performance was decided on the basis of a formula which, even by contemporary standards, was of a most fiendish complexity. It is given here in all its horrid splendour; a monument to misapplied genius:

$$\frac{(w \times 60 \times L) + (W \times h) + \dfrac{(W \times v^2)}{2}}{a \times n \times s \times \dfrac{(G)}{D\pi}}$$

when: w = laden weight of car in tons
L = length of hill*
W = laden weight in pounds
h = height of hill*
v = velocity in feet per second
a = area of piston in square inches
n = number of cylinders
s = stroke in inches
G = gear ratio in lowest gear
D = diameter of road wheel in feet

* Unit not specified; presumably both in feet.

Factors in other formulae might include price, horsepower and cylinder capacity. But there were almost as many formulae in use for determining overall merit, 'efficiency' and such like as there were clubs: each club, including the ACGBI, had its tame mathematician, of greater or lesser tortuousness of mind, who was appointed official handicapper. This diversity led to disaffection among sportsmen and trade entrants who were accustomed to taking in dozens of events all over Britain each year for the sake of sport or sales, for with such varying formulae it was impossible to arrive at any fair comparison of worth.

A club would even change its formula from one year to the next when using the same course. There was much talk in the motoring press of the need for a successful standard formula, and it was generally admitted that power and weight were the two most important factors, but how did you determine power without a dynamometer test, and when you had only the manufacturer's claims to rely upon? Horsepower might be minimised to improve the car's chances in contests where it was a factor; but the manufacturer's figure was still used in some formulae. *The Autocar* lamented the unsophisticated attitude of the public towards merit: 'Within very wide limits, in the eye of the motorist, the best car on a hill is the one which makes the best speed.' Speed rather than efficiency, spectacle rather than solid worth. No one need have been surprised. . . .

In the midst of such confusion, the second of the Nottingham AC's climbs took place on 28 May, when, as in 1903, Napiers taking part in the current Gordon Bennett eliminating trials ascended Kettleby at frightful speed. This constituted the open event of the day, S. F. Edge's 80 hp Napier climbing in 1m 35s. Mark Mayhew and Clifford Earp in their Napiers were second and third, only 2·4s apart, while in the closed event, restricted to club members, W. D. Wells' 28 hp Daimler was fastest, in 2m 15·8s. This is the earliest reference to 'open' and 'closed' classes in the modern sense which the author has been able to find. Until now, all events had been open to all comers, unless otherwise specified.

The ascent of Padley Wood Hill, Grindleford Bridge, by the Sheffield & District AC on 18 June was distinguished by a triumph for a very obscure make; F. Churchill's 10 hp Hallamshire climbing at 13·56 mph to set fastest time of the day, a 14 hp car of the same breed being best on formula. The timed distance of this course was a shade less than two miles, and second on time and formula was A. S. Fawcett's 15 hp Darracq. The 'Flying Fifteen' Darracq, a conventional car for whose superior performance there was no obvious reason, appears frequently at the top of tables of results at this time.

In the same year, 2 July saw the Yorkshire AC climbing Pot Bank, near Harrogate, between Beckwithshaw and Killinghall. This hill was 900 yd long, with sharp bends and a piece of 1-in-7. Albert Farnell's 28 hp Daimler was fastest, beating S. Kirk's 24 hp De Dietrich by 1m 13·4s to 1m 39·4s: a fine performance by a driver who was to become famous in hillclimbs and speed trials. The results were recorded by electrical timing and conveyed by telephone, both unusual indulgences for a provincial club at this time.

The combination of an Edge, S. F. this year, and Sun Rising, again produced protests, louder this year than in 1903. His Napier, ostensibly of 20 hp model rating and admitted to develop at least 30 bhp, was alleged to be a 45 hp 1903 Gordon Bennett chassis with a touring body, its live axle lending credence to the supposition. In other words, the story of 1903 was resurrected. This meeting of 23 July was for fully-equipped touring cars only, and Edge claimed that his car was a catalogued 127 × 127 mm 20 hp model; in fact, it appears to have been the prototype six-cylinder, live-axle touring machine.

The twenty-nine starters were all petrol cars, for the first time on record, steamers being excluded. The Midland AC thus recognised the fact that at this time, over short distances, steam cars could outclass petrol-driven cars with embarrassing certainty.

As it happened, Edge's time of 2m 48·2s was not all that much better than that of E. M. C. Instone on his 28 hp Daimler at 2m 49·6s. True, Edge was baulked by a slower car still on the course, almost colliding with it and running it off the road, but Instone was himself a very skilful works driver. Indeed, this meeting presaged the coming dominance in sprints of Daimler as a *marque*, for no fewer than four 28 hp cars were faster than Lionel de Rothschild's 60 hp Mercedes.

The cars ran over the same 1,000-yd course as in July 1903, and went through the same stop-and-restart test, but everyone was a lot slower, no doubt because of the wet surface. This was extremely treacherous, and Crowdy's 1903 28 hp racing Wolseley, which, it seems, was allowed to compete with cars calling themselves tourers, went into a series of wild, time-wasting skids in the course of a climb taking 5m 10·4s. Other less spectacular, if no less entertaining, incidents punctuated the climbs. *The Autocar* recorded that: 'A gentleman who signs himself "Esq.", resident in the locality, who does not approve of motor cars, signified his opinions by causing his manure carts to be driven up and down the hill most of the afternoon, but no one was any the worse.'

Indeed, popular feeling against the motorist, and especially the high-speed motorist, was growing faster than ever. The 1903 Motor Car Act had come into force on 1 January 1904, and was regarded by many motorists as a setback. The speed limit was raised from 12 to 20 mph, but this was of no practical advantage. The old limit was universally disregarded, while normal touring speeds of 20 mph and more were already commonplace. However, whereas generally the police and local authorities had previously taken only occasional and sporadic action against contraventions of the speed limit, they now treated the rise as an excuse for launching an intensive campaign to secure adherence to the letter of the law, and to gain revenue. Greatly increased use of traps and heavy fines embittered relations between motorists, police and the Bench. Also, of course, local authorities were still at liberty to apply for lower speed limits, as before. It had been hoped that the limit would be altogether abolished, so no wonder the outcome was looked upon as a defeat. The same Act compelled all drivers to be licensed and all cars to carry number plates, their owners registering them with the local authority and paying a pound for the privilege. These measures to make motorists easier to trace, and again to provide revenue, were thought to be a scandalous attack on the freedom of the individual, now forced to carry a number like a cabman!

These observations hold good as generalisations, but an example of the dangers of over-generalisation was provided by the 'unanimous' local support accorded to Earl de la Warr's proposal in June to hold annual speed trials at Bexhill. Mayner's views no longer ruled. Perhaps the jobmaster had converted his stables into garages. The three-day ACGBI meeting on August Bank Holiday was open to touring cars only, carrying a full load of passengers, but attracted no fewer than 112 entries and 89 starters, divided into classes by price. Competitors ran in pairs over the kilometre (finishing instead of starting at the top of Galley Hill), speeds were high and finishes were close; all things making for a good holiday's sport.

In the most interesting of the first day's heats, S. F. Edge's '20 hp' Napier of Sun Rising notoriety beat C. Cordingley's 60 hp Mercedes by a bare 0·8s, in an elapsed time of 52s. Cordingley, like others before him, protested at the miserly horsepower attributed to Edge's car. On the other hand, although Algernon Lee-Guinness' 'Sixty', in 50·8s, beat a 40 hp Panhard, this was not a surprising victory, the Panhard being smaller and less advanced in specification. Sidney Girling's 28 hp Wolseley unsportingly defeated a lady driving a third 60 hp Mercedes, but the Wolseley was a racing machine with a professional at the wheel. Although the event was supposed to be restricted to touring cars, the Wolseley's participation did not arouse comment, any more than it had at Sun Rising.

On the second day, the matching of cars in the heats drew strong protests, especially directed at Edge, who improved his time to 50·6s, finally beating a swarm of big Daimlers. However, Lee-Guinness and the Mercedes now came into their own, thrashing Edge in 47·8s in the class semi-final, and a 24 hp Bollée in 46·8s in the final. This was the fastest time of the meeting, representing a speed of about 48 mph. The finals of the other touring classes produced wins for H. O. Hall's 15 hp Darracq (in 61s), and Huntley Walker's 30 hp Darracq.

The Derby & District AC held their second hillclimb of the year on 20 August, this time at Hill Cliff Lane near Turnditch. The course was a mile long, with a piece of 1-in-7. Each of the seventeen entrants were given two runs, resulting in a victory on time for F. A. Bolton's 22 hp Daimler. Bolton, a Daimler dealer, was indeed to become the make's most successful sprint driver.

The ACGBI's important road event of the year was the Small Car Trials held out of Hereford at the end of August. Dinmore Hill, between Hereford and Leominster, was climbed twice, first on the 29th, when the south side was tackled.

A timed 1 mile and 20 yd with a worst gradient of 1-in-10 was ascended by a 6 hp De Dion Bouton at 16·5 mph; an impressive achievement. A 6 hp Wolseley was second fastest.

On the 30th, the cars twice attacked Frome's Hill between Hereford and Worcester. This was a much more serious proposition; so serious, indeed, for small cars that the last section, steeper than 1-in-7, was not included in the timed distance. The same De Dion

 A. W. Tate's Mercedes after ramming the railings at Shelsley Walsh, 1913

Page 52 (above) *Caerphilly hillclimb, 1914: a sports 12/16 hp Sunbeam;* (below) *Malcolm Campbell's Talbot at Spread Eagle hillclimb about 1921*

was fastest on the morning ascent. On the second climb later the same day, after the cars had returned to Hereford from Worcester via Bromyard, a 6 hp Wolseley was best with 11·8 mph. Speeds were so low that it was thought safe to allow several cars on the hill at once.

On the following day, the north side of Dinmore was climbed, resulting in another victory for the 6 hp Wolseley and a second place for the De Dion. The Wolseley ascended at 15·4 mph, which was quite a bit faster than its rival. If anything, the Wolseley, E. V. Fielder's car, put up a more meritorious performance than the De Dion driven by J. B. Bee, for at 12 cwt, it was 2 cwt the heavier.

A notable 'first' in 1904 was the Hertfordshire Automobile Club's climb of Aston Clinton Hill, near Tring, on 10 September. The timed distance was ¾ mile, with an average gradient of 1-in-9 and a chalk surface. The road, though public, ran through Alfred de Rothschild's estate, and lavish hospitality greeted competitors and officials whenever they gathered. S. F. Edge won another round of the Napier–Bollée duel in his 20 hp car, his time of 1m 27·6s easily bettering the performance of A. J. Dew on the 24 hp French machine. A telephone line was laid to accelerate proceedings and relay results more quickly.

The Western Region of the Scottish AC ran a climb up Kirkfield Bank between Lanark and Hamilton on the same day, cars being divided into classes according to the number of their cylinders. J. R. Richmond's 15 hp Darracq was fastest, at 14·69 mph. One of the rules forbade the use of results for advertising purposes, a practice that was growing among trade competitors, as can be seen by a glance at the motoring magazines of the day.

In August, the Kent AC's Detling hillclimb had been restricted to privately-owned cars driven by private individuals, and so was the Yorkshire AC's speed trial at Wentworth Woodhouse six weeks later. This rule in the Scottish AC's Kirkfield Bank event, and the Nottingham and Wolverhampton clubs' use of open and closed classes at Kettleby on 17 September and Gatacre Hill on the 24th, were symptoms of growing disquiet among the clubs at the way in which their meetings were being used by the trade to boost its products. Trade entries, present from the very beginning of history in the case of important sprints, introduced a hard-boiled professional atmosphere into club meetings, and the speeds they achieved with cars on which much time and money could be lavished usually outclassed those of their amateur competitors. Furthermore, it was regrettably true that the stretching, or even disregard, of rules defining touring cars, and much of the bitterness of the subsequent protests, were results of the incursion of the profit motive into the sport.

On the other hand, the organising club's aim in promoting a sprint was to make money as well as sport, and if entries were limited to club members the revenue from entry fees would be curtailed. Publicity was another consideration: demonstrations of skill and high speed attracted new members and their subscriptions; and the trade could always provide a more spectacular show than the local talent. The quality of its entries, too, could mean renown or obscurity for a club: it was gratifying to be famous. A real benefit accruing from trade interest was improvement in the organisation of sprints. The outcry for simplification and rationalisation of formulae in determining results was, as we have seen, one consequence. Others were the adoption of more exact timing methods, and devices to expedite the proceedings, such as telephones. Neither highly-stressed machinery nor professional drivers whose living was involved took kindly to prolonged waits on the starting line. In the coming years, many were to be the expedients resorted to by the clubs to have the best of both worlds: to satisfy both the trade and the private member. They will be noted as they arise.

Blackpool was the next of the seaside resorts to perceive the hitherto unsuspected financial potential of their splendid promenades. The ACGBI's second and much more important speed trials of 1904 were held there on what was regarded—after the corporation had specially widened it—as the fastest motor-racing track in England. There was well over a mile of road; straight, broad and level. Racing (1,000 kg) as well as touring cars were to compete in the two-day event scheduled for 14 and 15 October. The town was transformed; for the better or not depended on whether you were a motorist, a businessman or a lover of peace and quiet.

> Blackpool this weekend is alive with motor cars. The delightful odour of petrol gas is mingled with the salubrious sea breezes. The incessant hum of the motor engines greets the ear at every turn, whilst now and then, as some powerful racer flies past, one is startled by a series of explosions which very much resemble a volley of musketry. . . . The scene presented on the Promenade, between Victoria and Central Piers, early yesterday morning was one of intense interest and animation. Motor-cars of all sizes and makes flitted hither and thither with lightning-like speed, and the hum of their engines resembled a colossal bee-hive.

Thus wrote the *Blackpool Times* reporter on the days before the races. It is odd that the sound emitted by early cars was so commonly described by the lay press as a 'hum': no word could worse describe the medley of clatter, puff, whine and whir which they in fact produced.

On the first day, the standing mile events were contested. Winners of the first heats for the 1,000 kg class included A. Callan on a 96 hp Wolseley, who beat Algernon Lee-Guinness' 100 hp Darracq, but his relatively low speed of 58·1 mph gives the clue to Lee-Guinness' defeat: he stripped his differential at the end of the first hundred yards. G. Higginbotham's Wolseley beat the Gordon Bennett Darracq of A. Rawlinson at 64·28 mph, A. Fletcher on a 90 hp Mercedes at 62·28 mph, and saw off C. S. Rolls' 100 hp Mors. Our reporter found the Higginbotham-Rawlinson duel most alarming: 'Both men came down the course at a terrific rate, the ignited gas blazing from the exhaust chambers of their cars with a vivid glare.'

In the second round, Higginbotham beat Fletcher with a speed of 62·71 mph, and went on to win the final from Callan at 61·43 mph. Only Wolseleys had been left in the running; they had finally vindicated themselves.

The afternoon of the second day promised the real excitement of the meeting: the kilometre, with a flying start of 3 furlongs. Running stripped to the barest bones, mostly with bonnets discarded, Clifford Earp's 80 hp Napier, Rolls' Mors and Rawlinson's Darracq were fastest in that order, at 84·68, 84·04 and 82·8 mph respectively. Earp's speed was a British record for the distance.

In the standing mile for tourers, F. C. Noar's 15 hp Darracq, Huntley Walker's 30 hp Darracq, H. Martin's 40 hp Léon Bollée and L. Williamson's 60 hp Mercedes won their classes. In the flying kilometre, Hugh Kennedy's 15 hp Darracq, Huntley Walker, Martin and Williamson won again.

However, in spite of the excellence of the entry and the course, this meeting had been disappointing in some ways. As far as the spectators were concerned, the programmes were inadequate, speeds were not as high as expected, events were run off without reference to programme order, there was no easy way of ascertaining results, and there were few close finishes for the cinematograph operator to record. The competitors, however, had more to complain of.

The corporation committee who organised the event lacked experience, and ACGBI regulations were disregarded wholesale (there were, for example, no stewards at all: the committee, ignorant of rules and procedure, were the final arbiters of dispute; and to make matters worse this body consisted mainly of the trade—not, moreover, a fair cross-section of the trade, but representatives of a few firms only). Chaotic mismanagement was universal.

A plan to hold more speed trials—record attempts only—later in the year was abandoned, but the public must have thought well enough of the event to make it very profitable, for it was announced that the promenade was to be extended by a further thousand yards in time for the next meeting. Certainly the motorists among them were sufficiently inspired by what they had witnessed to gather in sheaves of convictions for speeding as they drove home. The 'Spectators' Grand Prix' is nothing new!

The eyes of organisers of speed trials, ever seeking new and still better courses less prone to the attacks of the objectors, now began to wander speculatively over the tempting stretches of sand revealed at low tide beyond the promenades. All ideas for sprint courses had so far come from the Continent; but this new one originated in Ireland.

The Irish Automobile Club had been first in the field this same year with very successful races on the Velvet Strand at Portmarnock (see Appendix), but investigations and discussions in club rooms on the other side of the Irish Sea had so far led only to the depressing conclusion that 'there were very few places where conditions were favourable'. These few included the sands between Redcar and Saltburn, which were found in the summer of 1904 to be smooth and hard in a northerly wind, but rippled, developing rivulets and wet patches, when the wind was in the south. Their advantage was that they provided a course 5½ miles long and 260 yd wide at low tide; broad enough for five or six cars to run together. They were also overlooked by gently-sloping cliffs ideal as grandstands for spectators. Further south, the Lincolnshire AC discovered the sands at Skegness to be suitable and, with the support of the Earl of Scarborough, promised speed trials for the summer of 1905.

Meanwhile, during October, a very much more modest event had taken place which, in its way, was almost as much of a landmark. A contest known as the Portsmouth Trials, apparently organised by a naval motor club, took in two timed hillclimbs on a run starting from Southsea. J. D. Siddeley's 40 hp Mercedes ascended Portsdown Hill in second gear in 2m 19s. Cars then proceeded to a hill on the Chichester–Petersfield–North Marden road which ran through the estate of Colonel the Hon Turnour Featherstonehaugh of Uppark. Its gradient on the steepest part was 1-in-6·7, its average was 1-in-12, and its name was South Harting. Mr Siddeley was again very much the fastest, with a time of 1m 5·6s.

* * *

If 1905 was a vintage year for sprints, seeing the first climb of Shelsley Walsh, the first Brighton speed trials and the first English sand races, it was also the first to show the symptoms of an over-crowded calendar: cancellations and single-figure entries. The car class of the Peterborough & Counties Automobile Club 'hillclimb' at Grimsthorpe on Easter Monday failed to win enough entries, so motor-cycles alone provided the sport. This event, run by a small club, may have been 'closed', so lack of members rather than of interest may have been the cause, but this could not have applied to some abortive meetings later in the year.

Though the events then piled up as never before, sprints proper were late in starting. The first of the Scottish AC's celebrated series of reliability trials covered 595 miles between 10 and 13 May, but the three hillclimbs included, Cairnwell, Cockbridge and Aberfeldy, were long—1¾, 2 and 3½ miles—rather than steep; tests of stamina rather than speed. Cairnwell, between Braemar and Blaisgowrie, was the reverse slope of the hill called the Devil's Elbow. The factors governing results were weight and petrol consumption as well as time on the hills, but the aggregate of times was given, Tom Thornycroft's 24 hp Thornycroft being fastest overall. A 20 hp Ariel won the Thornycroft's class on formula, however. Classes were determined by the archaic number-of-cylinders method, but in connection with its rule limiting entries to cars of under 35 hp, it is interesting to see that the Scottish AC, at least, was no longer taking manufacturers' statements on trust. An attempt was made to determine horsepower by formula, which had at least the advantage of being equally fair, or unfair, to all.

On 27 May, the Nottingham AC gathered at Kettleby. This is the earliest recorded 'invitation' event, the organisers inviting the Derby and Leicestershire ACs to send of their best to do battle for the Du Pré Challenge Cup. The encouraging result was that there were thirty-nine starters, of which the best, both on time and formula, was F. A. Bolton on a 36/40 hp Daimler, representing the Derby club. A second Daimler was next fastest, followed by a 14 hp Minerva; another make which was to enjoy some seasons of success in British sprints. Lord Brabazon of Tara, who later drove these poppet-valve tourers in sprints, describes them as a 'rough, but very fast'. Like

Daimler, they built up an entirely contrary reputation once they went over to sleeve valves. T. C. Pullinger, incidentally, gave one of the then new 16/20 hp Humbers an airing at this meeting.

The advantages of an invitation event were clear. The organising club gained revenue and prestige, while weak or ill-favoured clubs were saved the necessity of organising events of their own.

As the Midland AC had made itself unpopular on Sun Rising, it betook itself on 3 June to private ground, Middle Hill House, near Broadway, for its first climb of the year. The works 35 hp Daimlers of E. M. C. Instone and Percy Martin tied for fastest time with 4m 42·8s over the $1\frac{2}{3}$ miles, Sangster being next on his 30/35 hp Ariel. H. C. Holder's 30 hp Daimler was close behind, but the 'field' was nowhere. The handicap, based on time, horsepower and weight, mattered most in this event, and for all their thunderous strivings, the hares could not best the tortoise, a 10 hp De Dion.

Though South Harting had already been 'christened', its launching as a major course took place this year. On 10 June the ACGBI promoted a full-scale hillclimb up the winding mile between telegraph poles nos 49 and 29. The occasion was not a great success by contemporary standards. There were only forty-nine entries in the three price classes, no times, speeds or means of comparison were published, and delays between runs were endless. It was known only that Edward Manville's 30 hp Daimler (followed by Instone in another Daimler), T. C. Pullinger's 16/20 hp Humber, and F. W. Adams' 8/10 hp Humber driven by Louis Coatalen, its designer, were fastest in their classes. Those of the trade who were unplaced were annoyed by the absence of published times, speeds or marks, for the public were left ignorant of who was fastest after the first one or two in each class. Only speed counted in this event.

The latest campaign against publishing speeds had originated with the ACGBI. *The Automotor Journal* explained the reason for it. In the early days of hillclimbs, most competing cars were feeble and the law was not broken too flagrantly too often. Nowadays a felony was committed by pretty well every car on every hill. The engines of touring cars, let alone racing cars, were larger (size and not efficiency being still the fashionable producer of bhp); but there had been technical improvements as well, which made a car much easier to handle on a fast and tricky ascent, and which, given the same power and the same hill in 1900 and 1905, allowed better use to be made of the power and provided faster times. In the days of automatic inlet valves and tube ignition, one's engine was an inflexible, constant-speed affair. Its speed could not be adapted at a moment's notice to cope with a sudden change of gradient or surface, a bend sharper than anticipated or an unexpected hazard. Road speed could only be altered by braking or changing gear, and the latter was a time and attention-consuming operation because of this inflexibilty. By 1905, mechanical, controllable inlet valves and, better still, a throttle to control the mixture could regulate engine speed instantaneously. The adoption of electric ignition had allowed it to be so regulated. Quicker, tidier gear changes, too, were possible with the new flexibility of control. Most cars were also very much more stable, having longer wheelbases, lower centres of gravity and self-centring steering.

At last, in April of 1905, with the support of the responsible motoring press, the ACGBI made a rule that no times should be published by the clubs affiliated to it through the Motor Union. However, both the club and the papers were obviously being gnawed at by doubts from within. Although the ACGBI was said to be turning its face against speed on public roads, it still organised events such as South Harting. By simultaneously refraining from publishing times, it was in danger of antagonising both the anti-motoring public and the competitor. *The Automotor Journal* declared in one breath that public-road sprints should be stopped altogether, and that, 'Hill-climbing competitions . . . of course are not races at all, but merely tests of horsepower and efficiency of transmission'—a first-class piece of casuistry. The campaign was short-lived, and ineffective. Not for the last time, the affiliated clubs were to find that they could disregard the ACGBI's pronouncements with impunity.

Although the sands at Filey and Muston were described as 'ideal', the first English sand sprint meeting, held at Filey on 12 June, was an unmitigated disaster. This was not entirely the fault of the Yorkshire AC who organised it, because for once the condition of the sands was very far from ideal, but it was also true that there were long delays between runs, little or no information for the spectators, and a total absence of effective crowd control. Spectators used the course (a flying mile with a clear $\frac{1}{2}$ mile at either end) as 2 miles of promenade, irrespective of whether a competitor happened to be bearing down on them, while their feet churned the soft sand into a morass. Their wanderings made for dull racing, because although cars were originally to run in pairs, then in threes, they eventually had to be sent off singly for safety's sake. All the events, open and closed, were dreary except the open class for cars of any type or horsepower, but even in that, there were only two starters out of six entries, and the result, if not the speed, was unexciting. Cecil Edge's 80 hp Napier set up a speed of 71·42 mph, Huntley Walker's 70 hp Darracq being a lot slower at 62·5 mph. The open class for racing cars of up to 1,000 kg promised well, but only Edge was entered in it. Among the tourers, F. Churchill's 12 hp Hallamshire, Huntley Walker's 15 hp Darracq, Albert Farnell's 30 hp Daimler and H. Johnson's 24 hp FIAT all won their events.

Edge drove the huge Napier down from Filey to compete in the ACGBI's Bexhill speed trials on the 14th, but his presence could not conceal the fact that, although racing cars were eligible this year, the local public were taking far less interest than they had in 1904. Still, perhaps too few spectators were better than too many in the wrong places. It was a one-day event, run over a standing ½ mile only, there being no room to pull up at the far end of a mile now that speeds were mounting.

The class for racing cars of up to 1,000 kg was naturally the most exciting, Algernon Lee-Guinness and his 100 hp Darracq making the fastest aggregate of runs. His best time was 30·4s, compared with Edge's 32s. Sir Ralph Gore's 100 hp Mercedes was third, and J. E. Hutton on a 90 hp Mercedes fourth. No speeds were given, though knowing the distance and times, interested or evilly-disposed parties could work them out easily enough. As was now becoming usual, Daimlers carried off the class for the largest touring cars, Percy Martin's 30 hp setting a time of 50·6s. Edward Manville's similar machine was second best, among a flock of other Daimlers. Another touring class went to A. H. Bush's 28 hp Daimler in 55·6s.

Classes at Bexhill were divided according to chassis price, a classification which was attracting strong criticism. This was particularly the case at Bexhill, where there were only two classes: for cars costing between £350 and £650, and between £650 and £900. Some competitors complained that they were outclassed by bigger, faster, much dearer machines running as equals. Price classes were also open to abuse, for who could prove that a car was running exactly as sold to the public? The ACGBI was advocating classes consisting entirely of one make of car, so as to reduce scope for protest, and experimented with these at the Brighton speed trials. Although the BARC introduced them at Brooklands in later days as an occasional joke, the ACGBI made itself unpopular with the trade by taking the idea seriously. Such contests might allow individual sportsmen to show their prowess, but were useless to the industry. With between 50 and 90 per cent of entries in sprints now coming from this source, the search for the most practical classification, as for the most realistic standard formula, was avidly and tendentiously pursued. Clubs from the ACGBI downwards were continually harried not only by enthusiastic amateur theorists but also by those with a financial interest in results, disingenuously pressing the claims of ideas which would give their cars an advantage, and savagely reviling those suggested by competitors.

For its part, the ACGBI (as it appeared to contemporaries) occupied itself by enshrining long-established institutions in statute, promoting rules hated by the trade and impossible to enforce, and antagonising the provincial clubs. The new April rules stated that weight classes were still allowed (though in practice only used for racing cars), but that other classifications, including price, were to be recognised. The accepted definitions of 'open' and 'closed' were officially recognised as well. Then, as we have seen, no times were to be published following public-road speed events.

These rules might irritate, but it was another that caused the explosion. From now on, all closed events would need an ACGBI permit and would have to be run under ACGBI rules. Otherwise, there was no guarantee that this new type of sprint would be safe for spectators and competitors, or run in an orderly and discreet fashion. The provincial clubs were furious. They held that the organisation of contests run exclusively for their own members was nobody's business but their own. The ACGBI compounded its offence in their eyes by its tactlessness, presenting them with a coldly-worded *fait accompli* rather than allowing discussion of the matter. Neither can the clubs have been mollified by the resurrection of a rule abandoned in 1901, by which all handicappers were to be appointed by the ACGBI.

The clubs forming the Motor Union met at Leeds on 23 June to debate the new dispensations, and the heat generated was such that the ACGBI gave in. It was agreed that the rules should be suspended until they could be revised. There was in fact no noticeable change in the *status quo*. In spite of its prestige, and the commonly-felt need of motorists to remain united, it is surprising that the club exercised the control it did. The evidence suggests that there were differences not only between provincial and ACGBI interests, but between trade, works and private concerns. No doubt, too, there were some in the club who thought that splitting the motor movement at a time when opposition to it was still strong, even growing, was a worse evil than risking an increase in that popular opposition.

However, six days before this happening, the Nottingham AC had been disporting itself at Welbeck. Touring cars competed in a handicap and a scratch event over the flying kilometre, but rain caused all concerned to seek a speedy end to the proceedings and so the two events were run together. E. M. C. Instone's 35 hp Daimler was fastest, at 62·2 mph, with other Daimlers occupying second, third, fourth and fifth places. Spectators were invited to guess the competitors' speeds, many of the results being wildly inaccurate. Instone's speed was estimated at 46 mph, for example. If, as was suggested, one object of the competition was to help discredit eye-witness accounts of speed given in courts of law, the result was disconcerting. Of fourteen guesses, only two exceeded the actual speeds, and those by very little. A policeman who suggested that a car travelling at an average speed of nearly 24 mph was doing 11 mph was clearly a little too clever for those seeking to trap him.

On 8 July, the South Wales and Monmouthshire AC held a hill-climb on Buttrill's Hill, Barry. This, the earliest recorded sprint for cars to be held in Wales, was a closed event but attracted a formidable forty-two entries. There were three contests run over the 500-yd course, one of them confined to amateurs, but G. S. Seccombe and his 12 hp Wolseley won them all. His fastest run was in 1m 22·4s.

The Hertfordshire AC's climb of Aston Clinton on 15 July was a handicap, but on speed Tom Thornycroft's 24 hp Thornycroft beat Oscar Thompson's 18 hp Siddeley by 2m 7·4s to 2m 55s. There were only seven other starters. Perhaps an over-filled season was the cause, as this was an open meeting, but the trade was probably saving its strength for the far bigger prizes to be won on the front at Brighton in four days' time.

The ACGBI who organised it, Brighton Corporation who backed it, and the motoring world in general all anticipated that the Brighton speed trials would be the most spectacular and successful sprint meeting ever held in Britain. It was certainly the most ambitious. Extending over no less than four days, from 19 July to 22 July, the event was expected to attract a record entry, including, it was hoped, numerous foreign celebrities. Like Blackpool, Brighton went to great trouble and expense to provide a fitting course. The Madeira Road was specially resurfaced with tarmacadam for the occasion. Estimates of the cost varied, but it was about £4,000. There was room for a standing mile and a flying kilometre. Unlike the present practice, competitors were started from the eastern, Black Rock end of the road. Three terraces, the lowest covered in, already provided a splendid vantage-point for spectators, and these gathered in their multitudes. The *Sussex Daily News* commented that: 'Nothing quite like these immense lines of spectators stretched along the Madeira Road and the Marine Parade has been seen in recent years in Brighton, and the effect resembled that of a great national holiday.'

The weather was splendid throughout, and the whole meeting was exceptionally well organised and controlled. As today, the many classes made provision for motor-cycles as well as cars. Touring-car classes were divided according to chassis price, but each class sensibly catered for a narrow price range. Some of the less important races in the complex programme were devoted to single makes: Daimler, Darracq, White steam, and, curiously, New Orleans cars. The last-named were full-sized tourers; they had grown up since the days when they were replicas of the buggy-like Belgian Vivinus. Real speed was provided for by classes for 1,000 kg, Gordon Bennett, and 'unlimited' racing cars.

In the first day's heats for touring cars over the standing mile, J. Kelle's 15 hp Darracq won the £400–£500 class, and G. H. Warne's 28 hp Daimler the £700–£800 category. The final of the 1,000-kg race saw a win for Clifford Earp's 90 hp Napier in 47·6s. Highlights of the second day were two more Daimler wins in the £600–£700 and £700–£800 classes, by a 28 hp car and Percy Martin's 30 hp, and victories for Louis Coatalen's 8/10 hp Humber, E. Lewis' 16/20 hp Rover and H. B. Nearne's 30 hp Darracq. In this day's 1,000-kg final, J. E. Hutton on the 120 hp Mercedes beat Earp, who made a false start, in 48·4s.

On the 21st, the meeting began to warm up with the contest over the flying kilometre for the *Daily Mail* Cup, open to Gordon Bennett-type cars. In the final Earp, with a time of 24·2s and a speed of 92·88 mph, took the British kilometre record while beating Algernon Lee-Guinness' 100 hp Darracq and Hutton in his colossal Mercedes. Their speeds were respectively 88·01 and 86·64 mph. It had been hoped that Baron de Forest, holder of the cup since the Phoenix Park speed trials of the 'Irish Fortnight', would be present to defend his title, but he stayed away. Two interesting machines which put up disappointing performances were a 20 hp four-wheel-drive Spyker, and C. S. Rolls' monstrous 150 hp Dufaux. If it was not fast, this odd-looking Swiss vehicle certainly gave the crowd its money's worth of 'uproar and fiery terror'. In the words of the *Daily News*: 'Mr Rolls' car struck terror into the crowd at the Aquarium end of the course. It had no bonnet, and came in snorting and roaring and belching flames and smoke in a style alarming to those who did not know that it really meant no harm.' The Ladies' Handicap was won by Mrs Herbert Lloyd on a 30 hp Daimler.

Although the fourth day brought some grumbles concerning the handicapping and the delays between runs, incidents were plentiful. In the first heat for *The Autocar* Cup, run over the flying kilometre and open to any type of car, Earp twisted his crankshaft. He finished on one cylinder at 72·52 mph, then found time, before the third heat began, to repair the crankshaft and also to fit wire wheels. The latter was no small operation in the days of 'non-detachable' wheels, but his efforts were unrewarded. Lee-Guinness won the final at 89·35 mph, defeating Hutton (86·64 mph) and J. T. C. Moore-Brabazon's 90 hp Mors. Miss Dorothy Levitt, attired in a tulle gown, was fourth in her 80 hp Napier, but went on to win a handicap sweepstake for Gordon Bennett cars over the standing mile, with a time of 57·8s. Lee-Guinness failed to finish.

Moore-Brabazon (later Lord Brabazon of Tara) said of his car: 'She was a brute to start. We had to put an enormous box spanner on the starting handle so that the two of us could get hold of it to wind. At the start of one of the races she backfired as we were winding and lifted us up and pushed us both very firmly into the crowd.'

The *Daily News* reporter described the effect of another of the Mors' backfires on some of the spectators: 'The report . . . sent out by the 90 hp Mors driven by Mr J. T. C. Moore-Brabazon simply made highly-strung people jump into the air.' This Brighton meeting was the first occasion on which Moore-Brabazon had driven in a sprint, though he had ridden as mechanic to C. S. Rolls on the same car in Irish speed events. He had acquired his machine by the simple expedient of calling upon M. Mors and asking if he could borrow it. He was then twenty, and he had never driven a racing car before. He was unlucky at Brighton in several respects. The Mors was suffering from an air-lock which caused the engine to cut out, and on another occasion it was 'left' on the starting-line. Moore-Brabazon was waiting at the start with C. S. Rolls' Dufaux. The flag fell and Rolls moved off without his rival being aware of the fact. The volume of smoke produced by the Dufaux's exhaust was such that the Mors was completely enveloped in fog, through which the starter eventually loomed to inform its driver that Rolls had departed. Moore-Brabazon's ears could tell him nothing of what was going on: the din was too great.

If spectators tired of watching the bellowing monsters, they could follow the more sedate perambulations of the four racing motor-boats—three Napiers and a FIAT—which cruised up and down parallel to the shore.

These were only the highlights of a long and comprehensive programme, which was unanimously voted to be an enormous success. Not only was a repetition planned; it was proposed that the speed trials become an annual fixture. However, as at Bexhill three years before and at Blackpool later in the current season, a triumphant success was the signal for an uprising of local opposition. At Brighton, it was to be more effective. Even before the event, there had been reports of threatened injunctions. Now a story circulated that Brighton, far from having made money from the trials, had lost: that while the ACGBI had taken all the profits, Brighton was left to cover all the expenses, a major item being the £4,000 spent in resurfacing the Madeira Road.

It was proposed that the corporation should borrow the money from the local government board, repaying it by means of a charge on the rates. One Mr Shoesmith, a ratepayer, obtained a court ruling to the effect that the expenditure had been unnecessary and illegal. The corporation could not, therefore, recoup it from the ratepayers, and individual councillors found themselves personally liable for paying the bill. They appealed against the decision, and in April 1907 obtained a reversal of it. The charge was finally put on the rates, so the councillors could breathe again, but it seems that the experience was sufficiently nasty to discourage proposals for a repetition until eighteen years had passed.

The Blackpool speed trials on 27–28 July were the ACGBI's third important sprint meeting of 1905. Organisers and backers were out to exploit the enthusiasm engendered among spectators by speed; an object deplored by *The Autocar*. There was only one event for lower-powered machinery: a handicap for touring cars on the second day. The two touring-car classes were limited to chassis costing up to £1,250 and £1,500, and these cars were allowed to run stripped. There was one class for racing cars: those of up to 1,000 kg. On the first day, the events over 1½ miles from a standing start were run off. In the final of the class for the 'cheapest' tourers A. Birtwhistle's 35 hp Daimler beat Percy Martin's similar car in 1m 20·2s, both of them being faster than a 50 hp Itala, a 70 hp Darracq and a 40 hp Mercedes, handled by well-known professionals.

Apart from having an L-head, these side-valve, chain-driven, four-cylinder Daimlers were always of ordinary, even (as time went on) obsolete design. They were heavy, and made no concessions at all, ever, to aerodynamic efficiency. Yet for at least four seasons, 1905–8, they regularly met and beat, under all sprint conditions, cars not only of theoretically superior design, but also of greater attributed horsepower, driven by men of equal reputation. To this writer's knowledge, no convincing explanations have been offered, then or since. Absence of real competition, or its defeat by bad luck, the reasons behind many superficially surprising successes, are not among them.

In the £1,500 class at Blackpool, the story was the same. Birtwhistle led Instone home, improving his time by 0·2s. The 1,000 kg race saw Clifford Earp's 90 hp Napier return an average time for three runs of 38s; a mean speed of 94·73 mph. Algernon Lee-Guinness in the 100 hp Darracq was next best with 40·6s (88·67 mph), followed by J. T. C. Moore-Brabazon's 90 hp Mors at 83·72 mph. The Mors was now running better, though still backfiring. Miss Dorothy Levitt's time of 52s—69·23 mph—in the 80 hp Napier was deservedly applauded. Comparatively slow it may have been, but this unwieldly projectile must have needed courage and skill to hold at a speed which must have exceeded 80 mph at the finish.

The flying kilometre handicap on the second day, though unexciting, produced a splendid result: Louis Coatalen's 8/10 hp Humber defeated the terrible Birtwhistle. Neither did Birtwhistle repeat his previous triumphs in the flying kilometre scratch events to which most of the day was devoted. In the £1,250 touring class, Percy Martin, with a time of 30·4s—a speed of something like 75 mph—beat Huntley Walker on the 70 hp Darracq, and in the £1,500 class Huntley Walker had his revenge, beating Martin in 29·2s. This Darracq was, in fact, a 1904 Gordon Bennett racing car carrying a tonneau body. Among the undisguised racing cars, Earp's time of 22·8s, bettering Lee-Guinness' 24s and Moore-Brabazon's 26s, so encouraged him that he made an attempt upon the world's kilometre record. In fact, the Napier just equalled it, at 21·4s or 104·46 mph. Earp claimed that he would have beaten the record but for a bend in the course near the Central Pier, and asked the corporation to straighten it out before the next meeting, so that he could have another try.

There was only one accident at Blackpool, when Harvey du Cros forgot to strap down the bonnet of his Panhard. It flew up and knocked him cold in mid-career. Luckily for him, his last subconscious reaction was to put the gear lever into neutral and apply the brakes.

Paradoxically, one of the facts to emerge most clearly from this tremendously successful contest was that a third was unlikely to take place. As at Bexhill and Brighton, local opposition, reflecting nation-wide hostility to motorists in general and 'speed merchants' in particular, began after the event to shout down those favourably disposed towards it.

This summer, an announcement appeared in *The Autocar* to the effect that, 'The committee of the Midland Automobile Club have chosen a hill at Court House, Shelsley Walsh, Worcestershire, for their hill-climbing competition on 12 August.'

The Midland AC had had an excellent and sporting hill in Sun Rising, but they could not go back there. Where could they find an equally good course on private ground, untrammelled by the public's right of way? Mr M. C. H. Taylor, a club member who happened to be the tenant of Court House, offered an extremely narrow, rough, steep and twisty 1,133 yd on his land which was seen to have splendid possibilities. The gradient was eased a bit, so that its average was a shade worse than 1-in-10 and its steepest part 1-in-6·26, in time for the club's first assault.

Part of *The Autocar*'s 'Club Doings' column was devoted to results. It was said that Mr H. C. Holder's cup for fastest time of the day was won by E. M. C. Instone's 35 hp Daimler in 1m 17·6s. Other Daimlers among the thirty-eight starters occupied the next three places, A. Birtwhistle's taking 1m 18·2s and Percy Martin's 1m 29s; while H. R. Pope's 50 hp Itala was fifth on speed. The President's cup was awarded to the best car on handicap (a 6 hp De Dion), the formula being based on time, horsepower and weight.

From the Worcestershire hills back to the east coast, where Britain's second sand race meeting, on the 19th, was a better augury of the future than the first. It was a modest affair of two events, held by the Lincolnshire AC not at Skegness, which was to be used by another club, but at Mablethorpe, where the sands were said to be hard, fine and dry. Both standing kilometre handicaps, one run on a distance allowance, and the other on a time allowance, were won by Captain Newsum's 30/40 hp Daimler.

In the end it was the Nottingham AC who went to Skegness, where on 2 September they ran nine sprints for touring cars and motor-cycles, rounded off by an 'appearance competition'. The sands were thought too soft to withstand the wear and tear of racing cars. Classes were by price. Although the meeting was accounted very successful and all ran smoothly, only one event was really interesting:

the mile scratch race for cars of any horsepower. In the final, F. A. Bolton's 30 hp Daimler beat J. C. Wilson's 28 hp by 22s. Huntley Walker's 70 hp Darracq was unfortunately off form. Other scratch races went to J. Keele's 15 hp Darracq, J. W. Adams' 8 hp Humber and Spencer Downing's 10 hp Alldays. No times were given, though on a beach this might be thought an unnecessary precaution. However, Cecil Edge, not, of course, competing, put in some demonstration runs on his 90 hp Napier, and was reckoned to be travelling at over 90 mph when extended. The course lay between the Vine hotel and Gibraltar Point.

An event which should have been more important took place on the 27th, when the contest for the Henry Edmunds Trophy was run off by the ACGBI at Blackdown Park, Fernhurst, the Sussex estate of Mr F. S. Philipson-Stow. This trophy was first competed for during the 'Irish Fortnight' of 1903, but there had been no repetition the following year, and it never, in fact, became an occasion of much significance. The course at Blackdown Park was an exceptionally nasty one, consisting of 1,650 yd with a section of 1-in-4·5 on a sharp bend. The whole was very wet and 'heavy' on the day. Regulations stated that cars must be in full touring trim, carrying four passengers, and that their chassis price must not exceed £1,000. One way and another, it was not a popular occasion, only four starters out of seven entrants actually appearing.

The Rev F. A. Potts' 30 hp Daimler did best, followed by a 24 hp Itala and a 24 hp Rochet-Schneider. No times or speeds were published, but this was not to say that excitement was lacking: the over-enthusiasm of the driver of Huntley Walker's 70 hp Darracq caused him to burst a tyre on a bend, skid and clout a tree, buckling a front wheel and dumb-iron.

The season ended as it had begun, with symptoms of indigestion. The Midland AC was to have held speed trials on 30 September, but cancelled them at the last moment. The Yorkshire AC's second hill-climb of the year (see appendix to this Part for the first) suffered the same fate, the reason given being public feeling against motorists. Nor was anything further heard of sand races planned for Lytham St Anne's in September.

At the same time, the season had been more than usually productive of ideas and projects for special racing circuits. A tarmacadam circuit with 4-mile straights and loops at each end ½ mile in radius was contemplated for Clacton, and a course in Windsor Park was also mooted. In spite of the well-known predilection of King Edward

VII for motor-cars, it is easy to imagine that this idea was sat upon firmly at an early stage. Most sensational of all, however, was a project for a 40-ft wide banked track with a lap distance of $1\frac{1}{4}$ miles to be built in Central London, within 3 miles of Piccadilly. The proposed location was not given. As usual, none of these ideas materialised.

* * *

In 1906 the pace became hotter than ever. The season began on 28 April when the Essex Motor Club and the South Hertfordshire Automobile Club ran a joint open hillclimb on Lippett's Hill, High Beech, in Epping Forest. In the car class, E. H. Richards' 16 hp JP won on handicap over the timed $\frac{1}{2}$ mile. A four-in-hand also competed, with unrecorded results.

A week later the Nottingham AC, or rather the representatives of the motor trade, gathered once more at Welbeck. The flying kilometre handicap resulted in a tie between Dr R. Hogarth on one of the new 12/16 hp Talbots and Spencer Downing's 10 hp Alldays. It was decided that the tie should be resolved in the form of a mile handicap race at the same club's forthcoming Skegness meeting. Dr Hogarth was soon to become a famous exponent of the Clement-Talbot in sprints, and this motor-car, as redesigned by C. R. Garrard, was an extraordinarily successful machine of which more will be heard. Though its season of fame was to be much shorter, the two-cylinder 10 hp Alldays also extracted a surprising degree of efficiency from a conventional specification. Most cars ran stripped in the scratch race over the flying kilometre. F. Coleman's 18 hp White steamer, at 61·08 mph, was narrowly pipped by E. W. Wells' 35/40 hp Daimler, which achieved 63·15 mph. A 22 hp Minerva recorded over 52 mph.

The Derby & District AC assembled again at Hill Cliff Lane on the 12th, to take part in a contest which was exciting both for competitors and spectators. Each car was given a preliminary run up the hill. It was then allotted a time handicap according to its performance, and paired with a close contender. Drivers were put on their honour not to 'pull'. Close finishes were the result in the heats. Cyril Smith's 8 hp Rover, with a start of 2m 36s, kept ahead of F. A. Bolton's pursuing 30/40 hp Daimler to win the final. A week later the Nottingham AC used the same excellent system of handicapping in their first climb at Oakamoor. This course was 3 miles east of Cheadle in Staffordshire. The timed distance of 1,460 yd lay between

E

The Star at Oakamoor and The Three Lowes, Weaver Hills. Like the same club's spring fixture at Kettleby the previous year, this was an invitation event: teams of four from each of four clubs participated. In the final, J. A. Doran of the Leicestershire AC in his 22 hp Minerva, with a time of 3m 24s, beat G. F. Reading's 10 hp Wolseley, which ascended in 4m 22s.

The first 'big' event of the year was the Herefordshire AC's open climb of Frome's Hill, held on 24 May. Touring cars of up to 35 hp were eligible, so long as they were not steamers, which were excluded. There was a fine entry of sixty-seven, of which fifty-eight were starters. A course of 1,289 yd, rising to 1 in 7, was used. In theory, cars were sent off one at a time, but the next was usually started while its predecessor was still on its way. This was far from being an easy climb, the surface being 'heavy' thanks to rain, but poor times were more often than not the drivers' fault. They struck reporters as being generally a ham-handed crew. Besetting faults were premature upward gear-changes, not excused by a false crest, and over-lubrication, betrayed by huge clouds of smoke. However, the two 10 hp Alldays competing were both remarkably good, and fast. A 30/40 hp Daimler made the best time, but an Alldays and a 12/16 hp Talbot tied for first place on formula. No times were published.

Although it had gained a parallel success at the Nottingham AC's Welbeck meeting, the Frome's climb was held to mark the true beginning of the new Talbot's remarkable competition career, being a more important event. It was said that by the time of the Blackpool speed trials in October, the Talbot had won all of the dozen or so events in which it had started in the previous six months. Nine of these wins are recorded here; others were gained abroad. Its 2·7-litre T-head engine, of unexciting specification, was capable of sustaining 1,500 rpm, a high figure for a four-cylinder engine, and produced a surprising amount of bhp per litre. This efficiency derived from a conventional side-valve engine of modest proportions; a fact which distinguishes the Garrard Talbot as the first of that splendid line of British sporting tourers of two to four-and-a-half litres' capacity which were to dominate the sprints of the 1908–14 epoch: Talbot, Vauxhall, Sunbeam, Crossley, Singer, Star, Calthorpe and Straker-Squire; together with W. O. Bentley's adaptation of the 12/15 hp DFP, a French design. Unlike the earlier Daimlers, all depended on efficiency for success in competition, to make up for moderate size and conventional design. It was claimed for the Talbot that it won 106 cups and medals during 1907. At this time wins were rewarded with gold and silver medals as well as trophies. A gold medal usually denoted a class win on time or handicap, but the value of the awards naturally depended on the wealth of the donor.

The Talbot was virtually unchallenged in its class for two years, its supremacy maintained by the growing emphasis on devising formulae which gave truer indications of all-round merit. It was now generally accepted that there were only three ingredients that were essential in determining overall efficiency: time, weight and power. *The Autocar*, in pointing this out while supporting an appeal made by S. F. Edge, showed that simple clubmen need only use a simple formula. The basic principles of the formulae now in use at most events were:

$$\frac{\text{time in seconds} \times \text{horse-power}}{\text{weight in pounds}}$$

The old bugbear remained: how was horsepower to be determined? There were many different theories, which fluctuated between extremes, resulting in wins for either the most or the least powerful cars. Both eventualities caused discontent, which, as always, received a vigorous airing, the sufferers' livelihoods and commercial reputations being at stake. In their disgust, some lost interest in sprints. The Talbot company, its products being both small and extremely fast, was usually very happy.

Other factories and their dealers were driven to desperate expedients in their efforts to reduce weight and increase actual (as opposed to advertised) horsepower. 'Touring' bodies were short, narrow, cramped and stark to a degree which must have made driving in them to the meeting a torture. Gear ratios were changed to suit the course. Exhaust cutouts were fitted and various adulterants, such as oxygen, acetylene, picric acid, paraffin and naphtha added to the petrol, so as to screw a little more power from an allegedly standard touring car. Engines were enlarged without alteration of the manufacturer's stated horsepower as given on the entry form. Darracqs were among the worst offenders: their standard 20 hp engine had dimensions of 112 × 120 mm. The 'Twenty' entered in sprints was a square engine of 130 × 130 mm. If, as in the Fromes Hill event, the bore had specifically to be declared, this particular practice was discouraged, but in the absence of a universally-accepted formula for determing it, there was no means of checking stated horsepower.

Another way in which competitors tried to win an 'edge' over their rivals was to indulge in furtive practising before the company assembled. Practising for events on public roads was discouraged by the clubs for obvious reasons, but the trade in particular would naturally try to gain every possible advantage.

This wholesale evasion of rules underlined the growing importance of sprints to the trade, as S. F. Edge and others pointed out when attacking such sharp practice. The sordid atmosphere of trade-dominated sprints disgusted Charles Jarrott: to him, all sprints had become trade demonstrations in pursuit of profitable publicity and sales, devoid of the influence of the sporting amateur. He demanded more rigorous rules, rigidly enforced.

If competitors were, for diverse reasons, feeling increasing irritation, the same applied to the public in some parts of the country. The police turned out in such force at the North Hertfordshire Automobile Club's meeting on 31 May at Gravel Hill, Hexton, that the participants felt disinclined to open their throttles. The day's sport was spoiled. E. J. Blain's 10 hp Hallamshire was best on formula. An appeal made this year by the ACGBI to the provincial clubs, asking them to refrain from publishing times set up during closed events held on public roads, may have had a certain effect. It is hard to judge how great this was, because we are not always told when times were given. Also, it is sometimes impossible to say if an event was open or closed, because one is not told. The quality of the entry is no certain guide: the representative of a manufacturer or his dealer had only to join a provincial club in order to be able to take part in its closed events, unless he was specifically excluded from them.

Kidd's Hill, otherwise known as Pipingford Hill, was first used on 9 June by the Kent AC. Its full address was Coleman Hatch, New Bridge Mill, near Hartfield, near Crowborough. The timed distance was a mile exactly, rising to 1-in-6. Classes were defined by price. A time differential was used to give an idea of relative performances, for no times or speeds were given. F. W. Baily's 50 hp Napier was fastest with zero time, better than Huntley Walker's 20 hp Darracq by 39·8s. The idea was not new, having been used at Welbeck in 1903, but its revival now was perhaps prompted by a repetition of the suggestion in *The Autocar*'s colums. Nobody took kindly to the total suppression of the details of their achievements, unless they were unsuccessful.

No such concessions as time differentials were made by the Scottish AC after its 1906 reliability trials, which began on the 13th and ended on the 16th. As usual, speed was very far from being the only yardstick, but this year we are told only that on Birkhill, the climb used in the Thousand Miles Trial of 1900, a 40 hp Benz was fastest overall, beating a 30 hp Daimler; and that on Cairnwell, Bridge of Avon and Trinafour (near Tummel Bridge, between Trinafour and Dalnacardoch), Daimlers had their revenge. In the next class down, what was described with fair honesty as a 'Special' 20/32 hp Darracq defeated its class-mates on speed on all four hills.

Much more exciting to the followers of sprints was the Midland AC's second visit to Shelsley Walsh on 16 June. Thanks to the organising club, it was not as 'exciting' as it might have been, for £50 had been spent in easing the angle of the first bend, so that it would be safer for the fastest cars. Even so, a thunderstorm soaked the course, causing Dorothy Levitt's 50 hp Napier to begin a slide which nearly carried it over the edge of the road and into the valley. Sensation of a different kind was provided in the open event by the performance of Frederick Coleman's 18 hp White steamer, which ascended in 80·6s. E. M. C. Instone's 35 hp Daimler could approach no nearer than 86·2s. Other Daimlers were third, fourth and fifth on time. Cecil Edge's 60 hp Napier, having only three speeds in its gearbox, and none of them very suitable for the course, was well down, being beaten even by Dorothy Levitt's 50 hp car, which, however, was lighter. Although the time of the fastest was a paralytic 205·6s, three 10 hp Alldays led the field on formula. They also won the closed event, in which Instone set up fastest time.

On the same day but far away, the North-Eastern Automobile Association held its first climb on Ragpath Side, 2½ miles from Lanchester. This was a closed event, though the organising club, like some others who were prepared to be ruled by the ACGBI, announced that the parent club's rules would apply. The timed distance was only ½ mile, but the gradient was shocking; 1-in-4·75 at its worst. The average rise was 1-in-11·3. Classification was governed by cubic capacity; the earliest recorded instance of this practice. There were classes for cars of up to two, three, four, five and six litres. Bad weather killed the event, and there were only fifteen starters. Of these, the fastest was G. S. Barwick's 30 hp Daimler, 17s better than a 40 hp FIAT in the same class. Other classes went to a 10 hp Alldays and two epicyclic Wilson-Pilchers. Although specially classified for the event as an eight-cylinder petrol car, an 8 hp Stanley steamer won on handicap.

It was decided to re-run the event on 7 July. On this occasion there were thirty-five entrants, but an almost equally disappointing turnout of starters. Barwick was again fastest, the Stanley being second,

13·4s slower. The organisers found some recompense for their efforts in the numbers of spectators: it was estimated that about 1,500 watched the climbs. They were shepherded by a strong force of police, who, as was usual in the midlands and north, were much more helpful and co-operative than their southern colleagues. The north, with its predominant manufacturing and commercial interests, had always been more sympathetic towards mechanical innovations and technical progress in general. This background dictated the views of local society.

Because it was an ACGBI event, held in conjunction with the Sussex County AC, no times or speeds were published after the South Harting climb on 23 June, except in the case of the last contest of the day. However, it was a considerably more satisfying event than that of 1905, there being eighty-four entries, of which sixty-four arrived on the starting-line. Classes were by chassis price for fully equipped and laden touring cars. In the class for cars costing over £850, which included the most powerful, Edward Manville's 35/45 hp Daimler was fastest, in spite of being baulked. Instone in a similar machine was second, after sliding and mowing down some markers. In a very skilful climb, Cecil Edge came third in his 60 hp Napier; still, presumably, with only three gears. A Daimler also won the £500–£850 class, Dorothy Levitt being second fastest in the 50 hp Napier. A Darracq took third place in this class, but in the next cheapest category they swept the board completely, annexing the first five places. The highlight of the meeting was a petrol-versus-steam match; Frederick Coleman's 18 hp White against Dorothy Levitt's Napier. Coleman won, by a mere 1·8s, incidentally setting up fastest time of the day, but Dorothy Levitt had the satisfaction of beating Manville's earlier time by 0·2s.

The Herts County AC held its third open climb of Aston Clinton on 30 June. An entry of forty-four was thought excellent. The contest was a handicap, but there was also a prize for fastest time, which went to E. M. C. Instone in the 35/45 hp Daimler. Coleman's White was baulked by both a haycart and some officials, so was only seventh on time. G. D. Powell's Daimler was 4·2s slower than Instone, and Dorothy Levitt on her 50 hp Napier third. Following a successful protest against the sketchiness of the bodywork on Tom Thornycroft's 14 hp car, the formula prize went to H. Ramoisy's 14/22 hp Germain; beautifully-made, and, like the Thornycroft, a fairly efficient motor, in this case from Belgium. A 10 hp Alldays could do no better than come second on formula.

Numerous other quite important events were held on the same day. The Bristol and Gloucester AC climbed 1,900 timed yards of Birdlip Hill, Cheltenham, with its steepest gradient of 1-in-5·5, throwing open their list to any residents of Gloucester. No times or speeds were published, but we are told that J. S. Davey's 30/40 hp Daimler was fastest, a similar car being second. Humbers cleaned up two of the cheaper price classes, a two-cylinder 10/12 hp Talbot disposing of the remaining one. A single incident was reported: when a competitor missed his gear, failed to drop his sprag in time, and 'jumped' it. Other contestants were delayed while officials swept up the pieces.

The local authorities concerned with the Ipswich and East Suffolk Automobile Club's closed climb at Lawford Hill, Manningtree, on the 30th not only tolerated the law-breakers; they repaired the road and watered the surface to make conditions as favourable as possible for them. Eighteen starters, divided into amateur and trade classes so as to give the former a chance of glory, climbed the timed 760 yd, which averaged 1-in-10. The fastest of any was R. S. Laxen's 20 hp Talbot. Dr Moseley's 6 hp De Dion was best on handicap irrespective of class.

On 14 July, the Yorkshire AC held the first of their speed trials on the sands at Saltburn. This meeting was also the first important sand sprint to be held in Britain. It owed much of its success to the efficiency of the organisation: the Yorkshire AC were determined to avoid a repetition of the Filey fiasco, and arranged for over a hundred police to patrol the course. So alarmed were they by the previous year's disaster that they had deliberately postponed the event from Whitsun, when, it was thought, the spectators would be too numerous. This year, too, the timed kilometre of sand in the two miles between Agar's Gap and Marske was beautifully firm and smooth. There were horsepower and price classes for touring cars, a special class for steamers (otherwise excluded from the meeting, unless they were racing machines), and a class for racers of up to 1,000 kg. All the events were closed with the exception of one for touring cars not exceeding £800 in price, and the racing class. Winners among the touring cars included Albert Farnell's 30 hp Daimler, successful in two races, E. W. Leather's 24 hp FIAT, T. H. Woollen's 10/12 hp and 12/16 hp works Talbots (each with one win), Warwick Wright's 30 hp Darracq, two 16 hp Humbers and a 16 hp Rover. The class for steamers attracted only a 15 hp Stanley. Cecil Edge was present with the 90 hp Napier, but being unable to produce more than 74 mph on this occasion, he was beaten easily in the racing class by Warwick

Wright's 100 hp Darracq. Its speed was 96·5 mph. No other speeds were published, which seems a little illogical, as they must have been much less spectacular than the Darracq's.

The Coventry Motor Club's assault upon Newnham Hill near Daventry on the 21 July was spoiled by the spectators, who were all over the road, baulking the drivers. This was an open event, for which cars of up to 30 hp were eligible. Thirty-seven of a splendid eighty-two entries were cars; the rest motor-cycles. Seventy-one of them started. Fastest car time was set up by F. P. Prestwich on a 30/40 hp Daimler, Albert Farnell's similar car being second. Third fastest was a make new to England; Isotta-Fraschini. This was H. O. Hall's 28 hp car. W. Byron's 22 hp Minerva won on formula. Misunderstanding of the principles of aerodynamics is no new thing: the 16 hp Maxwell 'appeared to be coming up without any passengers in the tonneau, but these were found to be sitting on the floor to reduce wind resistance.' This practice, noted by *The Autocar*, was a common one. The hill, 1,136 yd in length, had a gradient of no worse than 1-in-8·2, but a 16 hp touring car of 1906 burdened with four passengers can hardly have gathered enough speed at any point to justify such an uncomfortable manœuvre.

Also on 21 July, members of the Motor Union had gathered on the Marquis of Bath's estate at Longleat. To mark the occasion fittingly, the Somerset Automobile Club organised a speed trial in the grounds with four price classes. Although F. A. Bolton's 35 hp Daimler made fastest time of the day over the timed mile, Mrs Herbert Lloyd's 30/40 hp Daimler, driven by herself, won the two most expensive classes on formula, and was only 9·6s slower. She beat A. Rawlinson's 20/35 hp 'trade' Darracq, which was 18s slower than Bolton. A 10 hp Alldays won the cheapest class. So ended what was virtually the only important West Country sprint to be held in these years.

The next of the galaxy of celebrated 'firsts' which 1906 produced took place on 25 July, when the North-East Lancashire Automobile Club climbed Rivington Pike, in Lever Park, near Horwich. This was a private road on Sir W. Lever's estate, so times could safely be published. The distance was a kilometre, most of it 1-in-10. There were no fewer than ten price classes, compressed below a ceiling of £1,000, which seems a bit unnecessary as there were only twenty-seven starters. Of these, A. Birtwhistle's 35 hp Daimler was fastest, in 1m 7·6s, followed by J. E. Baxter's 40/50 hp Wolseley with a time of 1m 12s. F. Birtwhistle's 50 hp Mercedes, slower by 0·2s, ran him very close. The new 40 hp Crossley which Charles Jarrott sold returned

1m 43s. We are told that although the club used the normal component parts for its formula, they calculated the horsepower ingredient by their own private method, as was the common practice. The win on formula of George Burton's 28/36 hp Daimler was not, therefore, as surprising as it might have been.

This year's Skegness sand races, run by the Nottingham AC on 8 September, were a more ambitious affair. Unfortunately, the weather was wrong and the sands were loose and shingly, so that the racing-car classes had to be dropped in favour of demonstration runs at the highest safe speed. There were compensations, however. Apart from a motor-cycle race, five 1-mile scratch events for touring cars and a mile handicap, attractions included a race for sand yachts and an appearance competition. Also, cars were to be run in threes or more, not simply against the clock, thus giving the contests a more race-like quality. Among the winners of the mile scratch races for the different price classes were Victor Riley's 9 hp Riley, R. M. Wright's 10/12 hp Humber, F. Wilkinson's 20 hp Stanley steamer, which surprised nobody by beating T. H. Woollen's 12/16 hp Talbot, H. R. Pope's 24 hp Itala (subsequently disqualified), and E. M. C. Instone's 35 hp Daimler, which proved that it could beat a 50 hp Napier, that of Cecil Edge, even on the flat. The final of the mile handicap was won by M. Ross Browne's 22 hp Tourist Trophy Minerva. Victor Riley's two-cylinder car made its first public appearance at this meeting and its opening win was to be repeated many times over.

Exhibition runs were made by Edge's 90 hp Napier, the Maharajah of Tikari's 130 hp De Dietrich, no fewer than three colossal Darracqs of 80, 100 and 200 hp, driven by Algernon Lee-Guinness and Warwick Wright, and, on a minor key, a 20 hp Stanley. This demonstration by the monsters spawned by the 1,000-kg formula, which by 1906 had reached the ultimate stage of galloping elephantiasis, must have provided an awesome spectacle.

The Manchester MC's ascent of Snake Hill, on the Glossop–Ashopton road, was distinguished by the 'arrival' of two new names: J. Higginson and his La Buire (sometimes called De La Buire). Although the La Buire was soon to become obsolescent, relying as it did upon unlimited cubic capacity for performance, in the hands of Higginson and others it would stand up to the coming generation of much smaller, more efficient motor-cars for several years, in almost complete isolation: the last of the dinosaurs. Higginson's first La Buire was rated at a comparatively modest 30/50 hp, which was enough to give him fastest time of the day on this 8 September, and a win on handicap in his price class. Humbers and Rovers monopolised the cheaper classes. Steamers were excluded. The police were friendly and helpful, which was just as well on this occasion, for a Mr Zorilla, being baulked at the top of the hill by another car and lacking room in which to regain control of his 25 hp JP, ditched himself violently. The worst gradient on this hill was 1-in-8.

A week later the Leicestershire AC ran what they were pleased to call a closed event at Kettleby, to which were invited the Nottingham, Derbyshire, Northamptonshire, Midland, Coventry and Wolverhampton clubs. Still, they had the grace to concede that they would adhere to the ACGBI rules. Classification was by number of cylinders (one, two, and more than two) and also by horsepower (under and over 20 hp). Class winners included Victor Riley, and Phillip Graham's 16/20 hp Rover. In the latter category, T. H. Woollen's 12/16 hp Talbot was best on formula and second on time. Another 12/16 hp was second on formula and third on time. In the class which included the biggest machinery, nobody was surprised when four Daimlers, led by F. A. Bolton, made the best times. Here, J. A. Doran's 22 hp Minerva won on formula.

The Scottish AC might load competitors in its reliability trials with inhibitions on speed, but to do it justice, its hillclimbs were glorious blinds untrammelled by formula or handicap. One such was the earliest recorded ascent of Rest and Be Thankful (between Arrochar and Inverary) on 29 September, when there was not even a horsepower limit. Only steamers were excluded: inevitably, *their* competition was held to be unfair. The distance was about a mile, rising to 1-in-7. Broome White's 60 hp Mercedes set up fastest time, with 2m 19s, followed by Thomas Shaw in his 28/38 hp Ariel in 3m 1s. H. M. Napier took full advantage of the general lack of restriction by running his 20/32 hp Darracq on naphtha, but his ingenuity was not rewarded.

As already mentioned, the Blackpool speed trials, the ACGBI's main speed event of 1906, ran into difficulties which almost killed it before birth. No sooner had the corporation given its blessing to the promoters (the ACGBI and the Blackpool and Fylde & District Motor Club) than some ratepayers objected to the closing of the promenade. Strictly speaking, it was illegal to close this road, and when an injunction was applied for, the corporation withdrew its support. However, when the law refused an interim injunction, it was decided to allow this year's races to proceed.

The programme was long and complicated, but except in the

handicaps, fastest time alone counted. In some contests, touring cars had to carry a touring body and full complement of passengers, but in others, they could run stripped and without silencers so long as two passengers were carried. Special awards were also offered for the establishment of any new world's record. At the opposite pole to the racing cars were the motor-buses, for which there were two events. At least one bus, a FIAT, was driven up from London for the occasion, though it was not the fastest present; a 40 hp Darracq-Serpollet steamer defeated it.

Everything considered, the public were promised plenty of entertainment, and in spite of a torrent of rain and sleet on the first day (Friday, 12 October), it was estimated that 40,000 people packed the barriers six or eight deep along the course. Luckily, all ran smoothly.

In the standing mile events for tourers, some winners in the various price classes were H. G. Day's works 12/16 hp Talbot (41·6 mph), and Warwick Wright's 30 hp Darracq, winning an exciting race in which it, another Darracq and Tom Thornycroft's 30 hp vehicle all finished within the same second. A. Rawlinson's 40 hp Darracq went on to provide real sensation by beating first Instone's 35 hp Daimler at 57·7 mph in one class, and then, astonishingly, E. E. Wadcoat's 100 hp Mercedes in another, at 57·9 mph to a mere 52·3 mph. Only Gabriel was ready to let his car out in the teeth of a blinding hailstorm, so the standing kilometres for racers were postponed to the 13th.

On Saturday the sun came out, and so did the racing cars. The standing kilometre for the up to 650 kg class was won by Huntley Walker's 80 hp Darracq at 55·3 mph, and the 1,000 kg, four-cylinder class by Warwick Wright's 100 hp car of the same make. His speed was 63·9 mph. J. E. Hutton's 135 hp Mercedes was second. The sensation of the day was supplied by the class for cars of up to 1,000 kg in weight but otherwise unlimited, in which Algernon Lee-Guinness' eight-cylinder 200 hp Darracq at first tied with Cecil Edge's 90 hp six-cylinder Napier at 66·5 mph, but then, in spite of a strong adverse wind, went on to beat him at 69 mph. Lee-Guinness's time of 32·4s was a new world's record for the standing kilometre. Built specially for sprints in 1905, his car was propelled by two of the 100 hp 11-litre engines in V-formation, modified in respect of overhead exhaust as well as inlet valves. Six other racing-car contests that day were all triumphs for Darracq; the standing miles in the 650 kg, 1,000 kg four-cylinder and 1,000 kg unlimited classes (the last won by the 200 hp Darracq at 78·9 mph), and three flying kilometre contests. Huntley

Walker won the 650-kg kilometre event with the 80 hp car at 73·5 mph, Wright the 1,000 kg, four-cylinder event with the 100 hp at 86 mph, and Guinness the unlimited 1,000 kg race race with the 200 hp machine at 106·4 mph. In the last-named contest, Dorothy Levitt in her 90 hp Napier set up a British Ladies' Record for the flying kilometre, with a time of 24·6s, or 90·88 mph. She equalled Edge's best time with the same car at the same meeting.

Gabriel was again unlucky. His 120 hp De Dietrich was off form, and could do no better than two fourth places and two fifths. A standing mile handicap for any type of racing car up to 1,000 kg rounded off events for racers. A. E. George's 16/20 hp Tourist Trophy Argyll, given 40s by the 200 hp Darracq on scratch, won at 43·3 mph. The handicappers were A. V. Ebblewhite, later of Brooklands fame, and F. Straight. Ebblewhite, as handicapper and timekeeper, had become a familiar figure at sprints long before Brooklands was heard of.

In these days, racing cars were usually driven to meetings, but if the prospect was too uncomfortable or the distance too great, wealthy drivers might hire a train: a dining-car in front followed by a string of flatcars on which the racers were stowed. A party consisting of Algernon Lee-Guinness, S. F. Edge, and probably J. T. C. Moore-Brabazon, Warwick Wright, J. W. Stocks and the rest, journeyed thus to one of the Blackpool speed trials. Edge's intensive salesmanship and dedicated professional attitude was not much liked by the younger, carefree amateur sportsmen. On arriving at Blackpool, Edge found that his Napier had vanished. Someone, never positively identified, had bribed a railwayman to put it on the last truck and leave the coupling undone!

In the flying kilometres for touring cars, the supremacy of Darracq was almost as complete. Although in one class Daimlers, led by Albert Farnell at 67·3 mph, occupied all places between second and ninth, they were beaten by Rawlinson's 40 hp Darracq at 67·7 mph. A Darracq won the flying kilometre for unrestricted touring cars, defeating Huntley Walker who, for once, drove a 100 hp Mercedes, and may have wished he hadn't. In another touring class, the 18 hp Germains of H. Ramoisy and Servais were first and third, Ramoisy's speed being 43·8 mph. Daimlers were first and second in a standing mile handicap for tourers, but this was little comfort for their general lack of success at Blackpool.

Nor did Daimlers show in the results at the Crystal Palace Automobile Club's climb of Kidd's Hill on 20 October. Although it was this new, ambitious club's first attempt at organising a sprint, the event was open, and attracted a handsome entry. There were thirty-eight starters, no delays and some excitingly close finishes. H. G. Day's 12/16 hp Talbot, H. Ramoisy's 18 hp Germain, and C. Glentworth's 50 hp Napier all headed their classes on speed, Cecil Edge's 60 hp Napier coming second to Glentworth. In the class for Tourist Trophy cars, John S. Napier's 18 hp Arrol-Johnston was fastest, followed by A. McCormack's 20 hp Gladiator, only 0·4s behind, and J. D. Siddeley's 18 hp Siddeley. Winners on formula in these classes were Victor Riley's 9 hp Riley (Day coming second), E. H. Arnott's 24 hp Minerva, Edge's Napier, and the Gladiator.

The year 1906 had seen at least two abandonments: the Leicestershire AC's Bradgate Park speed trials, to have been held on 30 June, and the Lincolnshire AC's Mablethorpe sand races proposed for 21 July. As usual, the year did not pass without a brand-new, abortive plan for an artificial racing circuit. This time the track, 6⅞ miles long with loops at each end connected by a 3-mile straight, was to be built between Eastbourne and Pevensey. Its width was to be restricted to a rather exiguous 100 ft.

At long last, however, the planners and the visionaries were about to be satisfied, for a 2½-mile concrete dish was rapidly taking shape near Weybridge, in Surrey. Soon, racing men who did not want to cross the sea would no longer have to make do with sprints alone.

* * *

There being nearly a third as many events again in 1906 as in 1905, and every promise of a still more crowded season to come, the absence of a uniform, simple horsepower formula was felt more acutely than ever. No one had given a generally acceptable lead, to the fury of the trade, who were devoting so much time and effort to sprinting. Then, early in 1907, the ACGBI (or the Royal Automobile Club, as it became this year) at last filled the need. The club rating was based on the formula D^2N, when D was the bore (D for diameter of the cylinders) in inches and N the number of cylinders. Thus a four-cylinder car with a bore of 4 in would be rated at 64 hp. This horsepower formula was compulsory only in RAC events, but was thankfully accepted by clubs running other important contests. It was becoming fashionable at this period to encourage efficiency by limiting bore size, and a maximum D^2N quotient of 125 was common in British sprints. At the same time, the clubs made life more difficult for themselves by adopting another RAC invention, a handicapping formula devised by Colonel Holden which, unlike the horsepower formula, was too complicated for most clubmen to understand:

$$\frac{D^2 3\sqrt{S \times N}}{5}$$

It, too, penalised bore.

The horsepower formula was first used at the Frome's Hill climb run jointly by the RAC and Herefordshire AC on 3 May, where there were classes for cars whose D^2N was less than 35, 50, 65, and 125. Last year's climb had been so successful that it had been 'promoted' to the status of an RAC event. The 1907 climb promised even better things. Both competitors and the public turned up in unprecedented numbers: there were 110 entries, the most ever recorded for a hill-climb, and the cars brought by the vast crowd of spectators out-numbered those of the competitors by three to one. Such was the public interest expected that the recently-formed Automobile Association arranged for its bicycle scouts to patrol the whole road between London and the course. The *Ledbury Free Press* issued a series of eighteen picture postcards commemorating the occasion. With one reservation, everything went off splendidly: the surface was in fine condition, and *The Autocar* stated baldly that, 'We have never seen a competition so well managed.' The snag was that there was not enough room at the top for cars to pull up, and the road was exceptionally narrow. The crowds were thick on either side, and the police, of course, could only ask them to keep out of the cars' way.

While setting up absolute fastest time of the day, a two-cylinder Rex motor-cycle broke the leg of a labourer who, with many other spectators, persistently strayed into the road, but unlike the rest, had not jumped out of the way in time. A whip-round was made for the sufferer, and the money placed in the keeping of the vicar of his parish, presumably so that he should not rashly dissipate it upon strong liquors. This generosity did not succeed in averting a local outcry, which was to kill Frome's Hill as a sprint course.

The Rex was no less than 21·2s faster than the fastest car. Quickest in the various classes were Victor Riley's 9 hp Riley, H. G. Day's 12/16 hp Talbot, Oscar Cüpper's 24/28 hp 'trade' Metallurgique, a 40 hp Berliet, and H. C. Holder's 35 hp Daimler. A British Thomson-Houston petrol-electric bus taking part in the Berliet's class, presumably as a publicity stunt, was 8 minutes slower. The city of Hereford's trophy for the best overall performance of the day on formula went to Day's Talbot. Talbots also carried off the team prize.

In April, *The Autocar* had complained about the large number of such open hillclimbs, with their large entries. It suggested that they should be limited to half a dozen a year in the interests of everyone, and at the same time advocated as many closed sprints as possible, these to be confined to amateurs. (A closed event which the trade could take part in by joining the club concerned could easily assume all the characteristics of an open contest, without having the benefit of RAC supervision and control.) The resources of the trade and the patience of the public would not thereby be so strained. The appeal went unheeded, with the result we shall see.

For a change, the Nottingham AC's speed trials at Welbeck on 11 May were blessed with fine weather. F. A. Bolton was both fastest and best on formula in the closed flying kilometre handicap, his 35 hp Daimler covering the distance in 35s dead. In the scratch race for 'unlimited tourers', Cecil Edge's 80 hp Napier was fastest in 36·8s, but Daimlers were second, third and fourth. The 1-mile standing-start handicap was not only closed, but also restricted to private members of the club; a counter-measure against the practice growing in the trade of joining every club that ran an interesting closed sprint. The event might not even be important, but if it were not, the opposition would be less and a win easier to come by. The public did not always discriminate between significant and insignificant successes. The epithet 'pot-hunter' was applied thus early to members of the trade who pursued this policy, by Charles Jarrott. F. A. Bolton, who must by now have ceased to deal in cars, was again fastest, in 1m 17·4s, but this time Dr P. E. Tresidder's 15 hp Talbot won on handicap. Disappointment was caused by the non-appearance of a special 60 hp sprint Humber, with six cylinders and a round radiator.

The Crystal Palace AC, organisers of the highly-successful Kidd's Hill climb of 1906, now over-reached themselves. Their Bexhill speed trials on 20–21 May were an unalloyed disaster. The organisation was appallingly lax, the delays between runs so prolonged that the spectators left in droves, and the handicapping was attacked even more bitterly than was usual. Although cars ran three at a time, some of the racing was dull to watch. The tragedy was that the meeting had all the makings of a resounding success: 110 entries, the same as at Frome's, and immense public interest. The standing $\frac{1}{2}$-mile scratch race for touring cars of unlimited price, won by Cecil Edge's 80 hp Napier in 35·6s from H. C. Tryon's 60 hp Napier, was fair enough, as were the event for cars conforming to the Kaiserpreis race formula (in which Edge on the 60 hp Napier won from a 90 hp Junior and a

30/35 hp Simms-Welbeck in 41·6s) and (best of all) S. F. Edge's breaking of all the course records in the Napier he had used for his recent Brooklands twenty-four hour record run, at a speed of 73·77 mph.

However, neither the drivers nor the crowd could work up much enthusiasm for a very peculiar three-fold contest consisting of a ¼-mile sprint from a flying start, a 110-yd 'slow' race in top gear, and a ½-mile top-gear sprint from a standing start, all run consecutively. The 60 hp Napiers of Sidney Smith and Cecil Edge won this misplaced test of flexibility. What with one thing and another, the *Sussex Daily News* felt constrained to describe the first day's racing as 'the worst farce ever conducted in the name of a motor-car race meeting'.

The second day's programme appears to have been a little more interesting, if no less ill-run. In the final of the handicap event for cars conforming to the Herkomer Tour formula, a 15/30 hp Spyker won from a 30/40 hp Spyker in 43·4s. F. G. Cundy's 50 hp Napier beat Captain Owen's 40 hp Junior in the final of the scratch race for tourers costing less than £700, his time being 42·2s; while in a second event for Kaiserpreis-type cars, Cecil Edge's 80 hp Napier beat Sidney Smith's 60 hp car in 37·8s. Officially, this time was recorded by both cars; the finish was so close that only the length of a bonnet separated the two. The organisers' many shortcomings provoked a scarifying correspondence in the motoring press, but in spite of this they proposed to hold another Bexhill meeting on 5 August. Not surprisingly, lack of entries killed it. The dearth of entries from famous factories, if not from obscure ones, noticeable even in May, was probably a symptom of growing selectivity among major manufacturers and their agents.

While most events at this time were held at weekends, it is an indication of the strength of the trade interest in sprints, and of the amount of leisure time available to those amateurs able to afford to run and race cars, that this was by no means invariably the case. Especially as the calendar became more crowded, important meetings might often be held on weekdays.

The Leicestershire AC added the Lincolnshire AC to the list of invitations to their Kettleby climb on 22 June, thereby increasing the number of participating clubs to eight. This year there were delays between runs, so that the meeting was not accounted as successful as it might have been. Victor Riley's 9 hp car, Dr P. E. Tresidder's 15 hp Talbot and Arthur Ford's 30 hp Daimler were fastest in their classes, at 2m 4·6s, 1m 39s and 1m 19·6s respectively. Cecil Edge, in the un-

Page 85 *A famous car on a famous hill: Archie Frazer-Nash's GN* Kim II *at South Harting*

Page 86 (above) *A pre-war racing car at the Southsea speed trials, 1922: Barlow's 84 hp Benz in action;* (below) *Southsea speed trials: an evocative paddock view, with a Bugatti in the middle distance and a Talbot behind it to the right*

successful 60 hp Herkomer Tour Napier, set the best time of the day in 1m 7s. The Du Pré Challenge Cup was also contested at this meeting, being won by G. H. Wait's 8 hp Clyde. However, Edge was fastest in this competition, in 1m 9·8s; the runner-up on speed being E. W. Wells' 30 hp Daimler. The best formula performance of the day, taking both events into consideration, was made by Captain B. Byron's 24 hp Minerva, whose times were 1m 23s and 1m 22·8s.

Two other very important events were held on the same day; a fact which cannot have improved their entry figures. In spite of a heavy surface, virtually awash after a downpour, speeds at the Yorkshire AC's second Saltburn speed trials were excellent, as was the organisation. Touring cars were dispatched over the standing kilometre in fours, using starting-boards laid on the sand to counteract its softness. They still suffered from wheelspin, for the boards soon became wet and sandy, but at least the starting-line was not turned into a morass. Ten of the thirteen events were for touring cars, and the remainder for racing machinery. Of the touring events, five were divided according to maximum cylinder bore and four by chassis price, while the last was for steamers.

During the racing events, contested over a flying kilometre by Algernon Lee-Guinness on the 200 hp Darracq and Charles Jarrott's 120 hp De Dietrich, the former raised what had become known as the 'Yorkshire record' for sand racing to 111·84 mph. The winners of the horsepower classes were H. G. Day's 12/16 hp Talbot, beating a FIAT of identical rating, H. Pickles's 12/14 hp Singer, J. E. Hutton's 22 hp Berliet, Albert Farnell's 30 hp Daimler (at an excellent 46·02 mph), and Hutton's 80 hp Berliet, the speed of which (48·63 mph) was more than F. A. Bolton's 45 hp Daimler could produce. We find two 15 hp Model 'N' Fords in the cheapest price class, the faster setting a speed (30·98 mph) which was better by 1·16 mph than Day's in the Talbot. The Model 'T' was to become known as a car susceptible to tuning and possessing good acceleration, but its predecessor was no slouch, either. Other price classes were won by P. Graham's 16/20 hp Rover, Farnell again improving his speed to 46·21 mph, and A. Rawlinson, whose 40 hp Darracq, at 48·2 mph, was faster than Bolton.

The Southern Motor Club's open climb, planned for Kidd's Hill this day, was saved from disaster by the resourcefulness of the organisers. Competitors, including important trade entries in force, arrived to find the police out with stop-watches, following local residents' complaints over the use of the hill for sprints. After hasty discussions at the Dorset Arms in East Grinstead, all the cars trundled off in convoy to Toy's Hill, which lay near Edenbridge, 10 miles away over the Kentish border and out of the clutches of the Sussex constabulary. Toy's Hill was not ideal, being steep (up to 1-in-6) and at the same time carrying a lot of local traffic. It was therefore much cut up by carters' drags, and there were delays to allow cattle, wagons and motor vehicles to pass. In the class for Tourist Trophy cars, Oscar Cüpper's 24/28 hp Metallurgique was fastest, beating a 25 hp Arrol-Johnston. Winners on speed in the other classes were Sidney Smith's 60 hp Napier, a 45 hp Mors, an 18 hp Germain, a 12/16 hp Talbot and a 9 hp Sizaire-Naudin. Miss Hinds' 24 hp Deasy was the fastest of the ladies' cars, for which three smaller-horsepower classes had been organised. On handicap, the winners were Sizaire-Naudin, Talbot (two classes), Daimler (two classes), and Cüpper in the Tourist Trophy class.

To descend from the heroic to the nearly ridiculous, and to demonstrate the pitfalls awaiting the amateur club mathematician, it now becomes necessary to report that when the North Wales Automobile Club told its handicapper to prepare for its hillclimb on the Llanwrst–Llangerniew road, that gentleman arranged that the scratch car should leave the line twenty-three days after the first. The disadvantages of the formula were discovered in time, and an RAC handicapper hurriedly called in, so that when the event took place on the 24th it occupied no more than the usual few hours. Fastest time of the day was set up by Gordon Chapman's 30 hp Daimler. His time was 3m 3·8s, beating another, 35 hp Daimler. Mrs Parry's 12/16 hp Talbot was third fastest, in 4m 3·2s, and won on formula.

The hillclimb of the New Forest Automobile Club held on 28 June at Stoney Cross is no more important historically than the foregoing, but similarly, is worth a few lines here rather than in the appendix to the Part for its humorous content. The police were all set to time the runs, so the organisers shortened the course to begin in the middle of their timed distance. Exeunt police, to grinding of teeth. The class winners were a 24 hp La Buire, which also made fastest time of the day by 14·4s, beating a 20 hp Talbot, an 8 hp Rover, and a 10 hp Gladiator.

Bad weather made the hills in this year's Scottish reliability trials, held between 25 and 29 June, a good deal more difficult than previously and therefore more important to the results. On Rest and Be Thankful, a 10/12 hp Swift, 24 hp Mass, and 28/38 hp and 30 hp Ariels were fastest in their classes. For Cairn o'Mount, a 'new' hill between

Fettercairn and Banchory, we are told only that a 60 hp Berliet was fastest of any. At Trinafour, an 18 hp Mass, an 18/22 hp CCC (Chassis Construction Company, of Taunton), a 30/40 hp Ariel and a 35/45 hp Ariel put up the best performances, the last-named being fastest of all. No results for Loch na Craige were given, though it was the easiest of the hills.

On the 29th the Bristol & Gloucester AC again assailed Birdlip, on this occasion reducing the timed distance to a mile and fixing a new starting-point on a stretch of 1-in-14. This was done so as to discourage the furtive practisers, whose selfishness had already roused bitter feeling locally. We are told that the surface was specially treated with 'Dustabato', and that it did what it said it did in a satisfactory fashion. Otherwise, though, the meeting was poorly managed and occasioned protests. Classes were by price, fastest being A. W. Healey's 15 hp Ford, E. C. Skurray's 15/20 hp Rover, the 15/20 hp Talbot of Viscount Ingestre, son of the Earl of Shrewsbury and Talbot, and G. A. W. Young's 45 hp Daimler, which made best time of the day. Class awards on formula went to J. F. Buckingham's 9 hp Riley, C. J. Newey's De Dion, H. G. Day's 12/16 hp Talbot, and Oscar Cüpper's Metallaurgique. Lord Ingestre put up the best performance of any car on formula. In later years, Buckingham was responsible for designing his own, very fast racing cyclecar.

On 10 July the RAC and the Sussex County AC again combined to run the South Harting climb. Forty-three cars were entered for the open 'Yellow Trophy' contest, so called after the magazine which presented the award, *The Automotor Journal*, commonly known as 'The Yellow Cover'. Cecil Edge's 60 hp Napier was fastest. Second, but by only 0·4s, was A. E. Harrison's Ariel-Simplex, which rather surprisingly beat Frederick Coleman's 30 hp White steamer, 4s slower than Edge. Winners in the two closed climbs were H. Ramoisy's Germain, in 2m 15·8s, and Lindsay Scott's Lindsay, in 3m 36·6s. Coleman had some consolation in finishing first on handicap in the 'Yellow Trophy' contest, with 24 hp and 18 hp Talbots pressing him close.

Not even the redoubtable A. Birtwhistle could stave off defeat for Daimler at the hands of La Buire when the monsters met at the Manchester Automobile Club's closed climb on Werneth Low, near Hyde. J. Higginson's 80 hp car was fastest, followed by H. Hollingdrake's 35/50 hp of the same make, 9·8s slower. Birtwhistle's 35/45 hp Daimler was 13·4s behind Higginson. Hollingdrake, the British agent for La Buire, was soon to become well known as the other great exponent of the *marque*. This course was extremely sporting, stiffening to 1-in-4·5 and full of twists and turns. On 13 July it was also wet, so that few of the twenty-seven entries turned up.

For its first hillclimb, held on the same day, the North Yorkshire Automobile Club chose 1,605 timed yards of Garrowby Hill on the York–Driffield road. Daimlers, led by G. S. Barwick's 45 hp car with a time of 1m 32s, occupied four of the first five places, split up by O. B. Pease's 60 hp Itala, which was third in 2m 52·8s. Meanwhile the Ipswich & East Suffolk AC's speed trials were being run off on private land: that of Sudbourne Hall at Orford. It was a closed event, with separate classes for amateurs and members of the trade. In the flying miles, the appropriately-named D. Mustard won two classes in 9 hp and 12 hp Rileys, his best time being 1m 37·2s. C. R. Garrard's 15/20 hp Talbot (a very special works car) won its class in 1m 20·8s, Lindsay Scott his in a 15 hp Lindsay, Mawdsley Brooke his in a 30/35 hp Brooke (incidentally setting fastest time of the day in 1m 10s), and G. H. Woods, perhaps the future Crossley driver, his with a 30/35 hp Simms-Welbeck. Lindsay and Brooke were both Suffolk makes, hailing from Woodbridge and Lowestoft respectively. The latter, better known for powered boats, had been one of the pioneers of the six-cylinder engine.

In the standing mile and flying kilometre events, speeds were given in preference to times. The flying kilometre results do, in fact, give a good idea of the speeds of which small cars were already capable. C. D. Castell's two-cylinder 10/12 hp Talbot achieved 56·16 mph, D. Mustard's 9 hp Riley 48·6 mph, and the same gentleman's 12 hp car, again with only two cylinders, no less than 59·07 mph. Standing miles went to Castell's Talbot, Scott's Lindsay, E. Marriott's 15 hp Talbot, Garrard's 15/20 hp and Woods' Simms-Welbeck.

The fact that the Midland Automobile Club still clung to its own formula for determining horsepower did not affect the popularity of its climb at Shelsley Walsh; nor did the fact that it was held on the same day as the other events just described: 13 July. As in 1906, rain had fallen, so that the surface earned the epithet 'wicked'. Neither were competitors helped by the presence of spectators on the road in large numbers; but even so, times were greatly improved over the previous year. In the open event, J. E. Hutton's 80 hp Berliet ascended in 1m 7·2s, Cecil Edge's 60 hp Napier coming second in 1m 9·4s. Viscount Ingestre's 15/20 hp car maintained the Talbot tradition by beating a number of larger cars, including Sidney Smith's 40 hp Napier, by 1·2s. A 20 hp 'La Hispano-Suiza' entered by W. H.

Weekes was rather slow. This Hispano was one of the earlier, non-sporting models. T. W. Bowen's 10/12 hp Talbot won the open climb on handicap. In the closed event, H. C. Holder's 35 hp Daimler, with a time of 1m 19·2s, beat Harvey du Cros's 60 hp Mercedes, while W. Stokes's 20/24 hp Talbot was best on handicap.

In order to discourage pre-contest practising, a habit which vastly increased the likelihood, and the vehemence, of public protest, the Coventry MC refrained from divulging the location of its climb planned for 20 July until the actual day of the event. The result was that the inhabitants of several neighbourhoods, instead of only one, suffered from noise and dust, for entrants worked their way through all the likely courses in the area. As it turned out, the organisers made things easy for themselves by using Newnham again. Cecil Edge won his class and set up fastest time of the day in his 60 hp Napier, beating F. A. Bolton's 45 hp Daimler. Mrs E. W. Lewis's 1905 Tourist Trophy Rover made the best speed in her class, followed by J. F. Buckingham's 9 hp Riley.

The history of the Crystal Palace AC's climb, intended for Kidd's Hill, was as stormy as that of the same club's Bexhill meeting. It had originally been planned for 15 June, a mere week before the Southern MC's event at the same place, but upon earnest representations from the RAC, it was postponed to 27 July. Then, when Kidd's Hill was denied to the Southern MC, the Crystal Palace club, too, had to find another course. Star Hill, between Dunton Green and Knockholt Pounde, was chosen. As a final blow, it was discovered that the climb now clashed with the Hertfordshire AC's open event at Aston Clinton, which had itself been postponed to avoid coinciding with the opening meeting at Brooklands, so that the Star Hill entry was much below expectations. Club secretaries were indeed beginning to find life difficult. In the end, J. Goddard's 35 hp Daimler was fastest by 37·8s, followed by another Daimler and G. S. Monck's 35 hp Horch, the German make which had won the 1906 Herkomer Tour.

For its part, the Hertfordshire AC's Aston Clinton meeting was more successful than ever. There were no fewer than fifty-one starters out of sixty entries, the weather was fine and there were no hitches. Fastest in the various classes were J. Browning's 9 hp Riley, Tom Thornycroft's 14 hp Tourist Trophy Thornycroft, with Victor Riley only 5·8s behind with a 12 hp Riley, R. Verney's 35/45 hp single overhead-camshaft Maudslay, and Guy Lewis's 120 hp Mercedes. The last-named enjoyed an easy win, as may be imagined. A Daimler, Oscar Thompson's 35 hp, was best on formula in its class and the best performance on formula irrespective of class was made by C. J. Newey's 10 hp De Dion.

The Cardiff Motor Club found a fitting course on which to hold the first open hillclimb in Wales. It lay on the Mountain Road at Caerphilly, was 1,194 yd long, averaged 1-in-8·6 and rose to 1-in-6·2. Two motor-cycle classes were included, but this was mainly a car event. Sidney Smith's 60 hp Napier made fastest time, followed by Barker Thomas's 35 hp Daimler. Otherwise, 11 September witnessed a Talbot benefit. The class winners on handicap were C. J. Newey's 10 hp De Dion, H. G. Day's 12/16 hp Talbot (with Talbots in the next two places as well), C. R. Garrard's 15 hp Talbot, again followed by two more in *its* class, F. Blake's 15/20 hp Talbot, and E. W. Lewis's 35 hp Deasy. On speed, the winners in these classes were J. F. Buckingham's 9 hp Riley, a much more efficient machine than the staid De Dion, Day, Garrard, Blake and Smith.

So finished a season in which, on average, nearly three sprints were held every weekend, totalling more than twice as many as in 1904. All but eight of them were run on the public road. More public road hillclimbs (over sixty) were held this year than in any season past or, indeed, to come. The interdiction on Kidd's Hill, Birdlip and Frome's, and the abandonment of at least one other event (the Sussex County AC's closed climb planned for 24 August, being cancelled due to police hostility) were symptoms of—in the south at any rate—growing public discontent. Motorists in general were increasingly unpopular, because they were multiplying so fast. The 1903 Act was due for revision. Further restrictions were mooted, and motorists and their clubs were nervous for the future.* Quite apart from this, most of the trade agreed on one point: there were too many sprints, and too much competition of all kinds. The expense of taking part in every event of any importance, a policy deemed necessary to keep in the public eye, was now too great for the small manufacturer, and had become increasingly irksome for even the big factory. Those who could still participate, even the successful ones, doubted that their expenditure would be covered by sales, and naturally the smaller or less successful men, unwilling that the former should be left with all the limelight, encouraged this train of thought voci-

* They had reason to be. The Finance Act of 1909–10 introduced the taxation of cars, on a rating based on the RAC horse-power formula, and also imposed a tax on petrol. The owner of a 16 hp car was liable for £6 6s tax (equivalent to about £30 at today's valuation) per year. A small car of under 12 hp cost £3 3s a year, but as a sop to the motorist, the Chancellor of the Exchequer promised that all tax revenue would be devoted to road improvement.

ferously. The year 1907 saw a slump in the motor trade, and when expenses had to be cut, competitions were the first area to suffer. Such were the real reasons behind a firm's attack upon competitions, behind its covering smokescreen of letters to the press claiming that the public were not interested in abnormal performances made by special cars.

It is hard to assess the effect of the opening of Brooklands on the decline in sprints that was to come. We can guess that it had an erosive effect on entries in events to which the trade might otherwise have gone in large numbers, and that it might draw away the larger and faster cars which were less controllable on a sprint course. However, the first season of Brooklands had been short and not particularly auspicious. Also, there was only one Brooklands, tucked away in one corner of the country; and long-distance racing, if more spectacular, was still much more expensive than sprints.

Propelled by mounting public unrest and encouraged by the trade's declining interest in sprints, the RAC acted on 21 December. It placed a veto on all open competitions on the public road. Closed events did not need a permit, so could not be stopped, but the club made it clear that it would do nothing to support them. After all, a closed event with trade support could be as big an affair as an open one, and would be quite uncontrolled. *The Autocar* was in favour of the move. Speeds were no longer 'inoffensive', as they had been, by and large, in the early days. Much worse, it considered, was the fact that 'the feelings of whole neighbourhoods have been outraged again and again by . . . wild, indescribable, irresponsible practising', and that after many events, disappointed entrants foregathered at the hills to try and show assembled journalists what their car should have done, but didn't, on the day. The result had been intense local irritation, 'the wholesale stirring up' of local government bodies, and the posing of questions in Parliament. Motorphobia generally was as strong as ever, and the movement could not afford any more ill-feeling.

Some clubs, and especially the weaker ones, protested bitterly at the ban. These lived for, and might depend financially on, at least one open sprint every season, and suitable private courses were few. The *Automobile Club Journal* had reported in the spring that the RAC was searching for a private hill of its own for its own events, but nothing more was heard of this project. There was a widespread move to reject the RAC's decision and, indeed, to shake off the authority of the club altogether. This was at a time when a united front was more vital than ever to the motor movement.

The RAC had shown signs of breaking up since at least November. The Motor Union had grown enormously in size and influence since its early days, when it had been a mere department of the ACGBI to which the provincial clubs were affiliated. While the ACGBI had concerned itself mainly with technical developments and the control of motor sport, thereby attracting a minority interest, the Motor Union had been the proselytising body: the legal crusaders and the political missionaries of the movement, fighting for the ordinary motorist in courts of law up and down the land; fighting his battles in the chambers of local government as well, and working all the time for better relations between a neighbourhood and its local motorists. In other words, the Motor Union provided the ACGBI with most of its character as a nation-wide club, rather than as a centralised, London-based body of well-to-do professionals.

By 1904 the Motor Union had gained for itself a kind of autonomy within the club, but as it grew it became more and more impatient of ACGBI policy, which, as always, was to limit the number of motoring organisations to one, in the interests of monolithic unity in the face of the enemy, and to restrict and control all independent activity. The Motor Union also felt that the ACGBI did not truly represent British motorists in that it was a trade-dominated body which did not have the interests of the private provincial motorist or club at heart. By late 1907, the Motor Union's self-confidence had burgeoned, for its membership included nearly a hundred clubs and 20,000 individual members, while the RAC's own membership stood at 3,375. In the autumn, the Motor Union launched a heavy attack on the Automobile Association, a new but flourishing body which duplicated a good many of the former's services to motorists on the road and in the courts. The Motor Union, in fact, was as intolerant of rivals as the RAC, disliking the AA the more because it felt that the latter was tied closely to the RAC. But the AA had 6,000 members by early 1908, and there was also a clash between the MU and RAC over the provision of touring facilities.

However, it was the RAC, strangely enough in view of its opinions on unity, which created an open split when it unilaterally terminated its association with the MU in November. The RAC subsequently announced that the provincial clubs had the choice of affiliation to the MU in its new, independent role, or of affiliation directly with itself. The club offered the inducement of all the benefits and services provided by the Motor Union. It had deliberately created two similar bodies where one had existed before, and entered into direct competition with its creation for the loyalty of the provincial clubs.

As had happened in 1905, the new ruling on sprints had only to excite sufficiently violent opposition—in this case to cause clubs to threaten a transfer of allegiance to the Motor Union—to be modified out of existence. Open events on the public road were far fewer in 1908, notable losses being the RAC's own two 'babies', South Harting and the Henry Edmunds Trophy meeting, but they were held by the affiliated clubs, and with RAC permits. The RAC's face-saving formula said that, after all, such meetings might be held if the organisers had consulted and come to an agreement with the local authorities—which they always had done, anyway—and provided that the speed limit was not exceeded. Comment is superfluous. The falling-off in the number and size of speed events that was to come must, therefore, be attributed principally to the disillusionment of the trade and to the trade recession.

In 1910, the Motor Union, unable to survive in competition with the name and reputation of the RAC, became merged, as was logical, with the Automobile Association.

APPENDIX OF OTHER EVENTS

(ST = speed trial; all others hillclimbs; FTD = fastest time of the day)

1904

16 April — Oxford & District AC, Dashwood. 1st in car classes: Dr W. J. Turrell, 6 hp Eagle Runabout, 2m 10·4s; Biscoe, 11 hp Clément, 2m 47·2s.

14 May — Derby & District AC, Hazelwood Hill, Duffield-Belper. Max. 1-in-7. FTD: M. J. Astle, 12 hp De Dion. 1st on formula: M. J. Astle.

28 May — West Surrey AC, Hindhead. FTD: Wilson Noble, 18/28 hp Mercedes, 6m 9s.

29 May — Cambridge University AC, Offley Hill?. ½ mile. FTD: T. R. Brooks, 24 hp Georges-Richard, 1m 9·4s. 1st on handicap: 10 hp Panhard.

4 June — Reading AC, Sulham Hill. 600 yards, max. 1-in-6. FTD: A. H. East, 16 hp Argyll.

16 June — Lincolnshire AC, Bully Hill, Market Rasen–Grimsby. 935 yd, max 1-in-7. FTD: W. S. Foster, 24 hp Richard-Brasier (new name for Georges-Richard), 1m 35s. 2nd, 12 hp Panhard.

23 June — Nottingham AC, Rockingham Hill. FTD: E. H. Joule, 12 hp Darracq, 2m 25·2s. Part of reliability trial.

13 Aug — Kent AC, Detling Hill, Maidstone–Sittingbourne. Just under 1 mile, max 1-in-8. FTD: H. O. Hall, 15 hp Darracq, 2m 36·8s. Restricted to privately-owned cars driven by private members.

27 Aug — Stockton & District AC, Yearby Bank. 1,174 yd. FTD: A. Hall, 20 hp Waddington & Hall, 13·95 mph. 1st on efficiency: L. Ropner, 12 hp Napier.

Sept (early) — Lincolnshire AC, Thonock Hill, Gainsborough. 1,009 yd, max 1-in-8. FTD: C. W. Pennell, 16/22 hp Martini, 1m 36·6s. 1st on formula: 'A canopied Royal Humberette.'

17 Sept — South Shields AC, Hedley Wood Bank, near Weldon Bridge. 1¼

miles. 1st in car classes: F. Turvey, Darracq, 4m 12s; G. Rumford, 12 hp Darracq, 5m 2·5s; R. Rigbye, Humberette, 5m 1s.

17 Sept — Leicestershire AC, Kettleby. FTD: T. R. Brooks, 24 hp Richard-Brasier, 2m 26·4s. 2nd, E. G. Mawby, 15 hp Darracq.

24 Sept — Wolverhampton & District AC, Gatacre Hill, near Bridgnorth. 808 yd, max 1-in-8·5. 1st open handicap: J. B. Dumbell, 10 hp Turner-Miesse, 1m 12·2s. 2nd, 20 hp Wolseley. 1st club handicap: Charles Sangster, 20 hp Ariel, 1m 11·6s. 2nd, 20 hp Wolseley.

Sept — Dorset AC, Bridehead, near Dorchester. Hillclimb and ST combined. 1 mile. FTD (both events): J. Bennett-Stanford, 18 hp Peugeot. ST time: 1m 48s.

1 Oct — Yorkshire AC, Wentworth Woodhouse. ST. ½ mile. FTD: H. R. Kirk, 60 hp Mercedes, 57·5 mph. 2nd, Albert Farnell, 28 hp Daimler, 51 mph. Restricted to privately-owned cars driven by private members.

1905

15 April — West Surrey AC, Hindhead. FTD: Wilson Noble, 18/28 hp Mercedes, 6m 37·8s. 1st on handicap: Sir A. Conan Doyle, 10 hp Wolseley, 9m 56s.

4 May — Oxford & District AC, Dashwood. 1,180 yd. 1st in car classes: J. Collier, 8 hp Humber, 3m 0s; Hon R. Bethell, 15 hp Panhard, 1m 45s.

6 May — County of Durham AC, Hedley Wood Bank. 1st in classes: Young, 6 hp Wolseley, 5m 30·2 s; Lockey, 8 hp Humber, 4m 8·4s; Hunter, 12 hp Argyll, 4m 12·8s; A. E. George, 16/20 hp Argyll, 4m 0·6s.

13 May — Derby & District AC, Hill Cliff Lane. FTD: F. A. Bolton, 30 hp Daimler, 2m 21s.

25 May — North-East Lancashire AC, Buckrow Brow, near Settle. Closed. 1,010 yd. FTD: Huntley Walker, 70 hp Darracq, 1m 16·2s. 2nd FTD: F. Birtwhistle, 18/28 hp Mercedes, 1m 32·8s.

27 May — Yorkshire AC (Huddersfield branch), Honley, near Huddersfield. 1,260 yd. FTD: W. Blamires, 24 hp Richard-Brasier, 2m 8·2s.

27 May — Edinburgh MC, Soutra Hill, Edinburgh–Coldstream road. Closed. FTD: J. C. White, 12/16 hp Peugeot, 6m 13·4s.

27 May — Wolverhampton & District AC, Gatacre Hill. 1st open and club handicaps: Charles Sangster, Ariel, 1m 19·4s.

6 June — Cambridge University AC, Offley Hill. FTD: A. C. Riley, 28 hp Daimler.

8 June — Lincolnshire AC, Bully Hill. FTD: C. W. Pennell, 14 hp Martini, 1m 28s. 2nd, 24 hp Richard-Brasier.

17 June — Herefordshire AC, Frome's Hill. FTD: M. H. Orr-Ewing, 28/36 hp Daimler, 3m 3·4s. 2nd, 15 hp Darracq.

1 July — Sheffield & District AC, Grindleford Bridge. FTD: F. Churchill, 15 hp Hallamshire, 8m 33s. 2nd, F. Churchill, 12 hp Hallamshire.

1 July — Scottish AC, Cairnwell. FTD: G. Macmillan, 28 hp Mercedes. 1st on handicap: Hunter Crawford, 10 hp De Dion.

8 July — Nottingham AC, Kettleby. Closed. FTD: Charles Hardy, 35 hp Daimler.

8 July — Sussex County AC, East Dean Hill, Eastbourne. FTD: G. H. Warne, 28 hp Daimler, 3m 55s. 2nd, G. Baxendale, 24 hp Thornycroft. 1st on handicap: 12 hp Peugeot.

8 July — Blackheath AC, Moat Hill, Ightham. ⅓ mile. Closed. FTD. S. T. Graves, Darracq, 15·3 mph. 1st on handicap: T. Marshall, De Dion.

13 July — Sussex County AC, East Dean Hill. FTD: H. O. Hall, 15 hp Darracq, 4m 33·8s.

12 Aug	Derby & District AC, 'near Derby'. FTD: F. A. Bolton, 30 hp Daimler. 1st on formula: F. A. Bolton, 15 hp Ryknield.
August	Leicestershire AC, Neville Holt. FTD: Edward Kennard, 40 hp Napier, 55·6s. 1st on handicap: G. H. Wait, 7 hp Clyde, 2m 20s.
2 Sept	North-Eastern Automobile Association, Satley Hill, near Lanchester. 1,518 yd. 1st in car classes: A. E. George, 10/12 hp Argyll, 4m 18·4s; G. E. Hunter, 12/14 hp Argyll, 3m 5s; E. Leather, 30 hp Darracq, 2m 14·6s.
16 Sept	Southern MC, Tilburstowe. FTD: F. C. Pattison, 9 hp Clement, 2m 41·4s. 1st on formula: ditto.
16 Sept	Scottish AC, Kirkfield Bank. 822 yd. FTD: Hugh Kennedy, 15 hp Darracq, 16·7 mph. 2nd, 15 hp Darracq.
23 Sept	Sheffield & District AC, Grindleford Bridge. 1st in handicap: C. D. Leng, 16/24 hp FIAT, 7m 4s. Amateurs only.
23 Sept	Manchester MC, Snake Hill, Glossop-Ashopton. 3 miles, max 1-in-8. FTD: Huntley Walker, 60 hp Mercedes. 1st in classes: Huntley Walker, 15 hp Darracq; Huntley Walker, 40 hp Darracq.
23 Sept	Somerset AC, Puriton Hill, Bridgwater. ½ mile, max 1-in-11. 1st in classes: H. Beauchamp, 30 hp Daimler, 52s; H. Armitage, 12 hp Bridgwater.
7 Oct	North-East Lancashire AC, course between Clitheroe and Slaidburn. FTD: A. Birtwhistle, Daimler, 1m 6·8s.
1906	
28 April	Mid-Staffordshire AC, Milwich. 1st on formula: C. H. Riley, 18/22 hp Daimler.
5 May	Essex County AC, Laindon Two Church Hill, Billericay–Gravesend. Max 1-in-6·5. FTD: Captain J. R. B. Newman, 18 hp Mercedes.
12 May	West Surrey AC, Tunnel Hill, Foxhills, near Pirbright. 1 mile, av 1-in-25. 1st in classes: A. C. Tessier, 12 hp De Dion, 1m 42s; R. McCaskill, 28 hp Pipe, 1m 33s.
26 May	Yorkshire AC (Huddersfield branch), Mill Moor Road, Meltham. (Moved from Honley because of illness of old lady living adjacent.) 1 mile 48 yd, av 1-in-13. FTD: Albert Farnell, 30 hp Daimler. 1st on formula: 10 hp De Dion.
9 June	South Hertfordshire AC, Hand Post Hill, Northaw–Newgate Street. 533 yd, max 1-in-7·5. FTD: Mrs Price, 7 hp Star. 1st on handicap Mrs Price. Amateurs only.
16 June	Blackheath AC, Hixey Down, near Ightham. 1,377 yd, av 1-in-12. Closed. FTD: W. Whiteway, 14 hp Regal. 1st on formula: T. Marshall, 10 hp De Dion.
16 June	Sheffield & District AC, Grindleford Bridge. FTD: Albert Farnell, 30 hp Daimler, 3 m 28·4s. 1st on formula: Albert Farnell.
18 June	Dorset AC, Milton Abbey. Hillclimb and STs combined. ½ mile ST: 1st in classes: L. Champion, 7 hp Star; Rev P. H. Milne, 16 hp Prunel; H. F. Weld, 35 hp Daimler. ⅞ mile ST: 1st in classes: as above. ½ mile hillclimb: 1st in classes: R. F. Glyns, 12 hp Peugeot; H. F. Weld, 35 hp Daimler.
23 June	Derby & District AC (or Nottingham AC?), Hazelwood. FTD: F. A. Bolton, 30/40 hp Daimler, 1m 14·2s. 2nd, 30/40 hp Daimler. 1st on formula and Du Pré Cup: Dr R. G. Hogarth, 12/16 hp Talbot, 2m 28s.
30 June	Southern MC, Tilburstowe. Closed. One car class. FTD: 10/12 hp Humber. 1st on handicap: 8/11 hp Panhard.

30 June	Somerset AC, Puriton Hill, Bridgwater. 1st: O. H. Bayldon, 22 hp Minerva.
7 July	Wolverhampton & District AC, Harley Bank, Shrewsbury–Much Wenlock. 1¼ miles. FTD: Tamagui, 20/24 hp Marchand. 1st open and club handicaps: G. H. Evans, 25/30 hp Austin.
12 July	Lincolnshire AC, Cawkswell Hill, between Horncastle and Louth. 966 yd, max 1-in-6. Handicap. FTD: Col J. S. Ruston, 30/40 hp Daimler, 1m 35s. Unofficial FTD: 16/20 hp Humber, 1m 26s.
14 July (about)	Edinburgh MC, Soutra Hill. 1st on formula: J. F. Duthie, 10/12 hp Whitlock-Aster.
14 July	ACGBI, Henry Edmunds Trophy, Blackdown Park. 1st, G. S. Barwick, 30 hp Daimler. 2nd, 30 hp Daimler, Rev F. A. Potts..
28 July	Derby & District AC, Hazelwood. Closed. 1st on formula: F. A. Bolton, 35 hp Daimler. 2nd, Daimler.
1 Aug	Northamptonshire AC, Castle Ashby. ST. 1 km. FTD: Lord Northampton, 40 hp Mercedes.
17 Aug	Nottingham AC, Hazelwood. FTD: Cecil Edge, 90 hp Napier, 1m 0·2s. 2nd, F. A. Bolton, Daimler. 1st touring car handicap, F. A. Bolton, Daimler, 1m 12·4s.
18 Aug	Lincolnshire AC, Syston Park. Closed. 660 yd, max. 1-in-7. FTD: Capt H. E. Newsum, 35 hp Daimler, 40s.
1 Sept	West Surrey AC, Blackdown Park. Closed. FTD: F. Houghton, 14 hp Renault, 4m 28·8s. Disqualified for improving on time set in handicapping run by more than 10 per cent.
15 Sept	Bury & West Suffolk AC, Woolpit Hill and Brookbridge Hill, near Rattlesden. 'Impromptu'. FTD on both: Dr Wood, 10 hp Darracq.
22 Sept	Mid-Staffordshire AC, Oakamoor. FTD: F. A. Bolton, Daimler, 1m 45·8s. 2nd, G. Brindley, 12/16 hp Talbot. 1st on formula: F. A. Bolton. Amateurs only.
29 Sept	Hertfordshire County AC, Durrant's Hill, between Boxmoor and Leverstock Green. Open to North and South Herts ACs. One car class. FTD: R. S. Grigg, 35 hp Daimler, accompanied by 'weird screeching of an electric siren' (*Automobile Club Journal*). 1st on formula: G. H. Gray, 6 hp Rover.
6 Oct	North Hertfordshire AC, Pegsdon Hill, near Hitchin. FTD: R. Selz, 18 hp Vauxhall, 100s. 1st on formula: Dr Day, 6 hp Rover.
6 Oct	Essex County AC, Bottledown Hill, Little Burstead–Billericay. Closed. FTD: E. A. Ferre, 24/40 hp FIAT. 1st on handicap: Rev E. T. Maw, 8/11 hp Panhard.

1907

4 May	West Surrey AC, Tunnel Hill, Foxhills, near Pirbright. 1st in classes: R. M. Wright, 28 hp Daimler, 2m 44·4s; G. H. Gill, 10 hp Victoria, 3m 46·8s. The Victoria was made in Godalming.
11 May	Yorkshire AC (Huddersfield branch), Mill Moor Road, Meltham. FTD: D. Stoner Crowther, 40 hp Napier.
11 May	Essex MC, Lippett's Hill, High Beech. Closed. FTD: E. H. Richards, 18/24 hp J.P. 1st on handicap: E. H. Richards.
18 May	New Forest AC and Hampshire branch Motor Union, Hill Top, Beaulieu. 1st in classes: Lord Montagu, 45 hp Daimler, 59·4s; Lord Montagu, 20 hp Rolls-Royce, 1m 21·6s.
19 May	Cardiff MC, Rhubina Hill. FTD: T. Gibbons-Brooks, 20/28 hp Darracq. 1st on formula: ditto.

23–5 May	Manchester MC, Sun Rising. FTD: 35/50 hp La Buire. Part of reliability trial.
25 May	South Devon AC, Moorshop Hill, Tavistock–Two Bridges. 1 mile + av 1-in-12. 1st on time in classes: Dr A. P. Drummond, 9 hp Sizaire-Naudin; Dr W. C. Hamilton, 10 hp Alldays; T. R. Perkin, 12/16 hp Talbot; Major A. L. Gallie, 30 hp Daimler. 1st on formula in classes: ditto.
25 May	Nottingham AC, Oakamoor. FTD: Charles Hardy, 45 hp Daimler, 1m 20s. 1st in final: J. M. Smedley, 24 hp De Dietrich, 2m 16s. 2nd, Dr R. G. Hogarth, 12/16 hp Talbot.
1 June	Motor Cycling Club, Sharpenhoe Hill, near Barton-in-the-Clay. FTD: S. F. Edge, 80 hp Napier. 1st on formula: P. Graham, 24 hp Deasy.
1 June	North Hertfordshire AC, Gravel Hill, Hexton. FTD: G. H. Hodgson, 30 hp Hodgson, 1m 47·6s, beat 15 hp White steamer, 2m 55·4s.
1 June	Welsh AC, Llangennech. 1,000 yd. Closed. Two events. 1st in both: Capt D. Hughes-Morgan, 28 hp Daimler. He donated cup, so latter went to: 10/12 hp Argyll.
5 June	Cambridge University AC, Sharpenhoe Hill. FTD: A. C. Riley, 28 hp Daimler.
8 June	RAC, Henry Edmunds Trophy, Carter's Hill, Underriver, Kent. FTD: G. S. Barwick, 30 hp Daimler, 1m 18·2s. 2nd, J. E. Hutton, 40 hp Berliet. Carter's Hill Cup: Oscar Cüpper, 24/28 hp Metallurgique, 1m 24·8s. 2nd, Ramoisy, 18 hp Germain.
8 June	Essex County AC, Laindon. FTD: Cecil Edge, 60 hp Napier. 2nd, J. Mason, 40 hp Darracq. 1st in handicap classes: Barnett Tabrum, 14 hp Argyll; J. Gurney Fowler, 35 hp Renault.
8 June	Derby & District AC, Hazelwood. FTD: Arthur Ford, 30 hp Daimler. 1st on handicap: 10/12 hp Humber.
8 June	Blackheath AC, Hixey Down. FTD: W. F. Burcher, 12/16 hp Talbot. 1st on formula: ditto.
8 June	Mid-Staffordshire AC, Weston Bank, Uttoxeter–Stafford. ½ mile. FTD: F. A. Bolton, 40 hp Daimler, 48·2s. 1st on formula: G. F. Brindley, 12/16 hp Talbot.
15 June	Derby & District AC, Uttoxeter, Marchington–Uttoxeter. FTD: F. A. Bolton, 45 hp Daimler, 50s. 2nd, Arthur Ford, Daimler, 59s.
15 June	NE Automobile Association, Ragpath Side. FTD: W. E. Galloway, 15/20 hp Stanley, 1m 15·6s. 2nd, S. F. Edge, 60 hp Napier.
15 June	Wolverhampton & District AC, Harley Bank. FTD: Charles Sangster, 35 hp Ariel-Simplex. 1st open handicap: C. J. Newey, 8 hp De Dion. 1st club handicap: Charles Sangster.
15 June	Ipswich & East Suffolk AC, Lawford Hill. FTD: Mawdsley Brooke, Brooke, 42·2s. Best amateur: J. Gordon Stewart, 15 hp Talbot, 50s. Best trade: E. Marriott, Talbot, 47·4s.
15 June	Sheffield & District AC, Grindleford Bridge. 1st in classes: Albert Farnell, 30 hp Daimler (FTD); J. F. Gregory, 24 hp FIAT; H. Beesley, 6 hp Wolsley.
20 June	Lincolnshire AC, Tetford, near Horncastle. FTD: Captain H. E. Newsum, 35/45 hp Daimler, 1m 13s. 1st on handicap overall: Dr R. G. Hogarth, 12/16 hp Talbot, 1m 59s. 1st in classes: Dr R. G. Hogarth; Sir Hickman Bacon, 6 hp Wolseley.
29 June	South Wales & Mon. AC, Buttrill's Hill, Barry. Closed. 1st in classes: W. Parker Thomas, 35 hp Daimler (two classes); Henry Webb, 40 hp Itala.

4 July	Somerset AC, Buncombe Hill. 747 yd, av 1-in-8. 1st on time in classes: C. P. Parker, 24/40 hp Weigel, 1m 0·6s; J. W. Aspinall, 16/20 hp Rover, 1m 31·4s. 1st on formula in classes: ditto.
4 July	Barnsley & District AC, Stainborough Lowe. 1,100 yd, max 1-in-6·5. FTD: W. H. Hanson, 20 hp Horbick, 2m 53·6s.
13 July	Yorkshire AC, Birk Brow. FTD: Stanley steamer .
13 July	Lincolnshire AC, Grimsthorpe Park. ST. 1 mile. FTD: Charles Hardy, Daimler, 1m 13·4s. 1st in handicap overall. Dr R. G. Hogarth, 12/16 hp Talbot, 1m 48·6s. 1st in class: Dr R. G. Hogarth.
14 July	Southend & District AC, Laindon. FTD: Perry, 15 hp Ford.
18 July	Naval MC, Hyden Hill, East Meon. 1st on formula: Lt Bruce, 15 hp Humber.
19 July	NE Lancashire AC, Rivington Pike. FTD: S. F. Edge, 60 hp Napier, 58·4s. 2nd, F. Birtwhistle, 60 hp Mercedes, 1m 6·6s.
20 July	Berkshire AC, Red House Hill, Wantage. Standing start. FTD: G. S. Monck, 35 hp Horch. Flying start: FTD: ditto. 1st in other classes: Dr W. B. Secretan, 9 hp Riley; Dr A. G. Paterson, 15 hp Mass.
20 July	Oxford & District AC, Irondown Hill, Deddington–Chipping Norton road. ½ mile. FTD: 9 hp Adams-Hewitt, 1m 40s. 1st on formula: J. W. Coxeter, 9/10 hp Swift.
20 July	Edinburgh MC, Firth House, Penicuik. Private ground. 605 yd, max 1-in-6. FTD: W. L. Sleigh, Berliet, 1m 8s.
27 July	Essex County AC, Bottledown. FTD: J. Gurney Fowler, 35 hp Renault. 1st on handicap: Sir Charles Locock, 16 hp FIAT.
17 Aug	Lincolnshire AC, Syston Park. 1,240 yd. FTD: Captain H. E. Newsum, 45 hp Daimler, 1m 6s. 2nd, Daimler. 1st in class: Dr R. G. Hogarth, 15 hp Talbot.
17 Aug	Harrogate & District AC, Briscoe Rigg, Stainburn.
17 Aug	One car class. FTD: G. S. Sayner, 14/16 hp Argyll.
24 Aug	Yorkshire AC, Greenhow Hill, Pateley Bridge–Grassington. 2,000 yd. FTD: Sidney Smith, 60 hp Napier. 2nd, F. A. Bolton, Daimler. 1st in class: T. H. Woollen. 15 hp Talbot.
24 Aug	Northamptonshire AC, Newnham. ¾ mile. FTD: H. Greening, 24 hp Minerva, 1m 22s. 1st on formula: H. Greening.
31 Aug	North Berkshire AC, Duxford Hill. 1st on formula: Mrs Viner Ellis, 12 hp Peugeot.
7 Sept	Hertfordshire County AC, Aston Clinton. Closed. FTD: E. Edwards, 24 hp Minerva, 1m 52·8s. 1st on handicap overall: Victor Riley, 12 hp Riley. 1st in classes: Riley; Tom Thornycroft, 14 hp Thornycroft.
14 Sept	Harrogate & District AC, Ripley. Amateurs only. 1st in classes: Scott, 6 hp De Dion; Peacock, 16/20 hp Mass.
21 Sept	Nottingham AC, Hazelwood. FTD: F. A. Bolton, 45 hp Daimler, 1m 12·4s. 1st in classes: P. Graham, 24 hp Deasy; Victor Riley, 12 hp Riley; P. L. Huskisson, 30 hp Daimler; Dr R. G. Hogarth, 12/16 hp Talbot. 1st overall on handicap: Dr R. G. Hogarth.
28 Sept	Southern MC, Tilburstowe. Closed. FTD: F. C. Goddard, 35 hp Daimler.
28 Sept	North Hertfordshire AC, Poynder's End Hill, near Hitchin. 1st in classes: Arthur Brown, 60 hp Napier; Dr J. H. Gilbertson, 7 hp Star. 1st on formula: Arthur Brown, 60 hp Napier.
28 Sept	Manchester MC, Bill o'Jack's, near Greenfield. 1st in classes: Sidney Smith, 60 hp Napier; W. Stone, Clément; R. Crossley, Belsize; R. H. Carlisle, Argyll; 6 hp Rover.

26 Oct Scottish AC, Fintry. FTD: J. Murray, 40 hp SPA. 2nd, J. H. Paterson, 30 hp Peugeot.

2 Nov Crystal Palace AC, Titsey Hill, Limpsfield–Warlingham. FTD: Cecil Edge, 60 hp Napier. 1st on formula: 10 hp De Dion.

PART FOUR

1908-1914: The Flight of Ignorance

If the pronouncements and prejudices of the RAC, the trade and the public were anything to go by, 1908 was to mark the virtual end of sprint motoring. In fact, it ushered in a new and technically more progressive era, even if the more important and better-known meetings suffered a period of decline in terms of numbers.

The Herefordshire AC was the first club to feel the result of the opposition to sprints which had just reached a peak. Their open meeting at Frome's Hill, planned for 15 May, was abandoned when the local RDC, alarmed by the previous year's accident, forbade them the course. The club then tried to obtain the use of Cockshut Hill, near Ledbury, but nothing came of this, and when at last they persuaded the local authorities at Frome's to allow them a climb on 11 July, so long as only small cars competed, the trade killed their prospects by witholding entries.

The Bristol and Gloucester AC's plans were similarly defeated. Forbidden to use Birdlip, they found a new hill whose whereabouts was only to be divulged a few days before the event, planned for 20 June, but nothing more was heard of it.

But the Two Thousand Miles Trial, held between 11 and 27 June, was an attempt by the RAC and the SMMT, its organisers, to meet the trade's desire for a greatly restricted and cheaper competition season, while still encouraging the improvement of the breed through sport and providing Britain with a competition of international status and appeal. Reliability, fuel consumption, brake efficiency, hill-climbing ability and all-out speed were to be tested in the 'One Big Trial', which was to concentrate within itself, in quantity as well as quality, all the features of a year's competition. The year's Scottish Trial course was to be included in it, the former event having

Page 103 (above) *Braidwood's GN at Syston Park;* (below) *The hazards of sand racing: a Three-Litre Bentley approaches a pylon at Porthcawl, 1922*

Page 104 *Porthcawl sands, 1922: Raymond Mays' Bugatti is followed by an Enfield–Allday*

slightly different regulations. Cars could compete in either or both. The Two Thousand Miles Trial was not only of unprecedented length, but also included no fewer than eleven timed hillclimbs and a 200-mile race at Brooklands to conclude the proceedings.

The hills timed were Cairnwell, Cairn o' Mount, Trinafour, Rest and Be Thankful (Glencroe), and Fintry—all in Scotland—and Dunmail Raise, Kirkstone Pass (between Windermere and Ullswater), Shap, Alston (near Penrith), Harley Bank (on Wenlock Edge and used for the preceding two seasons by the Wolverhampton Club) and Fish Hill, Broadway, in England. The feature of the event was the emphasis on time, and therefore speed. Not only involuntary stops, lateness and hillclimbs, but also petrol consumption, were translated into terms of time lost. The sporting bias was thus very strong.

The regulations were draconian, compared with those usually applied; and they were rigidly enforced. All spare parts and tools had to be carried on the cars, no outside assistance could be invoked, and axle ratios could not be altered during the event. Other regulations governed minimum frontal area, weight and distance between scuttle and rear axle, so that only cars with more or less bona fide touring bodies could take part. Classification was by RAC rating, ie, engine bore size. Because of the emphasis on time, the nature of the regulations, and the duration and severity of the event, the Two Thousand Miles Trial was a very tough proposition indeed.

In the cases of manufacturers who tackled the trial seriously and scientifically, these factors also produced some advanced motorcars, which with the precocious and until now lonely Talbot, marked the beginning of the dominance of comparatively small, efficient, conventional engines in British motor sport. The days of the powerful but wasteful Daimler and Napier were numbered. The problem in the trial was how to produce the best compromise; to deal with the conflicting demands presented by the rules and the course more skilfully than one's competitors.

The Talbots were familiar contenders, and as formidable as ever. Now with engines that could sustain 2,000 rpm instead of the 1,500 rpm of 1906, the Talbot had been considerably developed, but Tom Thornycroft's production was well known enough to be feared, too. There were two dark horses among the cars, later to be famous for efficiency; the 12/14 hp Singer, and the 20 hp Vauxhall. Produced by Laurence Pomeroy, Sr, specifically for this event, the Vauxhall would hold 2,500 rpm, a phenomenal speed then for a four-cylinder engine, and developed 38 bhp from its 3 litres at a period when two-thirds of this output would have been reasonable. At a time when a long stroke was fashionable for high-efficiency engines, owing to limitations on bore, Pomeroy believed in a moderate bore-stroke ratio (91 × 120·6 mm) and achieved his power output by efficient gas-flow and lightness of the reciprocating parts. A pressure-fed crankshaft accommodated the engine's high speed, and carefully-chosen gear ratios allowed the best advantage to be made of the power. Percy Kidner, then co-managing director of Vauxhall Motors, told the author that Ricardo had a hand in the design, and this was one of the very earliest engines with which he was involved.

The Vauxhall, in losing a total of 77 'minutes' 22·4 'seconds', amassed fewer penalties than any of the other forty-six starters. In its class, it was fastest overall on the hills, with six wins, leading 15 hp Talbot, 20 hp Daimler, and 18 hp Benz: none of them sluggards, although the Benz eventually broke its crankshaft and retired. The publicity attending the trial made its triumph the more famous.

The Singer won its class on general efficiency, and on speed on the hills. Before it crashed on Kirkstone Pass, the seventh timed hill-climb, the 18 hp Thornycroft had set second best time to the 25 hp Talbot in its class up five of the hills, and beat the Talbot on Glencroe. Although running with bad damage after its accident, it was second only to the Talbot on Harley Bank and Fish Hill, but the Talbot won this class, despite breaking a front spring on Shap, and was very easily fastest overall on the hills. Here its smaller, 15 hp brother was runner-up to the Vauxhall with five fastest times. Other class winners on efficiency (and on the hills) included Wilhelm's 30 hp German Adler (fastest up nine of the hills), and Platford's 40/50 hp Rolls-Royce Silver Ghost, which won no fewer than ten of its eleven timed climbs and averaged an incredible 20·2 mpg. A pair of the new 38 hp live-axle (though still poppet-valve) Daimlers were better on the hills than a 30 hp White steamer and a 25 hp Hillman-Coatalen which had made fastest lap in the 1907 Tourist Trophy, so the Daimlers were still a force to be reckoned with.

The times set up at Brooklands were little indication of the cars' potentialities, for in most cases the class winners were already so far ahead of their nearest rivals on time loss that they could afford to dawdle. However, the Adler completed one lap at nearly 69 mph in touring trim and with a full load, while the winning 38 hp Daimler set an average speed of 61·45 mph under the same conditions.

Of the firms taking part in the Scottish Trial only, Metallurgique and Swift were the most successful in terms of speed on the five hills. A 26 hp Metallurgique was quickest in its class on four of them, as was a 10/12 hp Swift.

As it happened, the Two Thousand Miles Trial was not to be repeated. It had attracted only twenty-six firms, while Napier, Riley and Mercedes all entered, but withdrew. This was a very expensive outing which, whatever might happen in future years, did not come in the middle of an empty season. The rules and conditions were so severe and searching that few manufacturers were confident enough to risk their reputations with their standard cars in an event which was to receive such wide publicity. Having decided to stay out, they naturally attempted to persuade their competitors to do the same. They declared by way of self-justification that the buying public were not interested in abnormal reliability, petrol consumption or speed, and that the general emphasis on time-saving was useless and deleterious sensationalism. It was a fact that, six months after vetoing open speed hillclimbs on public roads, the RAC had not only sanctioned but organised what amounted to eleven of them in rapid succession. Times might not be published, and speeds might be less than would have been the case had racing cars been involved, but they still made a mockery of the legal limit.

Although the trial generally went off well, there was a failure of organisation which the manufacturers resented acutely: the supply of information to the press. The system broke down badly, so that successful competitors lost much useful publicity. The race at Brooklands was to have been the culminating sensation but, as we have seen, there were no close finishes and therefore no excitement nor glory. Though this was nobody's fault, it induced a feeling of deflation and anti-climax.

Possibly because of the Two Thousand Miles Trial which ended that day, the Saltburn speed trials on 27 June attracted fewer contestants than in 1907: there were eighty-nine entries in the fifteen classes, which were by RAC rating and chassis price. The races began at 8.30 am in an effort to keep the number of spectators to a minimum. Naturally enough, interest centred on the four open events, in the course of which Algernon Lee-Guinness's 200 hp Darracq set up a new world's flying kilometre record of 18·4s, or 121·57 mph. Frank Newton's 90 hp Napier covered the distance at 102·61 mph, so this was certainly a spectacular meeting on the sands. Then, in the open standing kilometre event for racing cars, Lee-Guinness, with 66·7 mph, easily beat Newton's time on a 60 hp Napier. Finally, G. S.

Barwick's 58 hp Daimler was faster than a Metallurgique in the open touring car event.

The closed contests may not have been so exciting, but they held their own interest. J. E. Hutton's 26 hp Hutton (a disguised four-cylinder Napier), which must have been one of the team cars destined for the 'Four-Inch' Tourist Trophy race in September, was entered in the class for touring cars costing under £600 in chassis form. Not surprisingly, in view of the fact that it or a sister car was to win the TT, it saw off H. Pickles's 40 hp Austin. In racing trim, the winning Hutton lapped the Isle of Man TT course at over 50 mph. One wonders how this machine found its way into a class for production touring cars. H. R. Kirk's 40 hp Metallurgique and Barwick's Daimler set up fine speeds for the standing kilometre in winning their events, clocking 52·2 and 50·15 mph respectively, the Daimler beating Cecil Edge's 60 hp Napier which was being driven by F. G. Cundy. In the handicap races, Kirk's car, driven by G. R. Smith, pipped Albert Farnell's 30 hp Daimler, but was in turn defeated by T. Atkinson at the wheel of T. H. Woollen's 15 hp Talbot. Atkinson won another, scratch event, as did Hutton's 14 hp Berliet and the 20 hp and 15 hp Masses of W. G. Masser-Horniman and A. Masser. The latter beat a 16/20 hp Calthorpe in the process, and it should be noted that the 15 hp Mass had been fastest in its class up three of the five hills in the Scottish Trial, and was by no means a tortoise. Two Stanleys of 20 hp rating fought out the steamer's class between them, and that, largely, was that.

On the same day, the Bedfordshire AC were holding a hillclimb in the grounds of Luton Hoo, by permission of Sir Julius Wernher. This was really a speed trial as the average gradient over the 1,264 yd was only 1-in-20. H. Cotchin's 8 hp De Dion won on handicap, while J. Radley's 30/40 hp FIAT was fastest in 1m 12s. The Vauxhall of L. Walton, only 1s slower, was said to be the Two Thousand Miles Trial car, but this was impossible. The trial had only ended that day, and there was only one of the new cars in existence at that time. After the hillclimb, Guy Lewin's racing Hotchkiss gave a demonstration run, ascending in 49·4s, but this course, like Sutton Bank in Yorkshire, was to become much better known for motor-cycle meetings.

On 4 July, the Ipswich & East Suffolk AC climbed Hascot Hill between Battisford and Barking instead of their customary course, Lawford Hill near Manningtree, and it is significant that 1908, as well as 1907, saw a number of clubs changing their venues.

This suggests either that public opinion was driving them away from their old haunts altogether, or that they had taken the RAC's warnings to heart and were letting their usual venues lie fallow for a season or two. We know that the worst gradient at Hascot was 1-in-6, but the length of the course is not recorded. The meeting attracted a splendid entry of works cars, and saw fine sport. E. Marriott's 25 hp Talbot returned fastest time with 32s, but its time, together with those of D. Mustard's Vauxhall and C. R. Garrard's 15 hp and 25 hp Talbots, all occupied the same two seconds. This suggests that Mustard's car was an early replica of the 'Trial' Vauxhall, for had it been the famous works car, this would surely have been mentioned in reports. Mustard's 9 hp Riley was the best trade competitor on formula, G. Watson's 12/14 hp Singer gaining the same distinction among the amateurs.

Whatever happened at Hascot, the famous Vauxhall certainly came out at the Hertfordshire County AC's open climb of Aston Clinton on the 11th, when it won its class on time in the hands of Percy Kidner. Other class winners were J. Browning's 9 hp Riley, F. Browning's 40 hp Napier and S. F. Edge's 60 hp Napier (which beat Dorothy Levitt's similar car by 5·8s). J. Hedges's 15 hp 'Trial' Talbot, which had been second to Kidner on time by 15s, won the award for the day's best performance on formula irrespective of class. The fastest amateur was E. Edwards on a 24 hp Minerva. Famous names were here, but there were only thirty-seven starters this year. One reason was that the few trade competitors who had been willing to support the Frome's Hill event projected for the same day stayed away from Aston Clinton for this purpose, and when the Frome's meeting was abandoned, the cancellation came too late to help the Hertfordshire club. Practising was forbidden at this Aston Clinton climb, on pain of disqualification.

A week later the Coventry MC invited eight other clubs to its climb of Newnham Hill. They were the Bristol & Gloucester and Herefordshire clubs, who had lost their own hills, and the Midland, Nottingham, Derby & District, Leicestershire, Northamptonshire and Wolverhampton & District clubs. This was called a 'closed' event, but it was thought wise to obtain an RAC permit. Crowds were all over the course, so that the finish line had to be moved, and very careful steering was called for from the drivers. No times were given, but we know that of the forty-two starters, J. Browning's Riley, Oscar Cüpper's 26 hp Metallurgique, and W. Tryon's 60 hp Napier were fastest in their classes. G. S. Barwick was second to

Tryon in his 58 hp Daimler. The formula winners in the same classes were C. J. Newey's De Dion, J. Hedges's 15 hp Talbot, and G. Street's 38 hp Daimler. Mrs E. W. Lewis suffered the misfortune of breaking a universal joint on her 35 hp Deasy before the start.

Possibly to avoid clashing with the Clipstone and Style Kop events of the Nottingham and Mid-Staffordshire clubs, the 1908 Shelsley meeting had been postponed from 23 May to 25 July. In the open event, H. C. Tryon's 60 hp Napier set a time of 1m 5·4s, followed by G. S. Barwick's and E. M. C. Instone's 58 hp Daimlers with 1m 8·2s and 1m 11·4s respectively. In making fourth best time, Warwick Wright's 40 hp Metallurgique did well to beat a 40/50 hp Ariel, another 58 hp Daimler and a 65 hp Mercedes. Percy Kidner's performance with a 20 hp Vauxhall caused even greater astonishment, for his time of 1m 31·4s put a 38 hp Daimler, a 35 hp Deasy and a 25 hp Talbot all in the shade, among others, and won him first place on formula. F. A. Bolton's 40/50 hp Ariel was fastest in the closed contest, followed by Charles Sangster's similar car. C. J. Newey's 10 hp De Dion won this event on formula.

At the same time, but on the other side of England, the nomads of the Ipswich & East Suffolk AC held their speed trials in Rendlesham Park, on Lord Rendlesham's estate. Standing mile and flying kilometre courses were provided and amateurs and trade were catered for separately in this meeting. Talbot walked away with the trade class, C. R. Garrard's 25 hp car covering the mile in 1m 20·6s and the kilometre in 49·4s, two other 25 hp cars setting second and third best times in the names of E. Marriott and T. H. Woollen. In addition, an amateur class went to Gordon Stewart's 15 hp machine. A Mr A. D. Hepworth won his class with a mysterious device allegedly called a 14/20 hp VS & M 1d—and that was that.

On the other hand, the Lancashire AC's open climb of Rivington Pike on the 30th was a Napier benefit. W. Watson's 60 hp car made fastest time of the day with an ascent in 48·6s, and 40 and 60 hp Napiers entered in S. F. Edge's name won their classes in 57·2s and 49s. Other class winners on time were Victor Riley's 12 hp Riley (1m 55s), C. Bertrand's 15/18 hp Zedel (2m 15·4s), Percy Kidner's 20 hp Vauxhall (1m 14·8s), Oscar Cüpper's 26 hp Metallurgique (1m 12·2s). J. Dootson's 25 hp Talbot (1m 34s), Albert Farnell's 30 hp Daimler (1m 3·6s), and H. Hollingdrake's 40 hp La Buire, which climbed in 1m 5·6s. The meeting included both open and closed handicaps, and each car was allowed two runs, the best to count.

There were sixty entries and forty-nine starters in this increasingly popular event.

So far as important meetings were concerned, the 1908 season tailed off rather suddenly. F. G. Cundy and his 60 hp Napier were fastest at the Yorkshire AC's closed climb of Greenhow Hill, between Pateley Bridge and Grassington, on 12 September. This ascent, with a steepest gradient of 1-in-5·4, was unusually precipitous. Albert Farnell's 30 hp Daimler, Rowland Winn's 20 hp Humber and J. Hedge's 15 hp Talbot won their classes, the last gaining the distinction of beating Percy Kidner's 20 hp Vauxhall. It is uncertain whether these places were awarded on time or handicap, but deduction suggests that it was probably the latter. It was perhaps on this occasion that the high compression ratio of Percy Kidner's Vauxhall brought about pre-ignition, causing the car to stop in the last stretch of the 2,000-yd hill during practice.

A week later came the Scottish AC's hillclimb, traditionally an end-of-the-season affair. It was held this year at Cairn o'Mount and the trade, in the form of the Scottish Motor Trade Association, had a class to themselves. There were twenty-six official starters, of whom the fastest were T. Shaw's 40/50 hp Ariel with a time of 6m 7s, and Boyd McCrae's 25 hp Dundee-built Werbell, which not only ascended in 6m 37s, but was best on handicap irrespective of class. Actual fastest time of the day was made by a non-competitor, a 45 hp Sheffield-Simplex with what was described as an 'electro-magnetic clutch'.

Looking back on 1908, the effect of the trade's reduced enthusiasm for sprinting is obvious, but it also clear that firstly, most companies expressed their declining interest by entering fewer competitions rather than by withdrawing from them altogether, and secondly that the clubs were not yet discouraged either by this or by the strictures emanating from the RAC and motoring press at the end of 1907. Counting the Two Thousand Miles Trial as eleven sprints, the total number of recorded meetings falls by only 20 per cent. The decline was to be more gradual than had been expected. . . .

* * *

The most important meetings of the 1909 calendar did not begin until towards the end of May. On the 22nd, the RAC organised a tour of the New Forest, open to members of any affiliated clubs, which included a timed climb in the beautiful grounds of Palace House, Beaulieu. This consisted of a $\frac{1}{4}$ mile between the North Gate and the house, with a worst gradient of 1-in-6. Fastest time of the day was set up by Mr Rendell's Daimler, in 34·4s, runner-up being Charles Hardy's Knight-engined Daimler, only 0·4s slower.

The sleeve-valve Daimler had by this time arrived, and at the same moment the Daimler company's interest in sprints waned sharply. In future, silence and smoothness to rival Rolls-Royce was to be the company's objective: ferocity to match Napier was abandoned. However, the early, larger sleeve-valve Daimlers were fast cars by virtue of sheer size, as well as of the inherent efficiency of this type of engine, and they and the older cars still won sprints for their owners. Class winners at Beaulieu included G. Salter's 8 hp Rover, a works 15 hp Talbot which achieved 42s, J. F. C. Kimber's 25 hp Talbot, slow by comparison in 46·2s, and Hardy's Daimler.

The 1909 Scottish Trial, held between 14 and 19 June, was the last of the series: a circumstance which strikingly illustrated the decline of motor sport in this period. The five timed climbs used were Cairn o'Mount, Clash (between Kincardine and Lumsden), Gruinard, Glendoe (between Fort Augustus and Spean Bridge), and Fintry. All except Glendoe were triumphs for Riley.

Stanley Riley's 10 hp car and J. Browning's 12/18 hp were fastest in their classes on each ascent. W. G. Tuck's 10/12 hp Humber and Richard Lisle's 15 hp Star were almost as successful, each winning their classes on time on three hills. A 16 hp Humber was fastest up two, while A. J. Hancock's works 20 hp Vauxhall made best time in its class up two hills, and a 24 hp model did the same. Two Austro-Daimlers were entered in the trial, a year before the marque became world-famous for its success in the Prince Henry Tour. The smaller of the two, the 20/30 hp car of F. H. Ireland, won its class on one hill, but the 40 hp did not figure high in the results. As usual, of course, speed was only one criterion among many which affected final placings but, as before, the results on time are given here because they are more relevant.

On the last day of the Scottish Trial, the Lincolnshire AC held their speed trials, now properly so called, at Grimsthorpe. Sir Hickman Bacon's 60 hp Grand Prix Austin is described as being very fast, and probably made best time of the day over the flying mile. Dr Godfrey Lowe's Rover, W. G. Foster's FL, and Dr Hogarth's Talbot won their classes on handicap. Two runs per car were allowed, but in spite of this, the whole meeting, catering for twenty-five starters, was over in an hour and a quarter.

The Welsh AC were said to have 'discovered' Pendine Sands, but the first club to hold speed trials there was the Pembrokeshire Automobile Club. They attracted a very good entry of cars and motorcycles for their meeting on 24 June. In the scratch race, George Ace's 38 hp Daimler-Knight beat W. J. Tombs's 15 hp Deasy, but on handicap, Ace was defeated by H. A. Jones-Lloyd's 12/16 hp Talbot. Five miles of firm, smooth sand were available at Pendine, but only half of this stretch, albeit 150 yd wide, was used at this time.

The Lancashire AC and the Manchester AC combined to run an open meeting at Rivington Pike on 26 June. Fastest in their classes, which, as was now usual, were divided according to rated horsepower, were F. W. Hobday's 12 hp Sizaire-Naudin, in 2m 11·4s, A. J. Hancock's 20 hp Vauxhall, with 1m 32·4s (followed by G. H. Scutchbury's similar machine), J. H. Cordingley's 16 hp Humber, G. H. Woods's 40 hp Crossley, with 1m 44·4s, and J. Higginson's 80 hp La Buire. Higginson's time of 1m 5·6s was the fastest in the open climbs, and beat two Daimlers. H. Hollingdrake's 35/40 hp La Buire was best on handicap in this class. Hobday's Sizaire was only one of three cars of this make which occupied the first three places in their class. This meeting produced the first recorded success of the G. H. Woods/Crossley combination, and the first of a long string of Crossley wins in sprints. In this class at Rivington Pike, a 30/40 hp Daimler could do no better than third place on time. Hancock's performance on handicap was the best of the day irrespective of class. In a subsequent inter-club closed climb, Higginson improved his time to 1m 1·6s, but Hancock cut his to a fantastic 1m 18·2s. His performance that day outshone all others.

The Yorkshire AC's Saltburn meeting on the same day ran true to developing sand-race form in catering for innumerable classes—by horsepower, number of cylinders, and status of entries (private or trade)—and by using an exceedingly complex formula. This penalised stroke, the performance of the long-stroke cars in the 'Four-Inch' race and in Continental *voiturette* races having made a powerful impression on the organisers. However, the antiquated chassis-price classification was dropped this year, and entries were many and exciting, in spite of the clash with Rivington Pike.

The flying kilometre for unlimited racing cars as usual provided an easy win for Algernon Lee-Guinness's 200 hp Darracq, though his speed of 120·25 mph was slower than in 1908. A contest for cars of Grand Prix type was won by A. W. Tate's Mercedes at 93·2 mph, and to complete the panorama of racing types of the period, modern and obsolete, 'Four-Inch' race cars had their own event, won by G. C. Colmore's Darracq at 67·37 mph.

The other open events were for touring cars over the standing kilometre. While Hancock dominated Rivington Pike, Percy Kidner's car was doing the same at Saltburn. His 24 hp Vauxhall thrashed G. A. Phillips's 16 hp works Humber at 44·74 mph, and then Rowland Winn's 'trade' Model N Ford at 47·39 mph. Neither was negligible opposition. It seems that the Ford exercised Kidner more than the Humber; one would like to know its speed. But we do know that F. Scott's 38 hp Minerva, a Knight-engined 'four', saw off J. H. Haggis's 40 hp Mercedes at no less than 54 mph, A. Bray's 10 hp Sizaire-Naudin won two open events—in one beating T. Mitchell's 12 hp Calthorpe—and J. Hedge's 15 hp works Talbot and W. A. Foster's 28/40 hp SPA each collected one.

Very much the same group of entrants contested the closed races. In these Kidner again defeated Phillips, A. Bray again won two events (one from a 10 hp Delage) and T. Mitchell duly took his class. F. A. Bolton and his 58 hp Daimler took a sad beating, once from W. Blamires's 40/50 hp Rolls-Royce (40·96 mph) and once from F. Scott's Minerva, which achieved 41·11 mph. On the latter occasion Bolton uncharacteristically slipped up, and left his handbrake on.

N. F. Bayliss appeared on a 14/18 hp Sunbeam to win his class at 39·8 mph, this Sunbeam model, the first with a live axle and a machine capable of great development, having made its bow in the 1909 Scottish Trial. It was the first of Louis Coatalen's designs for the Wolverhampton concern, which was now to join the band of invincibles. Its driver came into the same category, on this occasion beating J. L. Kirk's 15 hp works Talbot.

On 16 July, the remoteness of Pendine did not deter the Motor Union from sponsoring a speed trial on its wind-swept, billiard-table sands. This meeting was closed to the Union's affiliated members and the Welsh AC. Mr T. J. Williams's 45 hp Daimler, Captain Hughes-Morgan's 35 hp Humber (which beat a 38 hp Mercedes), E. Lewis's 25 hp Vulcan, a Darracq and two De Dions won their classes, as did J. L. Kirk, whose company thought the event important enough to call for participation by his 15 hp Talbot.

In contrast, most of the famous names were present in the comparative cosiness of Shelsley Walsh the next day. So were 150 spectators' cars, their occupants present to see H. C. Holder's 58 hp Daimler win the open event in 1m 8·4s, and the Vauxhalls consolidate their already terrifying reputation by coming second and third with engines of less than half the Daimler's size. A. J. Hancock's 20 hp car was faster than Percy Kidner's 24 hp, perhaps owing to more suitable gear ratios: Hancock ascending in 1m 21s, Kidner in 1m 23s. Victor Riley's 12 hp car won on formula in 2m 20·4s, Holder was fastest in the closed contest as well with a time of 1m 11·6s, and a Riley, this time A. Cox's 9 hp, was again best on formula. The climb for the Henry Edmunds Trophy, due to be held the previous year in the Isle of Man at the time of the TT race, but cancelled, was contested at this Shelsley meeting. It was restricted to cars of less than 21 hp rating, and attracted only six entries. Hancock's 20 hp Vauxhall was the fastest, in 1m 13·4s, followed by J. Hedge on a 20 hp Talbot.

An odd occurrence may be mentioned here in defiance of chronological order. Early in September, the Midland AC held a second climb on Shelsley Walsh; an 'impromptu' closed affair which was won on formula by C. J. Newey's De Dion. Not until 1926 does another record appear of two hillclimbs being held in one year on this course.

Returning to the discipline of accurate order, Sir Hickman Bacon's 60 hp 1908 Grand Prix Austin made easily the fastest time at the Lincolnshire AC's Syston Park meeting on 17 July, also, of course, winning his class. His time was 59s, putting a Stanley steamer in the shade, among others. R. B. Purves's 12/16 hp FL, which ascended in 1m 45s, and Dr Hogarth's Talbot with 1m 18s also took their classes. This hill, 1,240 yd long, lay on Sir John Thorold's land.

The Hertfordshire County AC's open climb of Aston Clinton a week later was more successful than its predecessor. Arthur Cox's 9 hp Riley, G. W. Hands's works 12/14 hp Calthorpe and A. J. Hancock's 20 hp Vauxhall were fastest in their classes, while Percy Kidner's 24 hp Vauxhall and N. F. Bayliss's 14/20 hp Sunbeam dead-heated in their category. (This new Sunbeam, incidentally, was sometimes called a 14/18, sometimes a 14/20). From now until 1913, Talbots tended to be overshadowed by the newer arrivals, especially Crossley, Sunbeam and Vauxhall, as the latter marques grew faster and faster. The Calthorpe, although less prominent that the rest, was another example of the small to medium-sized, side-valve touring car with pretensions to efficiency. An earlier model, the 16/20 hp, had already distinguished itself in Ireland in the 1907 and 1908 seasons. On formula, the various classes at Aston Clinton were won by W. Jolly's 12 hp De Dion, Victor Riley's 12 hp Riley, Hancock, and Kidner.

The same day saw the Sheffield & District AC climbing Grindleford Bridge, an occasion remarkable for the performance of P. Richardson's 45 hp Sheffield-Simplex. It made fastest time of the day, and also set a new record for the hill, previously held by a larger-engined car, which had also had the advantage of a flying start, whereas the Sheffield-Simplex started from a standstill. Finally, it accomplished its run entirely in top gear. There can have been few more convincing demonstrations of low-speed torque and flexibility until the advent of the Trojan. On a less impressive note, L. Slater's 8 hp Jackson and E. F. Coupe's 35 hp Daimler were fastest in the other classes, while the handicap awards went to Slater, G. D. Flather's 12/16 hp Talbot, and B. Hinds's 12 hp Talbot.

On 18 September the Scottish AC held its annual closed hillclimb, again on Cairn o'Mount. Its 'purely private and sporting' character was emphasised and strengthened by the ban on using results for advertising purposes. No indication whatever was given of the speeds achieved, which must have detracted somewhat from the event's sporting nature, if not from its privacy. Two De Dions, two 38 hp Daimlers and, of all things, two 24/30 hp Albions led their classes on 'efficiency'. There was no more fitting monument to thumping, lumbering solidity than the Albion motor-car, designed as it was to last for ever on Scottish roads, flattening those irregularities it could not surmount.

This year the Yorkshire AC, out to attract the big names, included an open event in their Pateley Bridge climb; but some of the giants who drove north on the 25th may have wished they had stayed at home. It poured, and as the organisers had chosen the day of the cattle fair at Pateley Bridge for their meeting, the competitors got wetter than they need have done waiting for droves of sheep, cattle and farm carts to pass by.

Fastest time in the open event was set up by W. Bradwell's 'Four-Inch' Hutton, which ascended in 1m 27·4s. It was followed by L. Aspinall's 40 hp Metallurgique in 1m 44s, N. F. Bayliss's 16/20 hp Sunbeam and Percy Kidner's 24 hp Vauxhall. H. G. Day's and J. Hedge's Talbots were present, as was Richard Lisle's 15 hp Star, so there was sport such as the locals had never seen before, and Day won on handicap.

The closed event for which both amateurs and trade were eligible was won by the Hutton on speed (1m 25·8s) and by the Vauxhall on handicap, while the closed climb restricted to amateurs was entirely a Hutton benefit, with the rest nowhere. In this contest, the Hutton made fastest time of the day, with 1m 24s, and was best on formula as well. In the first of the closed events, the car met the same opposition as in the open climb, proving again that, to the manufacturers, a 'closed to club' rule was no discouragement if the occasion were worth the price of a subscription. At Pateley Bridge, as elsewhere, the clubs catered for their private members, who might otherwise be outclassed, by providing a purely amateur contest.

The last big event of the year was the Wolverhampton & District AC's 'stop-and-restart' meeting on Harley Bank on 2 October. Here the sensation was provided by Richard Lisle's 15 hp Star, basically another conventional touring chassis considerably 'hotted-up', which thrashed a field including Percy Kidner and A. J. Hancock on 24 hp Vauxhalls, a 60 hp Napier, and Louis Coatalen's 16/20 hp Sunbeam. When one is told that the Star's engine was turning over at 4,000 rpm while doing so, the achievement seems less surprising. This was a truly horrendous engine speed for 1909; though it was not suggested that the Star was capable of sustaining it. Winners on handicap in the various classes were A. Bray's Sizaire-Naudin, Hancock, Herbert Austin's 18/24 hp Austin, and G. F. Heath's 38 hp Minerva.

Apart from the steady decline in recorded numbers—18 per cent over 1908, 35 per cent over 1907—there were other indications during 1909 of the reduced popularity of sprints. The noticing of events in the motoring press begins to be sketchy and erratic; the secretary of the Motor Union says outright that 'hillclimbs have ceased to attract'. It is an interesting fact that this process, and its eventual reversal, is mirrored after 1908 in a parallel development on the Continent. The 1908 French Grand Prix was the last motor race of the old, heroic proportions to be held until 1912, when the prospects of the sport began to look up in Britain as well. However, motor sport refused to die. When the great Continental manufacturers withdrew their support from Grand Prix racing, new men developed a new type of racing car, the multi-cylinder *voiturette*, in contests of their own such as the Coupe de *l'Auto* and the Grand Prix des Voiturettes. When Grand Prix racing on the old scale was resumed in 1912, these cars had become so fast that they quite outclassed the giants, which found themselves obsolete.

Nor, in spite of similar discouragement, did racing expire in Britain. The forward-looking manufacturers who still supported sprints supported Brooklands as part of this policy, in their belief that high-speed testing helped sales and really improved the breed.

The conception of the second generation of British racing cars (the first being the Gordon Bennett generation) dates from the Talbot of 1906 and the Two Thousand Miles Trial cars of 1908; the conventional chassis already discussed. The new generation—the Vauxhalls, Talbots, Sunbeams and others—was born, took its form and was developed on Brooklands track. The newcomers were themselves used for sprints with simple modifications such as differing gear ratios; so if sprints helped the development of the British racing car, the benefits were mutual. These cars, with their high engine outputs from a small capacity, were made to measure for the earlier Continental *voiturette* races, as was illustrated by the triumph of the Sunbeams in the 1912 Coupe de *l'Auto* and Grand Prix.

After 1912 neither their side-valve engines nor, later, their feverish copies of the Peugeot could keep pace with the power output of the latest Continental *voiturettes,* whose makers had never been wedded to touring chassis. One firm at least—Calthorpe—entered high-speed four-cylinder side-valve racers in the Coupe de *l'Auto* as early as 1909, when four cylinders were *avant-garde* even in European *voiturette* circles and the single- or twin-cylinder engine of prodigious stroke still fashionable.

* * *

If sprints did not disappear from the face of Britain in 1910 and 1911, they reached a low that matched the figures for 1904 in terms of numbers, and which was unparalleled in our period in terms of interest. Many other events were projected, but they never took place.

Indeed, it seemed as if flexibility trials, slow-driving contests, gymkhanas and speed-judging competitions had taken the place of true sport. By the end of the 1910 season, all except two of the open sprints of 1907 had vanished: Aston Clinton, Frome's, Bexhill, the Henry Edmunds Trophy, Harley Bank, Kidd's Hill, South Harting, Rivington Pike, Caerphilly. Laindon, Sharpenhoe, Uttoxeter, Ragpath Side, Lawford Hill, Grindleford Bridge, Birdlip, Newnham, Bottledown and Syston, all sites of important closed events, were no more. The Scottish Trials were equally dead.

The promotion of Pateley Bridge and the discovery of Coalport, Pendine and Sutton Park (qv, 1910) were little consolation. In April 1910, the RAC reiterated its ambivalent views on events on the public road: competitors were bound to exceed the speed limit, so pure speed contents were 'injurious to the best interests of the automobile movement'. At the same time, the RAC was still willing to grant open permits for such contests, if all the local authorities were happy.

The Hertfordshire County AC's open and closed climb of Aston Clinton, planned for 17 September, was given a permit, but was killed by the trade's lack of interest. There were obviously no difficulties with the local authorities, for the club's closed hillclimb had duly taken place at the start of the season, on 23 April. Indeed, it was remarked that, for a course on a road close to London, it was still remarkably free of traffic. The two car classes, for vehicles under and over 15 hp, were won on formula by C. J. Newey's 12 hp De Dion and W. H. Bashall's 20 hp Vauxhall. Other Vauxhalls, entered by F. G. Carter, Percy Kidner and L. Walton, were second, third and fourth, while fastest time of the day was made by S. S. Barber's 40/50 hp Rolls-Royce.

Until this year of regression, the South Wales and Monmouthshire AC's closed climb on Buttrill's Hill, Barry, had been a very parochial affair, but this year, on 11 June, an intrusion of works cars promoted it into a position of greater importance; a circumstance perhaps attributable to the dearth of sprints elsewhere. The cars also ascended two abreast, adding greatly to the excitement. G. A. Phillips's light two-seater Humber with disc wheels and raked steering sounds more like a Brooklands car than a touring machine, but it beat a smaller-engined 16/20 hp Sunbeam, carrying four passengers, by a mere 3s. This duel rather overshadowed the fact that the Humber's time of 44·4s, fastest of the day, bettered that of a 30/40 hp Ariel. The fastest cars in the various horsepower classes were a 10 hp De Dion, J. D. Newton's 15 hp Talbot, Mrs W. G. Morel's 30 hp Napier, E. Brockett Groves's 16 hp Vauxhall, and P. M. T. Hill's 12 hp Talbot.

The Yorkshire AC's open and closed speed trials at Saltburn, held on 25 June, were practically unique in being an event which attracted more entries than in 1909. Conditions were ideal: fine weather, a dry course, and precious few spectators; the start being again timed for half-past eight in the morning. The meeting was thought remarkable for the number of freakish bodies worn by so-called touring cars: the low-slung, stark two-seater with acutely raked steering and precious little aft of the scuttle except two bucket seats; or the streamlined single-seater born at Brooklands in 1909. Unlike the bodies complained of in earlier years, when no attempt was made to lower chassis or rake steering, but merely to lighten touring cars of standard shape, this latest line was completely new and specialised, foreshadowing the true 'sports' coachwork of later years.

Talbots surprised no one by winning five of the standing-start events for touring cars, J. L. Kirk's 15 hp accounting for two, J. Hedge's 25 hp car for two more and a 12 hp for the last. However, a stripped 25 hp Talbot did particularly well to beat E. Hoyle's 1908 TT Hutton in another race. Although a Sunbeam won one event, this was not N. F. Bayliss's day, for he was beaten twice—once by Richard Lisle's 12 hp Star, at no less than 45·28 mph, and once by a formidable newcomer, G. O. Herbert. Indeed, the latter's 16/20 hp Singer went on to defeat Lisle's 15 hp Star, so was faster than either. The 12 hp Star chalked up another victory, making two in all. A 32 hp Metallurgique won two races, and G. H. Woods's 20 hp Crossley one. Wood's 20 hp Crossley was to become a very famous machine. It was said to develop 62 bhp at 2,000 rpm, but must surely have been capable of higher engine speeds than this. In the standing kilometre event for racing cars of up to 59·6 hp, complying with the 1908 Grand Prix regulations, Eric Loader's Itala won at 54·82 mph. The best of three runs counted. However, P. D. Stirling's Richard-Brasier won the flying-start 'unrestricted' racing-car event at 86·03 mph, Loader coming second at 84·09 mph and R. Wildegose's Itala third at 83·47 mph. These were the most interesting results arising from the twenty-three events of the northern sand meeting.

Meanwhile, whatever fate met other famous hillclimbs, Shelsley Walsh went on for ever. There were plenty of trade entries of the finest quality on 2 July and, although rain had fallen, the course was in excellent condition thanks to the skilful care of the Midland AC. Oscar Thompson's 40 hp Austin 'Pobble', driven by J. Hadley, made fastest time of the day during the open event, with 1m 10·2s. To help prove that the dinosaurs were not yet entirely extinct, H. C. Holder's 58 hp Daimler and C. A. Bird's 65 hp Napier gained second and third places. Richard Lisle's 12 hp Star won on formula, climbing in 1m 37·8s and followed by Kidner's and Hancock's 20 and 16 hp Vauxhalls. Cars competing in the open event had to carry a full load, whereas those entered for the Henry Edmunds climb, open to machines of up to 16 hp, were burdened with the driver only. This helps to explain the better times of the smaller cars, Lisle's 15 hp Star beating Hancock's 16 hp Vauxhall with 1m 30·6s against 1m 31·8s. The runners-up were Louis Coatalen's 16 hp Sunbeam, H. G. Day's 15 hp Talbot, and G. H. Wood's 16 hp Crossley. All had engines approximating to the popular dimensions of 80× 120 mm.

On 17 September, the Yorkshire AC repeated its successful open and closed meeting at Pateley Bridge: successful, that is, by the standards of 1910, with thirty-one entries and twenty-five starters. A TT Hutton, that of E. Hoyle, again made fastest time, and also won its class. A. J. Hancock's 20 hp Vauxhall and H. G. Day's 12 hp Talbot were best in their classes, while Hancock also established the best overall performance of the day to end one of the few major events of the year.

* * *

The 1911 season began with a climb on a course which was to become more famous and, finally, more notorious than any other: Kop Hill, near Princes Risborough in Buckinghamshire. Motor-cycles had climbed Kop at least as early as 1910, but the Motor Cycling Club's meeting on 13 May 1911 contains the first recorded reference to a class for cars. They were limited on this occasion to a 'ceiling' of of 30 hp, and the winner was J. van Hooydonk's 10/12 hp Phoenix. The timed distance on Kop was usually $\frac{3}{4}$ mile, the worst gradient being about 1-in-5. There were no bad corners; a fact which made for high speeds. These and a loose macadam surface made for excitement of the more hair-raising kind.

A week later, the Sutton Coldfield AC ran their closed climb of Coalport Hill, Ironbridge. The timed 1,000 yd included several nasty bends and steepened to a gradient of 1-in-7, while the surface was bad this year, too, so that some cars came unstuck on the hairpin and clouted the bank. This was a style all too reminiscent of Shelsley in later days. C. A. Bird won both the two car events on time in his 65 hp Napier, Cecil Bianchi's 12/14 hp Crossley and Seymour Smith's 12/20 hp Humber making the best formula performances. Bird and his Napier, like Higginson, Hollingdrake and their La Buires in the north, fought a long rearguard action against the new breed of sprint car. Bianchi, who had been Charles Jarrott's mechanic in the Paris–Madrid race of 1903, was to become a deadly exponent of the smaller Crossley in sprints. On this occasion G. H. Woods in the 20 hp model was second on time in the first event.

Back in Wales, the Cardiff MC's climb of Cross Hands Hill, near Usk, on the 20th was only briefly reported, but the stature of the entries shows that it was thought a fairly important occasion. Louis Coatalen at the wheel of a 12/16 hp Sunbeam made fastest time of the day, while Edward Genna's 16/20 hp machine was first on formula in the unlimited class. Genna had begun a spectacular career as a Sunbeam works driver in the previous season, and Coatalen was second to him on formula here, with a 15·9 hp Arrol-Johnston, possibly a Coupe de *l'Auto* team car, third. The fastest car in the touring class was the 12 hp Humber of J. Hunter, who was also best on formula.

The Lincolnshire AC's Grimsthorpe Park speed trials, as reliable a feature of the season nowadays as Shelsley Walsh, were held on 27 May, when R. Wright's 20 hp Singer, entered by G. O. Herbert, made fastest time in 1m 10s, and led on speed in the class open to amateurs and trade. The fastest amateur was T. Mays (father of Raymond Mays of ERA and BRM fame), whose 20 hp Vauxhall covered the course in 1m 20·6s. Formula winners respectively were W. J. Gilpin's 10 hp DFP (a make not yet transformed by W. O. Bentley), and O. Dixon's 14 hp Calthorpe. This car also ran in the 'open' class, and set a time of 1m 33·8s.

If any particular point in history can be chosen, it may be said that at this juncture, sprints had reached their lowest ebb. On 10 June *The Autocar* commented with truth: 'Hillclimbs have gradually dwindled until only a few remain . . . racing pure and simple has centred on Brooklands, with but one exception . . . the great Northern race meeting [Saltburn].' There was no sign that any climbs were going to be held at Kettleby or Hazelwood this year, let alone on lesser courses such as Buttrill's or Lippett's Hill. Reference to the appendix to this Part, under 1911, will show that the motoring press, reflecting what they believed to be their readers' feelings, hardly bothered to report small events at all. The later part of the season was to show the first signs of a revival, in quality if not in numbers, that would become manifest in 1912. During 1911, meetings would be renewed at Caerphilly, Style Kop and Bottledown, and at least two new major courses would come into use, but at this particular moment no such development could reasonably be expected.

Shelsley Walsh was 'the one classic open event of this kind of the year', and so 'one of the most valuable contests of the year'; but even this now appeared to be threatened, for the estate was up for sale. However, this did not affect the 1911 event, held on 10 June. The record for the hill, which had stood at 1m 5·4s since H. C. Tryon's Napier had set it in 1908, was broken in both the closed and the open climb by H. C. Holder's 58 hp Daimler, with times of 1m 2·2s and 1m 3·2s respectively. In this appropriately spectacular manner, the name of Daimler at last disappeared from among the winners of important sprints. C. A. Bird's 65 hp Napier was second in the open event with 1m 6·4s, followed by Holder's 40 hp Austin, which came up so fast that it went into a slide and almost turned over. It was remarked that the gradient, severe though it was, no longer worried the fast cars: the bends were the problem. High speed was the more dangerous when, as on this occasion, the public were allowed to run all over the course. The offenders were thought the more blameworthy because they were themselves mostly motorists, and should have known better.

The same placings on speed held good in the closed climb. A. J. Hancock's 16 hp Vauxhall was best on formula in the open contest, G. H. Wood's 12/14 hp Crossley coming second. In the closed event, G. O. Herbert's 20 hp Singer made the most creditable formula performance, followed by Arthur Cox's 12/18 hp Riley, but the competition for the Henry Edmunds Trophy had to be abandoned for lack of entries.

Hancock's Vauxhall contained a very special engine which had been endowed with a truly exceptional stroke of 200 mm in order to beat formulae which penalised bore. Its success was so convincing, or unconvincing, that officials were sure that the bore had been misstated. The car's performance was not even allowed for on Mr F. W. Lanchester's special rotary slide rule, and as it was unthinkable that Mr Ebblewhite's timing should be at fault, skulduggery was the only answer. Off came the sump, whereupon the bore was found to be precisely as stated: 80 mm! Mr Lanchester thereupon devised a new formula in time for the 1912 event.

Two days before the Yorkshire AC's Saltburn meeting of 1 July, H. F. Mills' monstrous 190 × 250 mm 300 hp FIAT went after the world's mile and kilometre records on the sands. The attempt, with Bordino at the wheel, ended somewhat ignominiously. Bordino got stuck in a soft patch of sand, and the car was caught by the tide. Amid great excitement, the huge FIAT's stern was afloat and water was over the hubcaps before horses managed to pull it clear of the clinging sand. A similar fate befell a couple of Talbots on the following day, but in the meeting itself, the FIAT won the flying-start event for racing cars at 116·5 mph, even if without much real opposition. Percy Lambert's 15 hp Brooklands Austin 'Pearly III' was second at 81·04 mph, followed by G. O. Herbert's Singer. However, the FIAT went on to attack the flying mile record once more, and took it at 116·2 mph in clouds of sand and fine spray.

The other open events went to 'Pearly III', G. H. Woods's Crossley, H. G. Day's 12 hp Talbot, and Edward Genna's 12/16 hp Sunbeam, each of which won two races. Their best speeds over the standing kilometre were 53·25 mph (Lambert), 51·54 mph (Woods), and 47·39 mph (Genna). Some idea of the speeds already being set up by stripped and tuned Model 'T' Fords can be gained from the fact that the humble £200 chassis-price class was won by Rowland Winn's car at 44·56 mph. Woods and G. O. Herbert's Singer each won two closed events; Day and Bayliss one.

Meanwhile, the Middlesex County AC were comporting themselves much more modestly on Hand Post hill, between Northaw and Newgate Street, rising to a 1-in-7·5 gradient. The organisers noticed sadly that, although their club had grown, the number of entries in their hillclimb had fallen; a complaint which must have found many echoes. J. H. Cummings's French 15·9 hp SCAR, with its dashboard radiator, made fastest time, while H. Fitch's 8 hp De Dion won on 'efficiency'.

There was near tragedy on 17 July when the extremely dry and rough condition of the course at Sutton Park on the occasion of the Sutton Coldfield AC's speed trials led to several accidents, and to the supposition, which was correct, that no further sprints would be held there. Though he was able to crawl clear of the wreckage, Edward Genna was badly hurt when his 16/20 hp Sunbeam skidded, burst a tyre, and somersaulted through the air to fall on top of him. Before this incident, which stopped the meeting, no very high speeds had been set up, for men of the experience of Woods, Herbert, Bianchi and C. J. Newey had been unwilling to extend their cars. Even at moderate speeds, they were sliding badly. Arthur Cox's 12/18 hp Riley was thought to have made fastest time over the standing mile, at 41·42 mph; a figure which proves how careful the others were.

This year the Manchester AC, like other clubs, found itself holding a more important meeting on 22 July than had hitherto been the case. Unfortunately, the 1,000 yd of its new course, Cornist Hall hill, averaging 1-in-10, was unsafe. The crown of the road on the bends was too high, and the finish was uncomfortably near a gate and a right-angled corner. In these circumstances, the spectacle of J. Higginson's 80/100 hp La Buire 'jumping from side to side of the road' on its way up must have been worth seeing. The second best time to Higginson's 49·4s was made by G. H. Woods's 20 hp Crossley. R. Wilkie's 20 hp Vauxhall ascended in 53·2s, and there was only 0·2s between E. Harding's 12/16 hp Sunbeam and H. Hollingdrake's 20 hp Vauxhall. Class winners included Harding, Hollingdrake and A. E. Barclay on his 12/14 hp Crossley.

More than a month later, on 25 August, the Yorkshire AC climbed Pateley Bridge. As was now usual, open as well as closed events were included in the programme. Also as usual, Higginson made fastest time of the day with his vast La Buire. However, J. Hedge's 15 hp Talbot was a mere 5·4s slower, followed by N. F. Bayliss's 12/16 hp Sunbeam, 9·6s slower. Bayliss won both the open and the closed events on formula. Three years old, E. Hoyle's Hutton was still making its presence felt. G. H. Woods would undoubtedly have figured high in the results had he not been disqualified for failing to weigh-in his car.

This process of weighing-in was a necessary preliminary to all sprints which included formula contests, as the formula always took weight into account. It was carried out at the nearest railway station which possessed a weighbridge. W. O. Bentley, who was to begin taking part in sprints in the coming year, has underlined the importance of weight to hillclimb entrants:

> The weighing-in on the doubtfully-accurate machine borrowed from the railway company would be followed with the closest interest by all the competitors, usually accompanied by critical remarks on the amount of chassis-drilling carried out by some enthusiast.
>
> I'm afraid sharp practice was occasionally resorted to, too. There was, for example, the driver who had an extraordinary run of success and was almost unbeatable in his class in the formula events until it was discovered that his car had a built-in concealed water tank, which was filled before the weighing-in and surreptitiously emptied on the way to the starting-line.

Kettleby was now lost to the Leicestershire AC, but the club found a splendid replacement near Loughborough, in the shape of Beacon Hill, Woodhouse Eaves. Its timed length was 1,433 yd, first climbed in anger on 2 September. The meeting, 'closed' to ten Midland clubs, formed part of a petrol consumption trial, but attracted an excellent entry of about sixty cars. C. A. Bird's 65 hp Napier won the class for cars of unlimited horsepower, in 65·4s. G. H. Woods's 20 hp Crossley was second in this class, in 70·2s, and first in the category for cars of up to 20 hp rating with a time 0·2s slower. N. F. Bayliss's 12/16 hp Sunbeam was second fastest, his time being 71·8s, and he won both classes on formula. The best performance by an amateur in either class was made by Sutton Clifford's 10/14 hp DFP. His time was 134·2s. Bayliss won the Du Pré Cup, a formula award, though fastest time in this event, and of the day, was the 64·6s of C. A. Bird.

On 23 September, the Coventry & Warwickshire MC followed the example of the Leicestershire and other clubs by pioneering a new hill. This was a memorable piece of nastiness called Saintbury, at Weston-sub-Edge, in the Cotswolds near Evesham. Its length was just over one and a quarter miles. The surface was bad, the bends were acute, and the steepest gradient of 1-in-6 applied to much of the course, notably the corners. Eight other clubs were invited to the meeting, and a class was laid on for steam cars. It is an interesting fact that four were entered, even though steam as a means of propulsion was held to be obsolete by this date. Fastest time of the day, and best overall performance on formula, was made by a works 12 hp Talbot. This savage little machine, said to develop 50 bhp, disposed of Saintbury in 2m 14·6s, a time equivalent to an average speed of over 35 mph. Not unnaturally, this feat provoked much awed comment. It is safe to say that, except in fundamentals, cars like this Talbot and the works 15 hp Star of two seasons before bore but little resemblance to their production touring sisters. It was at about this time that the motoring magazines began to interpolate disingenuously-phrased comments into their reports of sprints to the effect that this or that entrant of a 'touring' car seemed to have some difficulty in keeping his engine running smoothly, or running at all, while waiting on the starting line, and that it sounded unusually rough and raucous. At the same time, these cars were not 'specials' as the term is understood today: even most Brooklands cars were basically the touring product, highly tuned and modified; not a completely specialised 'one-off'.

Other classes at Saintbury were won on time by G. O. Herbert's 15 hp Singer in 2m 43·8s, and a 20 hp Stanley steamer in 2m 38·6s. Arthur Cox's 12 hp Riley took a class on handicap.

The Scottish AC's Tummel Bridge hillclimb (situated immediately south of Trinafour) held on the same day also included a class for steamers, but it attracted no entries. The day of the steam car was done. It was too complicated for the everyday motorist, and could no longer outclass most petrol cars in terms of sheer sprinting speed. Campbell Martin's 38 hp Minerva was fastest up the hill in the closed event, while the best speeds in the various classes were set by two Argylls—J. Anderson's 12 hp and John Blackwood's 15·9 hp—and by Martin J. Willison's 10/12 hp DFP. Blackwood, and Boyd McCrae's 20 hp Werbell won on handicap. Another 38 hp Minerva carried off the Scottish Motor Trade Association's event on time.

*　*　*

The trend of late 1911 continued into 1912, gaining momentum all the time. The total increase in numbers of reported events was small, but their quality improved. New courses were found, important events were revived, and the proportion of open competitions went up. This argues a certain increase in sprinting among rank-and-file motorists, perhaps attributable in part to the revival of motor racing on the Continent, and in particular to the success of the British Sunbeam in the Coupe de *l'Auto* and Grand Prix in June. The new trend also suggested a renewal of trade interest. In 1912 the representatives of four firms—Arrol-Johnston, Straker-Squire, DFP and Austro-Daimler—selling the same breed of car as Talbot, Vauxhall, Sunbeam, Crossley, Singer, Star and Calthorpe, sought to break the latters' monopoly of sprinting success. In the case of Arrol-Johnston, this participation was an extension of rivalry with some of the same firms in Continental *voiturette* races, and most of them competed directly at Brooklands. Five British firms entered teams in the 1912 Coupe de *l'Auto*. Four had done so in 1911, but only one in 1910 and 1909. The number of firms which were successful in a particular year is not a reliable guide to the number which entered in sprints, but a comparison of figures under the first heading in different years does give a rough guide to trends in this period. In 1910 it was about a dozen, but in 1912 the figure rose to at least twenty, matching that for 1908. There was more money about in the industry than there had been at the end of 1907, so makers who turned out cars which might have a chance in competition, and who believed that successes meant sales, were willing to chance their corporate arms.

The competitions of 1912 also reflected the beginnings of a much wider and more important movement; the development of the true economy car—the cyclecar, and the miniature big car—but the signs became significant only in 1913, and will be dealt with more fully under that year. Here we need only note two more new names: Mathis and GWK.

There was, indeed, a cyclecar class in the Essex MC's closed climb of Aston Clinton on 16 March, but it was equally a sign of the times that this was not filled. In the class for cars proper, G. D. Pearce-Jones's 1910 'Prince Henry' Vauxhall team car was fastest, in 1m 23·6s, and also won on formula. A. P. Howard's 15·9 hp Calthorpe was next best on time, with 1m 32·8s, and J. L. Kirk's 15 hp Talbot second on formula.

On 11 May, Rivington Pike was attacked for the first time since 1909, again by the Lancashire and Manchester ACs combined. The closed events were generally dull, except for the spectacle of J. Higginson making fastest time of the day with his La Buire in 50·8s. E. Hoyle's 'Four-Inch' Hutton continued to fox both opposition and devisers of formulae, for it made the best overall formula showing in the closed contests. In the open events, Higginson won the class for the biggest cars in 53·4s. No one else could get near his time: G. H. Woods getting closest with his 20 hp Crossley, in 1m 0·4s, taking his class on speed. J. S. Cordingley's 11·9 hp Arrol-Johnston (1m 47s) and Cecil Bianchi's 12/14 hp Crossley did the same in their classes. Each was also best on handicap. So were Cordingley's 15·9 hp Arrol-Johnston and Edward Genna's 12/16 hp Sunbeam (1m 31s) in Woods's and Higginson's classes.

Several entrants at Rivington Pike had been disqualified by the Lancashire AC for disregarding the rules defining standard production cars. Others were to meet the same fate at Aston Clinton, as we shall see. *The Motor* reported in June that the northern clubs in particular were becoming restive at the disparity between genuine touring cars and increasingly specialised works machines. Some new firms might be coming into sprints, but a lot more, they said, were staying away because their standard products had no chance at all. This had a deleterious effect on club finances and reputations. The RAC formula commonly used for handicapping also caused dissatisfaction. It was old-fashioned in that bore was penalised much more than stroke, so that a long-stroke car like the special 80 × 200 mm Brooklands Vauxhall had a great advantage. This car produced 80 bhp, compared with the 45 bhp of the 80 × 120 mm Vauxhall.

The Motor Cycling Club's otherwise obscure ascent of an unidentified hill near the Lambert Arms Hotel, Aston Rowant, Buckinghamshire, on 11 May is important to the historian for it saw the earliest recorded success of W. O. Bentley's modified 10/15 hp DFP. It was best on formula in the car class, and was probably fastest as well. Its 70 × 130 mm engine was very easily tuned, and Bentley's car was already capable of nearly 70 mph.

Since the decline in sprints, not so much was heard about public outcries against them, but as if to prove that prejudice was still strong, the police had made it clear to the Kent AC that they would stop that club's climb on Yorks Hill, Sevenoaks, scheduled for 18 May. Although the course ran through private ground, it was itself a public road, as was Aston Clinton. At this proof that the Kent County Constabulary was becoming as hostile as its counterpart across the border in Sussex, the club had naturally to cancel the event.

As for Aston Clinton, it regained its old splendour on 8 June, when the first open climb since 1909 was held there. The organising club's rather vague phraseology suggests that it had met much the same kind of trouble as the Kent AC in trying to promote this event. Speaking in 1912, the Hertfordshire County Automobile and Aero Club, as it then was, said: 'restrictions which prevented the running of the event' were now 'removed'. The timed distance had become shorter since 1904, and was now about a kilometre. The entry list of fifty-four, producing forty-six starters, was thought excellent.

Accelerating in fantastic fashion, G. H. Woods's famous 20 hp Crossley set up fastest time of the day in 58·6s, winning his class on time and formula, but otherwise the event was dominated by potent newcomers. Two of the formidable 27/80 hp, ohc Austro-Daimlers were second and third to Woods in his class, the faster only 3·6s behind him in spite of his speed. C. M. Keiller's works friction-drive GWK, one of the latest breed of light cars, hammered the De Dions in 1m 54·2s. W. O. Bentley's 12/15 hp DFP was both fastest and best on formula in his class, registering 1m 38·4s, while R. S. Witchell's 15 hp trade Straker-Squire made a phenomenal ascent, almost all the way in third gear. Its time of 1m 11·8s was no less than 8·8s better than that of a 20 hp Vauxhall. H. G. Day's 12 hp Talbot won this class on formula. Although it came only sixth on time in Woods's class, G. Vidler's 24 hp ALFA, the ancestor of the post-war Alfa-Romeo, was interesting for its novelty.

W. O. Bentley ascended with his fiancée in the passenger seat on this occasion, and his description conveys a fine impression of the atmosphere of a hillclimb of the period:

> One after another we watched the two-litre cars go away amid blasting exhaust roar and a scream of high revs that echoed against the high bank and rolled away through the beeches; and with each departure we moved closer to the starting line. . . . Because of the very steep initial gradient at Aston, it was the change from first to second a few yards from the line that counted. I had made a point of practising this frequently, and I snicked the lever back without touching the clutch and at revs for which the DFP was never intended. Once away, my nerve-storm and self-consciousness seemed to disappear, and as the track levelled off and I changed to third, I could see the first left-hander ahead. It was third gear all the time then, with the right foot hard on the boards: up the rising gradient, through the sharp right-hander, and on and up to the finish at the top.
>
> Leonie seemed to have enjoyed every wild second of the ride. When I pulled up she smiled through a mask of grey dust and congratulated me. In her innocence she even thought we must have broken the record.

Needless to say, many of these shattering performances were to the credit of cars much more highly-modified than the DFP. Two were disqualified after their climbs; one of them an 11·9 hp Humber which may have been W. G. Tuck's Brooklands 'Gold Bug' suitably disguised and geared. Unfortunately its time was not quoted.

Shelsley Walsh on 22 June, like Aston Clinton, was notable for its newcomers to the course, if not to sprinting. J. Higginson's 80 hp La Buire, which made fastest time in the open event and fastest time of the day, with 1m 8·8s, was the biggest car to attack the hill in our period. Its dimensions were 170 × 150 mm, giving a capacity or 13,619 cc. O. Tholander's 27/80 hp Austro-Daimler, dwarfed in comparison, was only a second slower, however. H. C. Holder's 40 hp Austin was third in 1m 11·4s and Cecil Bianchi's 15 hp Crossley won on formula, but the most admiring comment was reserved for the 6/16 hp Baby Mathis, a four-cylinder miniature car which was the smallest and lightest of those present, yet scuttled up the hill in 1m 44·4s. Five clubs entered the team event, won by the Midland AC's team of Holder, Arthur Cox's 12/18 hp Riley, and W. Stokes's 16/20 hp Sunbeam. Stokes won the closed event on formula, Holder being fastest in 1m 10·8s. Another Austin, a tuned version of the standard 40 hp, known as the 'Defiance' type, was second fastest in the hands of J. H. Dean.

But Saltburn speed trials, held on 6 July, were not the success they had been in earlier years. There were twice as many spectators as before, which was a doubtful blessing to start with, and they had much to complain of. There were fewer interesting cars than was customary, speeds tended to be poor owing to headwinds of between 25 and 35 mph, and the proceedings were prolonged by the large number of separate events and by the practice of arriving at fair handicaps by means of trial runs. The open class for cars conforming to the 1912 Grand Prix regulations attracted only G. O. Herbert's Singer 'Bunny VI', so there was no contest. A very mixed and second-rate bag contested the class for unlimited racing cars over the flying kilometre, which 'Cupid' Hornsted's 60 hp Benz won at 90·93 mph from O. Tholander's 27/80 hp Austro-Daimler; a stripped tourer. The finals of the open events for tourers were won by H. Atley's 10/12 hp Mass from a 12 hp Mercedes in 1m 3s, a runaway win; a Model 'T' Ford; Edward Lisle's 14 hp single-seater Briton, which beat a Sunbeam in 48·2s; G. H. Woods's 20 hp Crossley (43s); Bianchi's 15 hp Crossley (43·6s); Tholander's Austro-Daimler (42·8s); and R. S. Witchell's Straker-Squire (48·6s). Witchell, in fact, won two open events. G. O. Herbert's 15·9 hp Singer was off form, being beaten by the Ford mentioned, and in the closed events was vanquished by Cecil Bianchi's Crossley. This was really a Crossley day, especially among the closed contests, Bianchi also defeating H. G. Day's Talbot and Woods winning two more races, one from Tholander with a time of 45·2s. Other closed events went to Edward Genna and his 12/16 hp Sunbeam, W. G. Tuck's 11·9 hp Humber in 1m 1s from a 12·8 hp Benz, and J. Mortimer's 11·9 hp Arrol-Johnston, the time of which was 1m 7·4s.

After Shelsley and Saltburn (which were the year's most important sprints, both from the point of view of the contemporary and the historian), were the Caerphilly open and closed hillclimb and Porthcawl open and closed speed trials, run jointly by the South Wales AC and Cardiff MC. Held one after the other with a day's breathing-space in between, the Welsh 'double' was to become a classic occasion. This year the excitement began at Caerphilly on 18 July. 'Glorious weather prevailed, and the open banks along the course presented an animated appearance, a large and fashionable attendance being present throughout the six hours that the tests lasted': so wrote the *Western Mail* reporter. It sounds just like Ascot.

The twenty-two classes catered for cyclecars as well as their parents. G. H. Woods made fastest time with his 20 hp Crossley, in 1m 12·4s, while R. S. Witchell's 15 hp Straker-Squire won its class in spite of bursting a rear tyre, skidding wildly and having to finish on a 'flat'. Burgess's 15·9 hp Calthorpe repeated this performance, and its time of 1m 14·4s, second best of the day, was achieved after indulging in a terrific and time-wasting slide on the last bend. The Sunbeams of W. Stokes and N. F. Bayliss won these classes on formula. J. Dew's 15·9 hp German Oryx and W. G. Tuck's 11·9 hp Humber led their classes on both time and formula. Compared with all this excitement, the closed events were dull, winners including Miss Laura Starkey's 12/16 hp Sunbeam and J. A. Gibbs's 15·9 hp Arrol-Johnston.

The timed mile of sand at the Rest Bay, Porthcawl, was 150 yd wide and allowed cars to depart six abreast from their starting-boards. The boards were very necessary, for although the sands were usually hard, they were wet and heavy on 20 July, so that stationary cars sank to their axles. As was expected, all the starters in the later classes suffered from wheelspin on the boards, thanks to the accumulation of wet sand deposited by the earlier numbers. Edward Genna's Sunbeam seems to have made fastest time, with a speed of 57·5 mph. The Coupe de *l'Auto* Calthorpe running in the same class was in trouble, and came second, 1·6 mph slower. There were few starters in the classes for more powerful cars, so that these potentially exciting events became walkovers. Perhaps Caerphilly had thinned out the contenders? Whatever the reason, V. A. Cooper's Oryx won its class among the smaller cars, as did Tuck's Humber; but Tuck's victory at 41·57 mph was quite overshadowed by the extraordinary performance of G. F. Heath's Baby Mathis, which was only 1.57 mph slower. Closed classes went to Miss Laura Starkey's Sunbeam and H. West's 27/80 hp Austro-Daimler.

The Sutton Coldfield club, reappearing in a new incarnation as the Sutton Coldfield & Mid-Warwickshire AC, abandoned Coalport Hill this year because its condition was even worse than usual. They held their closed climb of 20 July on Hints Hill, near Tamworth, where there were also advantages in the shape of a complacent police force and favourable local opinion. It is uncertain if these happy circumstances would have survived a narrowly-averted collision between C. A. Bird's Coupe de *l'Auto* Sunbeam and a trap. As it was, Bird braked savagely, slid, missed the obstacle and went on to record fastest time of the day, 40·8s, for the ½-mile course. J. H. Dean's 40 hp Austin was second best with 46s, and won its class on formula as well as time, but Bird's class went to Cecil Bianchi's 12/14 hp Crossley on formula.

The Leicestershire AC's climb on Beacon Hill, Woodhouse Eaves, on 31 August is unique in one respect: it is the only instance the author has been able to trace of a stretch of public road being closed by the local authority (the Leicestershire County Council in this case) for a hillclimb. It was also a pioneer in another, lesser, respect in including a class for 'veterans'; these being classified as cars more than four years old. Nine clubs took part, so this was virtually an open event. G. H. Woods's 20 hp Crossley now proved itself one of the fastest, if not *the* fastest, road car in the country by beating two Coupe de *l'Auto* Sunbeams in the unlimited scratch event; this over a course which was so gentle that the latters' gear ratios, which would have put them at a grave disadvantage at most other venues, were insufficient excuse for defeat. Almost all the competitors covered a large part of the course in top gear. Woods's time was 59·6s, compared with the 60s of C. A. Bird's racing Sunbeam and the 65·6s of Louis Coatalen's car, which had been the Coupe de *l'Auto*-winning machine. Coatalen, in fourth place, was also beaten by J. Hedge's 25 hp Talbot, which came in third. Woods's average speed for the 1,433 yd was nearly 50 mph, and he and Bird each won another class, Cecil Bianchi's 15 hp Crossley coming first on formula in both cases. Even the Du Pré contest saw a remarkable performance in the defeat of such stalwarts as Cecil Bianchi, Dr Tresidder and J. L. Kirk by a lady, Miss Laura Starkey, whose time of 1m 28·8s in her 12/16 hp Sunbeam was better than anything they could do. She also won on formula.

This year, the 25 hp Talbot was redesigned by G. W. Brown and acquired an L-head. Hedge's car might have been one of the new type, which was to be so successful in 1913–14.

The Manchester AC, having found Cornist Hall unsatisfactory in 1911, resorted to the Manchester MC's hill at Heyden Bridge on the Woodhead-Huddersfield road for their event on 5 October. There was, however, a lot of traffic, causing delays in the programme. Higginson's La Buire was the only car in Britain which could see-off Woods's Crossley more often than not, but it seized a piston and retired, leaving Woods to make fastest time of 2m 37·4s. The sound of this mechanical cataclysm—the disintegration of four litres of piston—must have been something to tell one's grandchildren about.

Cecil Bianchi's 15 hp Crossley, which ascended in 3m 6s, was best on formula in Woods's class, that open to trade entries, but the best man on formula overall, as well as the second fastest up the hill, was A. Fillingham on a 20 hp Vauxhall. His time was 3m 2s, nearly half a minute slower than Woods.

* * *

To the contemporary, 1913 was the year of broken records and remarkable times. To the historian, it is much more important as the year when the new and rapidly-spreading cult of the cheap economy car—the spidery and light, single- or twin-cylinder belt-driven cyclecar and its more sophisticated relative the really small, compact four-cylinder—first impinged noticeably upon the competition world. The cyclecar age had begun in 1910, with the introduction of the four-wheeled French Bédélia and H. F. S. Morgan's first three-wheeler. Cyclecars enjoyed a spell of popularity in the years immediately before and after the first world war, but they were altogether too uncomfortable to be acceptable for general family use. The more substantial, rather more expensive but still very economical small 'four' of about 8 to 10 hp rating—the light car, which had begun to appear in 1912—was the true harbinger of the future; of the age of 'motoring for the masses'. The Morris Oxford, the Austin Seven and the Hillman Imp were and are of the same family.

Both these new classes promised much for the sportsman interested in speed. With few exceptions, the small car of an earlier age, typified by the De Dion single or twin, had little or no performance, combining the cyclecar's lack of power and smoothness with the small four's solidity. The cyclecar was the easier, more elementary answer: if your construction was extremely light and skimpy, your little engine did not need to produce much power in order to propel it at a fair pace. Of course, those cyclecar manufacturers who went in for competition seriously—notably GN, Buckingham and Morgan in 1912–13, followed by Carden in 1914—developed their engines until they had the best of both worlds. Comfort, of course, was of minimal importance in a sprint car.

Making the more substantial light car go reasonably fast was more difficult. Traditions varied among those who tried. Two of those who succeeded best, Singer and Calthorpe, already had wide experience of extracting the greatest possible power from side-valve engines of two to three litres' capacity: the twelves, fourteens and sixteens. Hillman, Mathis and Lagonda had made bigger cars, too, if not—usually—efficient ones. Bugatti and Morris were exceptions, in that they began their careers with miniature fours of considerably better-than-average performance. The GWK with two cylinders offered a parallel, while AC began life in the cyclecar class—the three-wheeler 'Sociable' of 1910 (not a car used for sprinting) and the earlier commercial Autocarrier—then went on to small fours.

The Light Car and Cyclecar, founded late in 1912, was quickly off the mark in promoting a competition: a climb of Alms Hill, Stonor, near Henley, scheduled for January of the coming year. This hill was a terror. It had been used by motor-cycles at least as early as 1912, but its gradient, varying between 1-in-3 and 1-in-5½, combined with its extreme roughness and narrowness to prohibit light car climbs until they had developed a lot more power in the twenties. Alms was really the first of the 'trials observed sections', found at a time when the term in its modern interpretation was unknown. In 1913 and later, it was enough to have got up Alms Hill at all. In this first attempt, when the surface was soft, only Messervy's Duo, a twin-cylinder cyclecar, succeeded out of over fifty cyclecars and light cars in attendance. A 40/50 hp Rolls-Royce, for example, failed miserably.

The Essex MC's first climb of Kop, not far away, on 15 March included only one car class, but enjoyed open status. A. G. Brown's Hispano-Suiza made fastest time of the day, and at one stage three of these cars, starting simultaneously, indulged in a neck-and-neck race up the hill. No one, however, seems to have condemned this irresponsible behaviour. L. N. Straight's 15·9 hp SCAR came first on formula. In the middle of April, Kop was to be used by the Motor Cycling Club for a climb which catered for cyclecars, but only two, the GWKs of J. T. Wood and V. Wilberforce, took part, and it is not known if times were taken. Incidentally, the definition 'light car class' or 'cyclecar class' did not mean that one type was admitted and the other excluded; this class in any event would include 'babies' of every variety.

On 3 May, the Lancashire AC, forsaking Rivington Pike, climbed Waddington Fells, near Clitheroe. The classes, open and closed, were differentiated by cubic capacity; the earliest recorded instance of this in a sprint. The limits were 1,639cc, 2,458 cc, 3,769 cc and over 3,769 cc. There was also a class for cyclecars, but the occasion was interesting historically for another reason: the maiden appearance of J. Higginson's 98 × 150 mm, 4½-litre 30/98 hp Vauxhall; a machine built for him by the company for the purpose of winning sprints. This it proceeded to do, when put into production, for the next twenty-odd years. Higginson must have come to the conclusion that the future lay with smaller, more efficient cars than the La Buire; with machines which had almost never actually beaten it, but had come very close to doing so with engines one-fifth of its size.

Although the course at Waddington Fells was wet and speeds curtailed, the Vauxhall made what was described as a 'sensational ascent', in a series of alarming slides. Its time in the open event, very easily best of the day, was 47·2s. Higginson had plenty of competition among the twenty-seven entries in the 'open', in the shape of Cecil Bianchi's 15 hp Crossley, which made second fastest time, W. G. Tuck's Humber, and two works Sunbeams, including that of the now-recovered Edward Genna. E. Hoyle's Hutton, now called a 25 hp Napier, and J. H. Brereton's 15 hp Straker-Squire set up the best time in the closed classes. Two 10/16 hp Stoewers won them on formula. G. W. Hands's 10/12 hp Calthorpe led the cyclecar class on time and formula. Now that Napier were making a four-cylinder car themselves, the 15 hp, it may be that they were no longer so insistent on disowning the old 'Hutton'.

Three weeks later the new 30/98 hp Vauxhall created another sensation at the Hertfordshire County AC's open climb of Aston Clinton. Watched, among others, by Dame Nellie Melba, it not only made fastest time of the forty-eight entries, but also set up a new outright course record. Driven by A. J. Hancock, this was a works car.

Cecil Bianchi, now on a 20/25 hp Crossley, was second fastest by 10·6s. S. S. Barber's 25 hp Talbot was first on formula in this class, while other winners on time were H. G. Day's 15 hp Talbot (with J. Barber-Lomax's 20 hp Vauxhall 2·6s slower), W. O. Bentley's DFP, and J. W. Lenanton's Baby Mathis. This Mathis and another were first and second on time and formula in their class, by a very large margin. Tuck's Humber and Bianchi's 15 hp Crossley won Bentley's and Barber-Lomax's classes on formula. The Humber was 7·8s slower than the DFP.

At Shelsley Walsh on 7 June the course record was beaten no less than seven times; and this without recourse to hair-raising slides. It was noticeable, in high-speed cornering, how much more stable cars had become over the years, and how general road-holding had improved. Only A. W. Tate's 60 hp Mercedes challenged this conclusion, by tearing up 10 yd of iron railing and suffering, among other damage, the loss of a hubcap. This was replaced by a loaf of bread, which kept oil in and dust out very effectively.* J. Higginson's 30/98 hp Vauxhall made fastest time of the day in the closed event in 55·2s, but the other remarkable times were confined to the open climb. H. C. Ansell, runner-up to Higginson in his 58 hp Daimler, managed only 1m 7·6s. Leslie Hands's 25 hp works Talbot ascended in 57·2s, to win the 'open'. C. A. Bird's 25/30 hp Sunbeam clocked 58·4s, A. J. Hancock's 30/98 hp Vauxhall being third. The other record-breaking runs were made by Bird's 12/16 hp Sunbeam, a 25/30 hp works, and Oscar Cüpper's 27/80 hp Alpine Metallurgique. R. Wilkie's 20 hp Vauxhall won the closed event on formula, and H. G. Day's 15 hp Talbot the open. Everyone who was anyone was there: Genna, Bentley, Bianchi, Kidner and Tuck as well as those mentioned. W. D. South's 8 hp Morgan was fastest in the cyclecar event in 1m 31·4s, followed by G. W. Hands's 10/12 hp Calthorpe with 1m 35·2s. The Calthorpe won on formula.

Hands's Talbot, a very special development of the standard G. W. Brown 'Competition' 25 hp, using a 12 hp chassis, was the twin of Percy Lambert's celebrated 'Hour Record' car. Their dimensions

* Other homely remedies for mechanical disorders were used. Porridge oats as an additive to a leaking radiator were popular, since the oats, having (one hoped) found their way into all interstices, there swelled on contact with the water. Care was needed, however. A Ceirano in which R. R. Jackson, the racing driver, was a passenger, having received this treatment, overheated again. The driver removed the radiator cap while the water was still boiling, and the resulting geyser of well-mixed, scalding porridge covered driver, passenger and car, and put the first-named in hospital.

Page 137 (above) *Madresfield: a very stark Morgan prepares to start;* (below) *Vauxhall on the sand: Humphrey Cook's 1922 TT Vauxhall*

Page 138 *Millership's very special racing Lanchester, usually seen at Brooklands, at Shelsley Walsh in 1923*

were the same as the production vehicle, 101 × 140 mm, but they churned out 130 bhp at 3,500 rpm instead of 75 bhp at 2,500 rpm.

Back in Wales, the Caerphilly-Porthcawl 'double' event of the Cardiff MC and South Wales AC was held on 19 and 21 June. A. J. Hancock's 30/98 hp Vauxhall was fastest up the Mountain Road in 1m 4·6s, but this performance, excellent though it was, was overshadowed by that of Leslie Hands in the new 25 hp Talbot. Sliding so wildly on one corner that he burst a tyre and nearly turned over, he went on to record 1m 13·4s; second best to Hancock. The fastest cars in the other open classes were W. G. Tuck's 11·9 hp Humber (1m 26·6s), the same man's 14 hp Humber with 1m 36·8s, Edward Genna's 12/16 hp Sunbeam (1m 20·6s), and H. G. Day's 15 hp Talbot (1m 18s). J. Thomas's 11·9 hp Arrol-Johnston won the first of these classes on formula. The latter included some interesting newcomers in the form of W. R. Morris's 10 hp Morris Oxford, which was rather slow, and P. O. Serck's 10 hp Bugatti, which was not a great deal faster. The other leaders on formula were Tuck's 14 hp Humber, and Day's 12 hp and 15 hp Talbots. As in 1912, the closed events were dull. G. Kemshall's 12 hp Talbot added a brace of firsts on time and formula to the Talbot score. R. F. Wakley's 11·9 hp Arrol-Johnston and Mrs W. G. Morel's 26/60 hp Metallurgique achieved the same double distinction in their classes, and E. M. Saul's 26/60 hp Metallurgique was fastest in its category.

On 21 June, the Rest Bay saw a reversal of fortunes in the Talbot-Vauxhall duel. E. Stokes's 25 hp Talbot registered 53·6s for the standing mile, Percy Kidner's 30/98 hp Vauxhall recording 55·2s. Stokes also set up fastest time of the day in another race, where he beat the 27/80 hp Austro-Daimlers of J. R. M. Stanfield and E. H. Lewis in 51·6s; an average speed of 69·76 mph. The nearest Austro-Daimler could do no better than 1m 2·2s. W. G. Tuck's 11·9 hp Humber beat J. Thomas's 11·9 hp Arrol-Johnston in two events, his best time being 1m 15·4s. H. G. Day's Talbots also won two races, the first with the 12 hp car against Edward Genna, whom he beat by 2·4s in 1m 3s, and the second with the 15 hp against J. H. Jones's 18 hp Minerva, in 1m 3·8s. Miss Laura Starkey won her closed event, her time in the 12/16 hp Sunbeam being 1m 17·8s. E. R. Insole's 15 hp Straker-Squire collected another first, and the cyclecar race was won by H. F. S. Morgan's Morgan at the very respectable speed of 49·58 mph from G. W. Hands's 10/12 hp Calthorpe, which achieved 43·26 mph.

It was remarked that the Nottingham AC's regular excursions to the Clipstone Drive were less interesting for the quality of their sport than in pre-Brooklands days. However that may be, Brooklands cars and drivers were not ashamed to be seen at Welbeck. Percy Lambert, driving the 'Hour-Record' Talbot, appeared there on 28 June and carried off the flying kilometre for any type of car in 22·6s, or 98·98 mph. Hancock's 30/98 hp Vauxhall was second on time in 23s, or 97·26 mph, while Percy Smith's 15 hp Straker-Squire covered the distance at 86·04 mph; such was the speed of the '30/98' Vauxhall even at this early stage in its history. The two flying kilometre handicaps for touring cars went to R. Wilkie's 20 hp Vauxhall on time and handicap. His time in one was 33·2s (67·38 mph). Wilkie also won the standing mile, again on both time and handicap, in 70·2s, a clean sweep, for he had won the unrestricted flying kilometre on handicap as well.

On the 28th, too, South Harting echoed to the crackle of open exhausts for the first time since 1907. The recently-formed Cyclecar Club organised this first major event for the new babies, and made it an open one. A. W. Lambert's Morgan single-seater won the class for 'monocars' in 1m 33·4s, setting up fastest time of the day in so doing. Best of the 750 cc four-wheelers was J. F. Buckingham's 'Chota', possibly a precursor of the Buckingham cyclecar, in 2m 29·4s. W. G. McMinnies' Morgan, which won its class in the 1913 Cyclecar Grand Prix at Amiens, ascended in 1m 43s, making best time among the 1,100 cc three-wheelers, while A. Frazer-Nash's GN, with 1m 50·8s, was better than Lionel Martin's Singer (2m 14s) among the 1,100 cc four-wheelers.

With their own magazine, and two clubs—the Motor Cycling Club and the Cyclecar Club—actively concerned for their future, the new breed of small car was well launched.

It is not strictly *apropos* in this context, but the story H. R. Godfrey tells of the 1913 Amiens race shows just how light-heartedly motor racing was sometimes approached at this time. Frazer-Nash was at the wheel of one GN, and Cecil Whitehead, 'a charming personality, but quite unmechanical' was to drive the other. Whitehead began to 'play the gallery' while waiting on the starting-line. He shouted to his mechanic (an equally unmechanical friend) to 'tighten all the nuts', handing him an enormous spanner for the purpose. The mechanic assailed the cylinder head nuts with such vigour that one head split clean in two. One wonders what Mr Frazer-Nash had to say.

Yet other competitors would go to almost any extremes to win. W. O. Bentley, speaking of sand racing at about this time, tells how:

One driver in particular had a special knack for persuading other competitors into the softer, damper sand, which had been carefully reconnoitred before. Another trick he had, which required some practice, was to swing the tail round hard alongside a fellow-competitor and spray him with sand like an excited dog scratching for a bone. This could be highly painful, as well as distracting, for the offended party.

Talking of sand races, the Yorkshire AC's Saltburn speed trials on 5 July 1913 were not an unrelieved success, in spite of attracting a record entry. The spectators misbehaved, wandering across the course in front of the cars, the sands were wet and soft, and for some reason hand timing was used, so that some surprising times were forthcoming. For example, in the flying kilometre for unlimited racing cars, Hancock, on his 30/98 hp Vauxhall, was said to have averaged 106·52 mph, and Percy Lambert 103·55 mph on the Brooklands Talbot. The conditions being what they were, these speeds were improbably high, by perhaps as much as 10 mph.

The contest for racing cars of up to 3,450 cc went to R. S. Witchell's 15 hp Straker-Squire at 86·7 mph. W. Masser Horniman's 15 hp Mass was second, beating R. Wilkie's Vauxhall. Other open races (the standing miles) were won by Cecil Bianchi's 15 hp Crossley, the 12/16 hp Sunbeams of Edward Genna and J. Mortimer, A. E. George's single-seater Model 'T' Ford (two events, at 49·26 and 51·3 mph), Hancock's 30/98 hp Vauxhall and Percy Lambert's Talbot. Lambert's speed of 60·78 mph bettered that of Leslie Hands's 25 hp Talbot and Hancock's Vauxhall by a wide margin, though, in the race he won, Hancock averaged 60·13 mph. Bianchi's and Genna's speeds were 49·05 and 53·51 mph respectively.

Bianchi, Genna and Hands also won their closed events, Hands doing so twice. His best speed was 55·92 mph, which was more than Higginson's 30/98 hp Vauxhall could achieve, in second place on each occasion. T. S. Rowlandson's 10/12 hp Mass was another 'closed' winner. As with most of the major events of 1913, an open cyclecar race was also organised. It was won by J. C. Stringer's 8 hp Winco at 36·53 mph after a much faster 10 hp Singer broke down.

Through misfortune or mismanagement, the Mersey Motor Club held their Colwyn Bay open speed trials on the same day as Saltburn and an important Brooklands meeting. The result was a very poor entry. The conditions militated against much excitement in the way of speed: the piece of road which was used, squashed between the promenade and the railway, was painfully narrow and heavily cambered. Also, there was only enough of it for a flying ½ mile and a standing kilometre. The spectators were very vulnerably placed as well, so initially, the RAC would only grant a permit if the meeting were restricted to cars of under 2 litres; but in the end this order was rescinded. The three capacity classes were divided at 1,639, 2,458, and 3,769 cc. In the course of winning two ½-mile events, W. Watson's single-seater 20 hp Vauxhall covered the distance in 28·2s, or 63·8 mph. G. W. Brown's 11·9 hp Arrol-Johnston did so in 36·2s, to win its class. Among the standing kilometre events, Watson again won two and Brown one. Brown's best time was 44·6s and Watson's only 0·2s better: a fine performance. N. H. Brown's 10 hp Austin won its ½ mile and its kilometre in 44·8s and 67·2s. There were no exciting dices.

The Leicestershire AC's Beacon Hill contest was run three weeks later. There were no fewer than eighty entries, but this year there was no talk of the hill being closed to the public. The presence of numerous and uncontrollable spectators and passers-by led to two incidents, one of them rather funny. One cannot do better than quote the deadpan account of *The Autocar*:

> At one period a motor char-a-banc stuck on the steepest portion of the hill and completely blocked the road for a considerable period, the length of which may be judged from the fact that the driver removed sparking plugs, cleaned and replaced them, and attended to other deficiencies of his charge in a manner by no means suggestive of haste.

However, it was very far from amusing when an old lady stepped across the road in front of Higginson's 30/98 hp Vauxhall, causing him to brake hard, spin and knock her flying, putting her into hospital. Higginson was estimated to be doing over 60 mph at the time of the accident; not at all the sort of figure it was wise to publish in the circumstances. Raymond Mays, only a boy at the time, was a witness.

In the end, Percy Lambert's 25 hp Talbot set up fastest time of the day, his 49s bettering Higginson's best time by 1·4s. The length of the course was the same as in 1912. No wonder that this was regarded as a year of fantastic speeds: the Vauxhall and the Talbot, the year's fastest cars, were 10 seconds faster on Beacon Hill than Woods's Crossley, one of the two best of 1912. The other feature of the day was the performance of W. E. Bullock's 10 hp Singer. This little car won two classes on time, in 1m 12·6s and 1m 11·4s, but had little opposition here: its greatest achievement was to come second to H. G. Day's 12 hp Talbot in a third contest; slower, in 1m 15s, by a mere 2·2s, and actually beating Cecil Bianchi's 15 hp Crossley, which could not get below 1m 32·2s. Day also won another class, in 1m 11·8s.

This year the Yorkshire AC's open and closed meeting at Pateley

Bridge attracted an exceptionally large entry of forty-five, all of whom, miraculously, turned up at the start on 13 September. In spite of an irritating wait while a flock of sheep passed by, and several near-accidents, involving R. S. Witchell's 15 hp Straker-Squire and Higginson's Vauxhall, which lost a tyre, the record for the hill was broken no less than three times. Leslie Hands, driving Lambert's Brooklands Talbot, made fastest time of the day, followed by Higginson's 30/98 hp Vauxhall. H. G. Day's 25 hp Talbot, also driven by Hands, was third. On reflection, it would have been surprising if the record had stood, for all the cars in this, the open event, ran in racing trim. In the closed contest, three 20 hp Vauxhalls gained first places on formula, but the 15 hp Mass of H. Dunnington beat them all on time. The name of Mass recurs in leading positions over a number of years at this period, yet there was no apparent reason why this obscure French car should be faster than its competitors. Like La Buire, DFP and some other foreign products imported before 1914, it was a pedestrian machine of little sporting merit or renown in its own land, simply 'hotted-up' by its British agents for the speed events that were thought to sell cars in this country.

Returning to the beaches, the Somerset AC's speed trials on the beach at Weston-super-Mare on 4 October, held in conjunction with the Bristol MCC, are important in the sense that any new sand race meeting attracted attention at this time. In any case, it included open events, even if these did not lure the big names. There was a respectable entry of twenty-one, and though rain made the timed mile of sand soft and slushy, the day was deemed a success. There was no restriction on bodywork or absence thereof, but the use of 'dope' in any form was forbidden. It is probable that the 25 hp Talbot which walked-over in its class made fastest time of the day among the cars. Other class winners included Miss Laura Starkey's 12/16 hp Sunbeam, E. S. Pink's 15 hp Talbot, a 12 hp Talbot, and W. Wilson Douglas's Douglas light car.

* * *

Nineteen-fourteen was to be a short season for reasons all too well known. In character, it followed 1913, with perhaps an even greater emphasis on light cars and cyclecars, their new importance underlined by the fact that the RAC gave over its major event of the year to them. This, too, was the first important sporting road event which the parent club had held since 1908; and by a coincidence, it was also to include eleven timed hillclimbs.

The RAC's Light Car Trials were very tough indeed for the small cars of that period, for they required the contestants, with a minimum of maintenance, to cover 1,010 miles of hilly north-country roads, including the eleven timed climbs, in six days: from 4–9 May. The factories were well represented among the successful entrants; and among those, AC and Singer outshone all the others. S. C. Westall's 10 hp four-cylinder AC made absolute fastest time on seven of the climbs: Wass Bank, Greenhow Hill (Pateley Bridge), Arkengarthdale, Scarth Nick, Kidstones Pass, Heaton Woods and Garrowby. His times were 2m 43·2s, 3m 12s, 1m 24·8s, 5m 57·4s, 4m 51·4s, and 2m 30s. S. Rollason's 10 hp Singer put up a similar performance on Sutton Bank (twice: on each occasion this famous motorcycling hill was attacked), Blue Bank and Brownstay Ridge, in 3m 6·2s, 3m 14s, 2m 26s, and 2m 19·2s. Rollason was runner-up on 'Westall's' hills, in 2m 50·2s, 3m 26·8s, 2m 9·8s, 1m 27·4s, 6m 15·2s, 5m 31·4s and 2m 36·2s, so on sheer speed these two cars were unbeatable.

In its class, C. L. Scott's AC, a lighter four-wheeler, made an even more consistent, if not quite so rapid showing by coming first on time in no fewer than ten of the eleven ascents, Robinson's Salmon spoiling a clean sweep. In a third class, J. T. Woods's GWK was fastest up six hills, and Armstrong's Gordon on the other five. The Gordon was a 10 hp four-wheeler chain-driven 'twin' made in Beverley, Yorkshire. Rollason's Singer made best overall performance of any car during the trials, taking into account all considerations, including speed.

J. F. Buckingham's 12 hp Buckingham was fastest in its class at the Hertfordshire County AC's open climb of Aston Clinton a week later. This belt-driven cyclecar weighed only 6¾ cwt, and with its vee-twin ohv 1,100 cc engine, had understandably fierce performance. Buckingham beat Lionel Martin's 10 hp Singer by 3·8s, though the latter won on formula. Both of them, and even a GWK, were faster than any of three Bugattis. J. Withers, driving W. O. Bentley's 1914 Tourist Trophy DFP, made best time in the next class, with Bentley himself second fastest by 0·8s in the same car. Bentley was first on formula. E. Stokes's 15/20 hp Talbot led its class on both time and formula, as did Leslie Hands's 25/50 hp Talbot. These 1914 works '25s', now brought to meetings inside vans, had a lengthened stroke of 150 mm, and represented the ultimate development of this car. F. W. Shorland's 20/30 hp Talbot, second by 7·4s, was also beaten by Hands on formula, though the latter's was the bigger car. In this class, incidentally, Talbots were first, second, third and fourth on speed. In spite of drought, the course was kept clear of dust by a convenient cross-wind. The spectators, however, were so numerous that there were not enough marshals to check their movements.

Although there were only nine starters, and the chalk surface was wet and slippery, Kop on 23 May was the scene of a momentous event: the first of the memorable series of so-called 'Inter-Varsity' sprints.

T. S. Coates's 10 hp Singer put up a truly incredible performance by beating J. W. Read's 25 hp Vauxhall, now described as an ex-Hancock works car with a racing body, by 56s to 63·6s. This, too, was in character, for the 'Inter-Varsity' events were to become notorious for excitement and fine sport. Motor dealers had a habit of bringing along their latest sporting cars to give demonstration runs before wealthy undergraduates, which gave these meetings still more variety and appeal. On this occasion, W. Scott's 15·9 hp Th. Schneider was best on formula. Naturally T. S. Coates won the cyclecar class, with a time of 57·4s.

Oxford were the winning team, however, which was not at all a foretaste of the future. Oxford were always at a sad disadvantage, for their university authorities were in general far harsher towards motor sport than their Cambridge counterparts, forbidding, from time to time, not only organisation of and participation in speed events, but also the ownership of 'racing cars'. The Oxford University motor clubs tended to be ephemeral bodies, dying from lack of interest caused by lack of sport, then being resuscitated briefly by a new generation of undergraduates. Never did they have the time, or build up their reputations sufficiently, to raise their events to the status enjoyed by those of their rivals. In the later days, inter-club sprints were usually organised by the Cambridge club, on a 'Cambridge' course; and once, in 1934, an Oxford-run event on an Oxford course had to be taken over by Cambridge at the last moment, the Oxford club having incontinently expired. To this rare humiliation was added the constant one of seeing the Cambridge team, its drivers allowed experience and its cars tolerated, carry off the honours wherever they might be. And Cambridge could even hold eliminating sprints to decide who would represent them at the inter-club event!

On the same day as the Kop climb, 23 May, the Lancashire AC again met on Waddington Fells. The open events were divided into capacity classes, and Leslie Hands won the unlimited class, and made best time of the day, his 25/50 hp Talbot ascending in 46s. Humphrey Cook's 120 hp Isotta-Fraschini and F. W. Hobday's 120 hp Mercedes were fast, but not handy enough for a course with bends. This was Cook's earliest recorded success in sprints, achieved in spite of the loss of his undershield *en route*. H. G. Day's 20/30 hp Talbot was best on formula.

In the other classes, G. Knox Gilchrist's 10/16 hp single-seater racing Stoewer was best on time and formula, as was E. Mercer's 12/15 hp DFP. E. Stokes's 15/20 hp Talbot was fastest in its class, but J. Hedge's similar put up the best overall formula performance of the day as well as leading Stokes's category in this respect. J. Higginson's 30/98 hp Vauxhall won the event which was closed to amateurs in 50·4s, while J. A. Barber-Lomax's 20 hp Vauxhall was first on formula. Buckingham's 12 hp Buckingham was best on time and formula among the cyclecars.

Leslie Hands went on to make fastest time of the day in the sand races at Weymouth and Weston-super-Mare on 27 May and 13 June. It could truly be said that, by 1914, Talbots had regained their old supremacy in sprinting, challenged and on occasion beaten only by Crossley, Sunbeam and Vauxhall. Now, not only was the works 25/50 hp Talbot in any case the fastest thing on the road, but its nearest challengers, the works Vauxhalls, had disappeared.

The Essex MC was to run splendid sprint meetings at Westcliff in the twenties, but its first open speed trials, held on the Chalkwell Esplanade on 25 June 1914, were almost a disaster. The course—a mile of excellent surface, 40 ft wide—the weather, and the turn-out of spectators were all first class, as was the prospect of no fewer than seventy-five events on the programme, but most of the famous names were on the other side of the island, climbing the Mountain Road at Caerphilly. B. Haywood with his 10 hp works Singer was the most distinguished racing man present. He won the flying ½ mile for 1,100 cc cars. The 1,500 cc standing kilometre event went to F. L. Scholte's 8 hp Bugatti, and the 1,100 cc division to Miss Addis-Price's 10 hp Mathis, while H. Nelson Smith's 9 hp Hillman collected firsts in the standing kilometre and ½ mile in all classes up to 3,000 cc and 2,100 cc respectively, foreshadowing Raymond Mays' early triumphs. 25 hp Berliets won two events, as did A. Bovier's 15 hp Th. Schneider. D. C. Sykes's Model 'T' Ford and L. M. Sanford's 22 hp Bedford-Buick won theirs. There was only one minor accident, which, in the words of the local newspaper, occurred 'during the afternoon, when Francis Henry Burr, of independent means, was riding on a motor-cycle from the direction of Southend towards Westcliff, and did not notice the rope across the Esplanade. . . .'

At the same moment, spectacular things were, as usual, happening at Caerphilly. Sliding wildly, Leslie Hands's 25/50 hp Talbot made fastest time of the day in 1m 6·6s with R. S. Witchell's 15/20 hp Straker-Squire second fastest, 5·4s behind. Witchell did even better in the class for 1914 Tourist Trophy cars, climbing in 1m 10·6s while winning it. He was also best on formula in Hands's class. It is interesting to read that Lionel Martin's time of 1m 22·2s, gaining him his class on time and formula with his 10 hp Singer, was better than W. O. Bentley could do in the two-litre DFP with 1m 25·4s. This time, however, gave Bentley a similar double win in his class. J. I. Walters's 12/16 hp Vermorel put up a time of 1m 31·8s, thereby winning his class on speed, but M. Neal's 14 hp Humber won on formula. The time of E. R. Insole's 16 hp Sunbeam—1m 19s—was just good enough to beat E. Stokes's 15/20 hp Talbot, but Stokes carried off the class formula award. Similarly, Richard Lisle's 20 hp Tourist Trophy Star, with 1m 17s, was too good for the formula winner, H. G. Day's 20/30 hp Talbot. The closed events are of interest only for the wins of E. R. Insole and H. Taylor, both in 16 hp Sunbeams, and G. D. Pearce-Jones (25 hp Vauxhall), on time and formula in each case except that of Taylor, who won on formula alone.

After a clear day's recuperation, competitors assembled on the 27th at Porthcawl, where the sands were firm and smooth for once. Leslie Hands was again faster than all comers, his speed of 68·97 mph over the standing mile being much too quick for R. F. Wakley's 25/35 hp Zust, more than 10 mph slower. A. Bertelli's 30/98 hp Vauxhall, at 52·63 mph, beat J. H. Jones's 18 hp Minerva. Could this have been A. C. Bertelli, the future designer of Aston Martins? In the race for TT cars, a 15 hp Straker-Squire driven by F. C. Clement, who was certainly the man later to become famous at the wheel of various Bentleys, pipped Cecil Bianchi's 15/20 hp Crossley by just 0·2s, at 58·25 mph. In another event, Bianchi was more heavily outclassed, this time by E. Stokes's 15/20 hp Talbot, which won at the remarkable speed of 62·72 mph.

In his class, H. G. Day with his 20/30 hp Talbot again beat Richard Lisle's TT Star, with 62·07 mph. Talbot's sprint cars were making Tourist Trophy racers look rather foolish. In the classes for smaller machinery, C. L. Scott's 12 hp AC was surprisingly faster than Lionel Martin's much-modified Singer, defeating him by 1·6s at

42·15 mph. W. G. Tuck's 11·9 hp Humber so easily saw off W. O. Bentley's DFP, with 51·87 mph, that the latter must have been sick, but Bentley went on to win the next class at 48 mph. As was her habit, Miss Laura Starkey won her closed class in her Sunbeam, as did Miss L. Cooper on a 40/50 hp Rolls-Royce, and Mrs W. E. Jones's 25 hp Vauxhall: a clean sweep for the ladies.

The Mersey MC did not repeat their mistake of 1913, so their Colwyn Bay speed trials on 4 July attracted some excellent works entries. Leslie Hands was there to make fastest time of the day with his Talbot: 32·8s for the standing kilometre. He won another event in 34·6s, and H. G. Day's 20/30 hp car one in 36·8s. H. Nelson Smith's 9 hp Hillman did extremely well to tie with W. O. Bentley's DFP at the head of their class, with 43·2s. In the next class down (for cars of up to 1,500 cc), Smith was second to B. Haywood's 10 hp Singer, which won in the splendid time of 40·4s.

Saltburn a week later was perhaps the most exciting and interesting meeting to take place since the series began. Haywood's performance in the racing Singer 'Caruso' was sufficiently sensational, for he won four open classes up to 1,850 cc with his 1,056 cc engine, competing against another Singer and H. Nelson Smith's 9 hp Hillman. Smith, however, went one better, collecting the 2,500 cc class award with his 1,357 cc machine. He beat the formidable Cecil Bianchi in his 15 hp Crossley, though giving away a litre. No more convincing proof of the 'arrival' of the light car in competition was needed. E. Stokes's 15/20 hp Talbot and R. A. Constantine's 12/16 hp Sunbeam won two classes each. Kenelm Lee-Guinness's 1914 Grand Prix Sunbeam beat J. W. Hedge's 25/50 hp Talbot, but had to give best to Leslie Hands's similar car, while E. Remington's 15/18 hp Bedford-Buick and G. H. Maynard's 10/15 hp Nardini won their classes. Humphrey Cook's 120 hp Isotta-Fraschini won its handicap.

In the flying start events for racing cars, R. S. Witchell's 15/20 hp Straker-Squire defeated Richard Lisle's faithful 20 hp Star with a speed of 73·6 mph against 71 mph, while Dario Resta's 9-litre, 12-cylinder Brooklands Sunbeam just managed to pip Leslie Hands. In spite of having an engine of nearly double the capacity, Resta's speed of 104·5 mph was only 1 mph better than that of the fine Talbot driver. Resta then tried for the world's flying kilometre record, setting a mean speed of 111·05 mph in successive runs, but he and all the other competitors had to contend with a very strong headwind and a course which was not quite dry, so their times were not of the best. The closed events brought victory to Stokes (twice), J. Hedge's

25/50 hp Talbot (twice), W. O. Bentley's DFP and Miss Laura Starkey's 12/16 hp Sunbeam.

On a miniature scale, there was just as much excitement at South Harting on 18 July, when the Cyclecar Club met. In the touring classes, A. Frazer-Nash's GN was best with 1m 51·8s. D. H. Cohen's Bugatti, the best time of which was 1m 55·4s, won on formula. James Radley, the Rolls-Royce driver, and A. M. Holzapfel in his Carden provided different kinds of 'diversion'. Radley made an impressive demonstration ascent in an Alpine Eagle 40/50 hp Rolls, while Holzapfel overturned his cyclecar in avoiding spectators in the road. In the racing class, J. V. Carden himself made fastest time of the day with 1m 25s, as Frazer-Nash could do no better than 1m 30·8s against him.

The Essex County AC's climb of Laindon, scheduled for the same day, was cancelled for lack of entries, and it is possible that this was a result of the increasing menace of the international situation, but the event was as usual closed, so it may simply have died from 'natural causes'.

No such fate, however, befell the Leicestershire AC's climb of Beacon Hill a week later. As was customary, the times established on this fast hill were excellent. A. H. R. Fedden (the present Sir Roy Fedden) was the sensation of the day, his 15/20 hp Straker-Squire climbing first in 60·8s, beating two 15/20 hp Talbots (H. G. Day's being the nearest, with 70·2s). He then set a time of 58·8s, again better than the Talbots. H. G. Day won each event on formula, however. Algernon Lee-Guinness's twin ohc 1914 Grand Prix Sunbeam made fastest time of the day with 43·6s, but Fedden pulled out still more speed, to register 53s and take second place.

Among the cyclecars and light cars, the 12 hp Buckingham of J. F. Buckingham shattered its rivals, also winning on formula, with a time of 82·4s. No one could get near him, the most successful being J. Mather with his 11 hp Lagonda, whose time was 127·8s. M. Ross-Browne's Baby Mathis beat Miss Addis-Price's similar car, but his time was only 130s, while the results of the Du Pré Cup contest were delayed, and eventually 'lost' in the hubbub of war.

On the same day, the RAC ran another, much less ambitious light car trial near London, for cars of between 1,100 and 1,400 cc. Partly because of the clash with Beacon Hill, and partly on account of its light-alloy racing body, Westall's AC met only feeble opposition. It climbed Star Hill, at Dunton Green in Surrey, in 1m 46·2s and Cudham Hill in 41·6s, making very easily the fastest time on both.

Important events, open or otherwise, had clashed before, and the fact had been duly noticed and deplored. But by 1914, this lack of proper co-operation and, more importantly, co-ordination, between the clubs had become intensely irritating. The main sufferers were the organising clubs and the trade. If co-operation had been tried, it had not achieved any notable success thus far.

But by 4 August, most of the world was at war, yet the carefree atmosphere which had ruled motor sport did not die immediately. Shelsley Walsh, planned for 22 August, was cancelled, but as late as 29 August, the desire to 'carry on' was strong enough to let the Coventry & Warwickshire MC hold their climb for motor-cycles and light cars on Style Kop, with nearly a hundred entries. This hill, near Rugeley, had a maximum gradient of 1-in-8, and four light cars and cyclecars contested their class, W. R. Morris's 10 hp Morris Oxford being best on time and formula. Then the full privations of a country embroiled in bitter war fell upon the motorists, and motor sport went into an enforced hibernation for four long, dark years.

APPENDIX OF OTHER EVENTS

(ST = speed trial; all others hillclimbs; FTD = fastest time of the day)

1908

2 May	Motor Cycling Club, Sharpenhoe. FTD: S. F. Edge, 40 hp Napier. 2nd, J. W. Stocks, 24 hp De Dion. 1st on handicap: W. V. Jolly, 10 hp De Dion.
9 May	Manchester AC, near Blaenau Ffestiniog. FTD: H. Hollingdrake, 35/50 hp La Buire, 43·4s. 1st in amateur class: H. W. Lee, 24 hp Lanchester, 56·4s. Part of reliability trial.
16 May	North Middlesex AC, Cat Hill, Cockfosters, Southgate. Closed. FTD: Max Graddon, 16/24 hp FIAT. 1st on handicap: 10 hp De Dion. Permission of Commissioner of Metropolitan Police obtained,
16 May	Cardiff MC, Rhubina Hill. FTD: W. H. Jackson, 40 hp Austin; 2nd. P. M. T. Hill, 30/40 hp Ariel. 1st on handicap: E. M. Griffiths, 12/14 hp De Dion.
16 May	Essex MC, Lippett's Hill. 1st on handicap: Victor Riley, 9 hp Riley.
23 May	Nottingham AC, Clipstone. ST. Closed. Flying km handicap: 1st, Ross-Browne, 40 hp Napier. Fastest E. M. C. Instone, 58 hp Daimler, 74·02 mph. Standing mile handicap: 1st, Dr Tresidder, 15 hp Talbot Fastest, Captain Newsum, 45 hp Daimler. Flying km scratch: 1st, Frank Newton, 60 hp Napier, 109·4 mph. 2nd, G. Street, 58 hp Daimler, 87·5 mph.
23 May	Mid-Staffordshire AC, Style Kop, Rugeley. 1,200 yd, max 1-in-8. FTD: F. A. Bolton, 40/50 hp Ariel, 63·2s. 1st on handicap: A. G. Harley-Jones, 15/20 hp Talbot.
30 May	Devon & Cornwall AC, Moorshop Hill, Tavistock. Closed. FTD:

T. Paddon, 30 hp Daimler. 1st on formula in classes: Dr W. Crosbie-Hamilton, 10 hp Alldays; W. E. P. Bastard, 10/12 hp Argyll; T. R. Perkin, 12/16 hp Talbot; T. Paddon.

May (ca) Yorkshire AC (Huddersfield branch). Course unknown. FTD: Daimler.

6 June Welsh AC, Philadelphia Hill, Carms. Approx 1,333 yd. FTD: Captain Hughes-Morgan, 45 hp Daimler; 2nd, T. J. Williams, 28 hp Daimler.

13 June Essex AC, Bottledown. 1st in closed handicap: W. Guppy, 20 hp Humber.

13 June Lincolnshire AC, Grimsthorpe. ST. FTD: R. M. Wright, 40 hp Napier. 2nd, Captain Newsum, 58 hp Daimler. 1st in classes: W. Nissler, 20 hp Talbot; Dr R. G. Hogarth, 25 hp Talbot; Dr E. H. Craggs, Baby Peugeot.

13 June Inter-club competition (Derby, Leics, Notts), Oakamoor. FTD: M. Ross-Browne, 60 hp Napier, 1m 9·6s. 1st in final: A. G. Harley-Jones, 15 hp Talbot.

13 June Blackheath AC, Hixey Down. FTD: W. F. Butcher, 12/16 hp Talbot; 2nd, W. Whiteway, 16/20 hp Calthorpe. 1st on formula: W. F. Butcher.

20 June North Hertfordshire AC, Pegsdon Hill. Closed. FTD: G. H. Hodgson, 30 hp Hexton, 55s; 2nd, 30 hp Humber, 88s.

25 June Barnsley & District AC, Stainborough Lowe. Closed. 1st on handicap: Dr Howell, 10 hp Alldays.

27 June South Wales & Mon AC, Buttrill's Hill. Closed. FTD: W. Graham, 35 hp Daimler.

27 June New Forest AC and Hampshire Motor Union, Hill Top, Beaulieu. FTD: Daimler, Lord Montagu. 1st in classes: J. W. Davis, 6 hp Jackson; P. B. Ironside-Bax, 11 hp Gladiator; F. Scorer, 20 hp Talbot; C. J. Haydon, 38 hp Napier.

27 June Derby & District AC, Holly Lane, Ambergate. $\frac{3}{4}$ mile, max 1-in-4. FTD: F. A. Bolton, 40/50 hp Ariel, 1m 11s. 2nd, Arthur Ford, 30 hp Daimler. 1st on handicap: M. Ross-Browne, 15 hp Mass.

11 July Leicestershire AC, Kettleby. FTD: F. A. Bolton, 40/50 hp Ariel, 1m 2·2s. 1st overall on handicap and Du Pré Cup: Dr Tresidder, 15 hp Talbot. 1st in classes: Stanley Riley, 9 hp Riley; M. Ross-Browne, Mass; Mrs H. A. Hamshaw, 60 hp Napier.

11 July Wolverhampton & District AC, Coalport Hill, Ironbridge. 1,000 yd, max 1-in-7. FTD: S. F. Edge, 45 hp Napier. 1st in classes: T. W. Bowen, 10 hp Talbot; G. A. Phillips, 10/12 hp Humber; A. G. Harley-Jones, 15 hp Talbot.

18 July Derby & District AC, Uttoxeter. FTD: F. A. Bolton, 40/50 hp Ariel, 46·2s. 2nd, Joseph Keele, 40 hp Weigel. 1st on formula: H. Jefferson, 9 hp Riley.

18 July Sheffield & District AC, Grindleford Bridge. Closed. 1st in classes: W. Hunt, 6 hp Wolseley; G. D. Flather, 12/16 hp Talbot; Albert Farnell, 30 hp Daimler.

18 July New Forest AC and Dorset AC, Melbury Abbas, Blandford–Shaftesbury road. (Probably Zig Zag Hill—*qv* 1909—conceivably Spread Eagle.) Closed. 1st on handicap in classes: G. H. T. Barlow, 42 hp Daimler; F. W. Lacey, 20 hp Talbot; Viner Ellis, 18 hp Peugeot; R. F. Glyn, 9 hp Sizaire-Naudin.

18 July Oxford & District AC, Irondown Hill. Distance now 678 yd, max 1-in-7. FTD: W. R. Morris, 40 hp De Dietrich, 55·9s. 1st on formula

in classes: G. H. Jones, 10 hp De Dion; W. H. Follett, 14 hp Germain.

18 July — Manchester AC, 'near Manchester'. FTD: J. Newton, 60 hp Napier, 45·2s; 2nd, H. Hollingdrake, 35/50 hp La Buire, 1m 6s. Unofficial 2nd FTD: 22 hp 'Four-Inch' SCAT, 54s. 1st in classes: F. W. Hobday, 7 hp Sizaire-Naudin, 2m 0·4s; T. Rothwell, 20 hp Rothwell, 1m 31s. 1st on handicap overall: F. W. Hobday.

25 July — Somerset AC, Wraxall Hill, Shepton Mallet. FTD: G. S. Lysaght, 35/45 hp Daimler. 1st in classes on formula: G. H. Temple, 9 hp Riley; K. J. H. Wilkinson, 15 hp Humber; W. G. Tilley, 20 hp Humber; J. W. Aspinall, 16/20 hp Rover; G. S. Lysaght.

15 Aug — Lincolnshire AC, Syston Park. FTD: Captain H. E. Newsum, 58 hp Daimler, 60·2s. 1st in classes: Dr R. G. Hogarth, 7 hp Clyde; R. M. Wright, Talbot; H. G. Nalder, 30 hp Germain.

19 Sept — Sheffield & District AC, Grindleford Bridge. 1st in classes: Albert Farnell, 30 hp Daimler; L. Slater, Jackson; E. Wilson, 12/16 hp Talbot.

19 Sept — Harrogate & District AC, Stainburn Moors. Amateurs only. 1st in classes: J. Yates, 20/30 hp Belsize; J. A. Little, 14/20 hp Renault; H. W. Breave, 10 hp Adams.

25 Sept — Pembrokeshire AC, Arnold's Hill, near Haverfordwest. ¾ mile, av 1-in-9. FTD: J. Thomas, 18/25 hp Siddeley. 1st on formula: H. A. Jones-Lloyd, 12/16 hp Talbot.

26 Sept — Southern MC. Course unknown. 1st in class: C. J. Newey, 10 hp De Dion. According to *The Autocar*, this club was holding *monthly* hillclimbs at this time.

26 Sept — North Berkshire AC, White Horse Hill, Woolstone. Private ground, Mr & Mrs Butler. Max 1-in-7. FTD: W. G. James, 20 hp Rothwell. 1st on formula: Mrs Viner Ellis, 12 hp Peugeot.

Sept (end) — Manchester MC, 'in Cheshire hills'. 2 miles, max 1-in-5. FTD: H. Hollingdrake, 35/50 hp La Buire. 1st in classes on formula: H. Hollingdrake; F. C. Hunt, 20 hp Humber; L. Stone, 16 hp FN; P. A. G. Bell, 16 hp Bell; J. A. Bennett, 6 hp Rover.

1909

1 May — Manchester MC, on 'borders of Cheshire & Yorkshire', 1½ miles, max 1-in-4½. 1st in classes on formula: G. H. Ward, 15 hp Lancia; Wilfred Stone, 40 hp Napier.

9 May — Richmond & District AC, Pitch Hill, near Ewhurst. 1st in car class: A. Carpmael, 12/18 hp Riley.

15 May — Manchester AC. Course unknown. FTD: J. Higginson, 80 hp La Buire, 48·2s. 1st in class (amateurs only): J. Newton, 22 hp SCAT, 58s. Part of reliability trial.

22 May — Blackheath AC, 'near Sevenoaks'. FTD: A. Jackson, 18/24 hp Mutel. 1st on handicap: Leonard Beadle, Lacoste & Battmann.

29 May — Cardiff MC, Rhubina Hill. 1st on handicap: E. M. Griffiths, 15 hp Lancia.

29 May — Derby & District AC, Hazelwood. 1st on formula: Dr R. G. Hogarth, 25 hp Talbot.

June (early) — Manchester AC, Dinas Mawddwy. FTD: G. H. Ward, 20 hp Lancia. Speech House, Coleford–Cinderford, Forest of Dean. FTD: P. A. G. Bell, 20 hp Bell. Part of reliability trial.

5 June — Four Midland clubs, Oakamoor. FTD: A. H. Faulkner, 30/40 hp Daimler. 1st in final: Dr Tresidder, 15 hp Talbot.

5 June — North Middlesex AC, Stag Hill, near Potter's Bar. FTD: W. A.

Vincent, 4-cyl 10 hp Delage, 58s. 1st on handicap: C. T. Culter, 8 hp Jackson, 1m 16·2s. Handicap results were given less than five minutes after the last run.

12 June — Nottingham AC, Clipstone. ST. Flying km handicap: 1st, J. A. Doran, 40 hp Metallurgique. Fastest, F. A. Bolton, 58 hp Daimler, 65·2 mph. Standing mile handicap: 1st, Dr Tresidder, 15 hp Talbot. Fastest, F. A. Bolton, 50·56 mph. Flying km scratch: A. Baker-White, Napier, 80·04 mph. 2nd, A. Baker-White, 90 hp FIAT.

19 June — Manchester MC, on 'borders of Cheshire & Yorkshire'. Start on 1-in-4½ section. FTD: J. Looker, 38 hp Minerva-Knight.

24 June — Oxford AC, Steepness Hill, Chipping Norton–Deddington road. 1 mile approx. FTD: Dr G. Horatio Jones, 10 hp De Dion, 3m 8s.

26 June — Hampshire AC, Beaulieu. FTD: W. H. Thompson, 30/40 hp Brasier, 1m 42·6s. 1st in classes: W. H. Thompson; F. W. Ramsay, 22 hp SCAT, 1m 49·4s.

3 July — Hampshire AC, The Grange, Alresford. Estate of Lord Ashburton. Closed. FTD: G. C. Colemore, 'Four-Inch' Darracq, 30·6s; 2nd, 60 hp De Dietrich, 35s. 1st in classes: J. W. Davis, Jackson, 44·4s; G. H. Cox, FIAT, 46·4s; J. B. Robinson, Star, 49·6s.

3 July — Mid-Staffordshire AC, Style Kop. Closed. FTD: A. G. Harley-Jones, 25 hp Talbot, 72s. 1st on formula: F. Riley, 15 hp Talbot.

3 July — Ten Midland clubs, Kettleby. Closed. FTD: F. A. Bolton, 58 hp Daimler, 1m 20·6s. 1st on formula and Du Pré Cup: A. Boulter, 15 hp Star. 1st in classes: H. Jefferson, 9 hp Riley; N. F. Bayliss, 14/18 hp Sunbeam; F. A. Bolton.

10 July — Southern MC. Course unknown. 1st on formula: — Pole, 8 hp De Dion.

24 July — Manchester MC, Longdendale Valley, near Woodhead, 'as usual'. Same hill as Sept 1908, 1 May 1909, 19 June 1909? Or Heyden Bridge (*qv* Part Four, 1911)? FTD: J. Higginson, 80 hp La Buire. 1st on formula: J. Oliver, 12/14 hp Calthorpe.

31 July — Manchester MC, Dinas Mawddwy. FTD: H. Cunliffe, 20 hp La Buire, 3m 34s. Part of reliability trial.

- July — Dorset AC, Zig-Zag Hill, Melbury Abbas. 1½ miles. 1st in classes on handicap: N. S. Hind, 40 hp Berliet; W. Mackintosh, 25 hp Talbot; Mrs Bradburne, 12 hp Berliet.

14 Aug — Sutton Coldfield AC, Coalport Hill. FTD: J. L. Kirk, 15 hp Talbot, 1m 35s. 2nd, N. F. Bayliss, 14/18 hp Sunbeam. 1st on formula: J. L. Kirk.

4 Sept — Derby & District, North Staffs, Mid-Staffs clubs, Uttoxeter. FTD: F. A. Bolton, 58 hp Daimler, 58s. 1st on formula: J. L. Kirk, 15 hp Talbot.

4 Sept — Manchester MC. Course unknown. FTD: J. Higginson, 80/100 hp La Buire. 1st in classes on formula: J. Oliver, 12/14 hp Calthorpe; F. Settle, 15 hp Lancia; J. G. Looker, 38 hp Minerva.

11 Sept — North Berkshire AC, Blowing Stone Hill. 1st, Hargeaves, 22 hp Daimler.

18 Sept — NE Automobile Association, Ragpath Side. 1st on handicap: J. Turvey, 12 hp Talbot.

25 Sept — Hertfordshire County AC, Aston Clinton. Closed. FTD: A. J. Hancock, Vauxhall. 2nd, Oscar Thompson, 40 hp Austin 'Pobble'. 1st on handicap: A. J. Hancock.

26 Sept — Southern MC, Tilburstowe. 1st on formula: H. Billing, 10/12 hp Humber.

1910

7 May	Sutton Coldfield AC, Coalport Hill. FTD (unofficial): C. A. Bird, 65 hp Napier, 1m 7·8s. 1st on formula: J. L. Kirk, 15 hp Talbot.
16 May	Scarborough & District MC, Filey. ST. FTD: T. Armstrong, 12 hp Star.
26 May	Pembrokeshire AC, Arnold's Hill. 1st on formula: H. J. P. Thomas, 12 hp Humber.
4 June	Manchester AC, Blaenau Ffestiniog. FTD: A. E. Barclay, 12/14 hp Crossley. Part of reliability trial.
4 June	Derby & North Staffs AC, Hazelwood. FTD: Edward Genna, 16/20 hp Sunbeam, 1m 22·4s. 1st on formula: H. Jefferson, 9 hp Riley.
11 June	Middlesex County AC, Hand Post. FTD: H. McMullen, 16/20 hp Sunbeam. 1st on handicap: W. Holmes, 12 hp De Dion.
11 June	Manchester MC, Longdendale Valley, near Woodhead. FTD: G. H. Woods, 20 hp Crossley. 1st on formula: G. H. Woods, 12 hp Crossley.
18 June	Northamptonshire AC, Rockingham. 1st in classes on handicap: R. S. Parris, 15 hp Star; J. C. Hannah, 12/14 hp Crossley; F. C. Parker, 38 hp Minerva.
18 June	Nottingham AC, Clipstone. ST. Flying km handicap: 1st J. L. Kirk, Talbot. Fastest, Richard Lisle, 15 hp Star, 40s. Standing mile handicap: Fastest, J. L. Kirk, 1m 19s. Flying km scratch: 1st, Richard Lisle. Other flying km: 1st, J. Mather, 12/14 hp Calthorpe, 51·2s.
23 June	Pembrokeshire AC, Pendine. ST. FTD: J. V. Colby, 16/20 hp Sunbeam. 1st on handicap: W. H. Greenish, 20 hp Humber.
25 June	Lincolnshire AC, Grimsthorpe. ST. FTD: G. A. Dyas, Sunbeam, 77s. 1st on handicap overall: R. M. Wright, F.L. 1st in classes: G. A. Dyas; C. Holland, 24 hp Vauxhall.
2 July	Four Midland clubs, Oakamoor. FTD: A. G. Harley-Jones, 15 hp Talbot, 84·6s. 1st in final: C. J. Pearson, 20 hp Vauxhall.
14 July	Blackheath Centre, Motor Union, Hixey Down. FTD: Cann, Ford 2m 47·4s.
16 July	Leicester & District AC, Kettleby. FTD: G. H. Woods, 20 hp Crossley, 1m 4·4s. 2nd, F. A. Bolton, 58 hp Daimler, 1m 14·8s. 1st on formula and Du Pré Cup: Edward Genna, 16/20 hp Sunbeam. 1st in classes: Arthur Cox, 12/18 hp Riley; G. H. Woods; J. A. Doran, 38 hp Minerva.
16 July	Essex MC, Lippett's Hill. 1st on formula: A. P. Howard, 10 hp De Dion.
18 July	Sutton Coldfield AC, Sutton Park. Closed. ST. 1 mile. FTD: C. A. Bird, 65 hp Napier, 1m 4s.
21 July	Somerset AC. Course unknown. FTD: L. R. Price, Vauxhall, 2m 1·6s; 2nd, 40/50 hp Darracq, 2m 1·8s. 1st in classes on handicap: J. Aspinall, 12 hp Sizaire-Naudin, 3m 6·8s; Dr Porteus, Renault; L. R. Price.
25 July	North Berkshire AC, Sparsholt Firs Hill. 1st on handicap: Mrs Hippisley, 14/18 hp Alldays.
August	Manchester MC, Dinas Mawddwy. FTD: N. Crosland, 12/14 hp Calthorpe. Part of reliability trial.
10 Sept	Wolverhampton & District AC, Coalport Hill. FTD: C. A. Bird, 65 hp Napier, 1m 9·8s. 1st on handicap overall: Louis Coatalen, 12/16 hp Sunbeam. 1st in classes: Louis Coatalen; Edward Genna, 16/20 hp Sunbeam; Arthur Cox, Riley; Edward Lisle, Briton.
11 Sept	Newcastle MC, Corby's Bank, near Alnwick. 1st in car class: J. R. Atkinson, 12/14 hp Armstrong-Whitworth.

Page 155 (above) *Parry Thomas in his Leyland Eight in full flight on Kop, 1924;* (below) *Kop hillclimb, 1924: Parry Thomas in the Thomas Special*

Page 156 (above) *Ralph Millais's AC at the Inter-Varsity hillclimb, Aston Clinton, 1925;* (below) *the scene of one of the two last public-road speed trials, held on 4 April 1925: Hereford, the Whitecross Road. A Morgan in action*

17 Sept	Northamptonshire AC? Rockingham. 1st: J. C. Hannah, 12/14 hp Crossley.
24 Sept	Manchester MC, near Cat & Fiddle Inn, Macclesfield–Buxton road. A new hill. ¾ mile, av 1-in-7. FTD: G. H. Woods, 20 hp Crossley. 1st (amateurs): L. Swain, 14 hp Darracq.
24 Sept	Scottish AC, Tummel Bridge, Perthshire. FTD: Campbell Martin, 38 hp Minerva. 1st in classes on formula: Dickie, 8 hp Rover; Mrs Burnside, 16 hp Minerva; Edward Genna, 16/20 hp Sunbeam.
1 Oct	Southern MC. Course unknown. Closed. 1st on formula: H. W. Toler, 25 hp Talbot.

1911

13 May	Manchester AC. Course unknown. 1st in classes: R. Wilkie, 20 hp Vauxhall; G. Rhodes, 18/24 hp Austin; W. C. Jones, 22 hp SCAT; N. Crossland, 12/14 hp Calthorpe. Part of reliability trial.
20 May	Hertfordshire County AC, Aston Clinton. Closed. FTD: G. O. Herbert, 20 hp Singer. 1st in classes: G. O. Herbert; W. G. James, 12 hp Vermorel.
27 May	Manchester MC, Longdendale Valley, near Woodhead. FTD: G. H. Woods, 20 hp Crossley, 2m 49·6s. 1st (amateurs): J. Higginson, 80 hp La Buire, 3m 5s.
27 May	Inter-club competition, Oakamoor. FTD: N. F. Bayliss, 16 hp Sunbeam, 69·2s. 1st in final: Dr A. D. Hunt, 11 hp Richard-Brasier.
7 June	Dorset AC and Hampshire AC, Puddletown Heath. FTD: K. K. Horn, 20 hp Vauxhall, 1m 3·4s. 1st on handicap: E. J. Underwood, 13·5 hp De Dion.
27 June	Sheffield & District AC, 'near Matlock'. FTD: G. H. Woods, 20 hp Crossley, 1m 26·8s. 1st in classes: G. H. Woods; L. Slater, 15 hp Star; V. J. Watson, 12 hp Talbot; B. Hinds, 12 hp Talbot.
1 July	Welsh AC, Swansea. Course unknown. 1st: H. G. Davies, 12 hp Talbot.
1 July	Somerset AC, Shipham Hill, near Axbridge. FTD: G. W. S. Gwyer, Darracq, 1m 26·2s.
8 July	Three Midland clubs, Style Kop. FTD: N. F. Bayliss, 12/16 hp Sunbeam. 1st on formula: N. F. Bayliss.
8 July	Essex County AC, Bottledown. 1st in classes: P. Seabrook, 18/20 hp Seabrook-RMC; Frank Christy, 18/20 hp Seabrook-RMC; Hull, 12/16 hp Calthorpe; Fasey, 65 hp Napier.
15 July	Manchester MC, Heyden Bridge. 1 mile. FTD: J. Higginson, 80/100 hp La Buire, 1m 35·2s. 1st on formula: N. F. Bayliss, 12/16 hp Sunbeam.
15 July	Nottingham AC, Clipstone. ST. Flying km handicap: 1st, J. Mather, 14 hp Calthorpe. Standing mile handicap: 1st, J. L. Kirk, 15 hp Talbot. Flying km scratch: 1st, Percy Lambert, Austin 'Pearly III', 26·8s; 2nd, C. A. Bird, 65 hp Napier, 27·2s.
22 July	Wolverhampton & District AC, Coalport Hill. FTD: C. A. Bird, 65 hp Napier, 67·8s. 1st in classes: Louis Coatalen, 20 hp Sunbeam; A. J. Hancock, Vauxhall; H. G. Burford, Humber.
29 July	North-Eastern Automobile Association, Quarrington Hill. 1st in car class: S. Wilson, 6 hp Sizaire-Naudin.
9 Aug	North Berkshire AC, White Horse Hill, Woolstone. 1st on handicap: Mrs Hippisley, 20 hp Vauxhall.
2 Sept	Essex MC, Chinnor Hill, near Princes Risborough. Approx 1 mile. FTD: L. R. Ridley, 16/20 hp Adams. 1st on formula: L. R. Ridley.

16 Sept — Manchester MC, Heyden Bridge. 1½ miles. FTD: J. Higginson, 80/100 hp La Buire. 1st in class: R. Wilkie, 20 hp Vauxhall.

16 Sept — Bradford AC and Huddersfield AC, Mill Moor Road, Meltham. FTD: G. H. Woods, 20 hp Crossley, 1m 22s. 1st in class: E. Hoyle, Hutton, 1m 26·6s.

14 Oct — South Wales AC, Mountain Road, Caerphilly. Closed. 1st in classes: P. M. T. Hill, 12 hp Talbot; 25 hp Talbot; Dr Naunton Davies, 15·9 hp Arrol-Johnston; W. Graham, 35 hp Daimler (2 classes).

1912

5 April — Cardiff MC, Speech House, Forest of Dean. 1st on formula: 12 hp Argyll.

4 May — Manchester AC, near Sportsman's Inn, between Denbigh and and Bettws-y-Coed. FTD: E. Harding, 25/30 hp Sunbeam. 1st on formula (trade): R. Wilkie, 20 hp Vauxhall; 1st on formula (amateurs): W. C. Jones, 20 hp Vauxhall. There were classes for American cars, and saloon cars. Both were becoming popular. Part of reliability trial.

4 May — Derby & North Staffs AC, Hazelwood. FTD: Edward Genna, 12/16 hp Sunbeam, 1m 9·8s. 1st in classes: E. G. Newey, 12 hp Star; J. Hedge, 12 hp Talbot; Edward Genna; F. A. Bolton, 40/50 hp Rolls-Royce. 1st overall on formula: J. Hedge.

11 May — Hampshire AC, Brook Hill, Bramshaw, New Forest. FTD: D. Hanbury, 40/50 hp Rolls-Royce, 38·4s; 2nd, 25 hp Berliet, 44·8s. 1st in classes: Renault, 103·6s; C. E. S. Gillett, 12 hp Talbot, 47·6s; Miss Laura Starkey, 12/16 hp Sunbeam, 43·2s.

18 May — Manchester AC, Heyden Bridge. FTD: J. Higginson, 80 hp La Buire, 2m 21·6s. 1st in classes: G. H. Woods, 20 hp Crossley; E. Hoyle, Hutton.

May — Manchester MC. Course unknown. FTD: G. H. Ward, 20 hp Lancia, 1m 40s. Model 'T' Ford, 1m 46·2s, beat 20 hp White steamer, 1m 56s. Part of reliability trial.

1 June — Devon & Cornwall AC, Moorshop Hill, Tavistock. FTD: W. L. Woollcombe, Model 'T' Ford; 2nd, C. C. Brodrick, 16/20 hp Sunbeam. 1st in classes: M. Hay-Chapman, 12/16 hp Sunbeam; De Dion.

1 June — Dorset AC, Weymouth. ST. 1 km. 1st in class: H. F. W. Farquharson, 16 hp Sunbeam.

8 June — Middlesex County AC, Hand Post. FTD: H. W. Toler, 25 hp Talbot, 51·6s. 1st on formula: A. Page, 6 hp De Dion.

8 June — Derby & North Staffs AC, Oakamoor. FTD: E. H. Lees, 26 hp Metallurgique, 68·6s. 1st in final: R. Wilkie, 20 hp Vauxhall.

20 June — Pembrokeshire AC, Arnold's Hill. FTD: Eric Green.

20 June — Model 'T' Ford, 62·2s; 2nd, Stanley steamer, 63·2s.

22 June — Sheffield & District AC, Holly Lane, Ambergate. 1st in classes: A. M. Spender, 12 hp Talbot; G. H. Woods, 20 hp Crossley.

29 June — Bristol & Gloucester AC and Somerset AC, Weston Hill, Bath. 1,818 yd, av 1-in-10·8. 1st in classes: G. H. Woods, 15 hp Crossley; Bridges, 25/30 hp Sunbeam; Graves-Knyfton, 12 hp Sizaire-Naudin.

June — Edinburgh & District MC, Soutra Hill. FTD: 38 hp Daimler.

6 July — Devon & Cornwall AC, Moorshop Hill. FTD: Dr Simpson, 10 hp Briton.

13 July — Nottingham AC, Clipstone. ST. Flying km handicap: Fastest, G. H. Woods, 20 hp Crossley, 79·32 mph. Flying km scratch: Fastest, G. H. Woods. 1st overall on formula: R. Wilkie, 20 hp Vauxhall.

18 July — Welsh A. & Ae. C., Philadelphia Hill. 1st on formula: E. E. Fletcher, Talbot.

20 July — North Berkshire AC, Litcombe Bassett Hill. 1st: Mrs Hippisley, 20 hp Vauxhall.

27 July — Somerset AC, Wraxall Hill, near Shepton Mallet. Closed. FTD: G. W. Gwyer, Darracq. 1st in classes on formula: Graves-Knyfton, Sizaire-Naudin; C. B. Hillyar, Alldays; A. E. Taylor, Fafnir; Miss H. Garnett, 40/50 hp Rolls-Royce. 1st on formula overall: A. E. Taylor.

27 July — Mid-Staffs AC, Style Kop. FTD: G. H. Woods, 20 hp Crossley. 1st on formula: Cecil Bianchi, 15 hp Crossley.

July (ca.) — Stanley AC, Hand Post Hill, Northaw. FTD: A. C. Baker Ewers 12 hp Star, 1m 5·6s. 1st on formula: C. H. Clement, 10 hp Star.

10 Aug — Yorkshire AC, Greenhow Hill, Pateley Bridge. FTD (joint): J. Higginson, 80 hp La Buire; Louis Coatalen, Coupe de *l'Auto* Sunbeam. 1st on formula: R. S. Witchell, 15 hp Straker-Squire.

22 Sept — Manchester Hundred MC, Axe Edge, Buxton. 1 mile. FTD: S. Knott, Model 'T' Ford. 1st on formula: C. Horkheimer, DFP.

28 Sept — Scottish AC. Trinafour. FTD: C. J. Waldie, 25 hp Talbot, 100·4s. 1st in classes: A. H. Betts, 11·9 hp Arrol-Johnston; Boyd McCrae, 20 hp Werbell.

Sept — Streatham & District MCC, Titsey Hill. 1st in cyclecar class: J. T. Wood, GWK.

23 Oct — Derby & North Staffs AC, Hazelwood. FTD: J. Higginson, 80 hp La Buire, 59·4s. 1st in classes: H. Jefferson, 40 hp Berliet; A. Fillingham, 20 hp Vauxhall and Colin Ling, 20 hp Vauxhall (tie); Hedge, Talbot.

1913

March/April — Cambridge University AC, Orwell Hill, near Biggleswade. 600 yd. FTD: J. W. Read, 25 hp 'Prince Henry'-type Vauxhall, 24s.

20 May — North Berkshire AC, Letcombe Regis Hill, near Wantage. FTD: Mrs Hippisley, 16/20 hp Sunbeam. 1st on formula: T. R. Hargreaves, 25 hp Mors.

24 May — Hampshire AC, Brook Hill, Bramshaw. Closed. FTD: C. W. H. Braun, 40/50 hp Rolls-Royce. 1st in classes: J. H. Bradford, Model 'T' Ford, 38s; J. G. Birch, 16 hp Vauxhall, 34·4s.

24 May — Cardiff MC, Rhubina Hill. FTD: E. W. Lewis, 27/80 hp Austro-Daimler, 53·4s. 1st in class: E. M. Griffiths, 10 hp Bugatti, 1m 13·6s.

31 May — Manchester AC. Course unknown. FTD: E. Mercer, 20 hp Vauxhall, 50s. 1st on formula: R. S. Owen, 20 hp Argyll. Part of reliability trial.

31 May — North Staffordshire AC, near Longnor. FTD: J. A. Prendergast, 30 hp Daimler. 1st on formula: Stanley Goodwin, 15·9 hp Crossley.

6 June — Dorset AC, Weymouth. ST. 1st in class: Edward Genna, 12/16 hp Sunbeam.

14 June — Mid-Staffs AC, Style Kop. FTD: H. G. Day, 15 hp Talbot. 1st on formula: H. G. Day.

28 June — Lancashire AC, Course unknown. FTD: W. Jones, 25 hp Vauxhall. Vauxhalls also 2nd, 3rd, 4th. Part of reliability trial.

29 June — Somerset AC, Wraxall Hill, Shepton Mallet. 1st on handicap and in class: Miss Laura Starkey, 12/16 hp Sunbeam.

12 July — Sheffield & District AC. ? course. FTD: Cecil Bianchi, 15 hp Crossley. 1st in classes: H. Morton, 11·9 hp Arrol-Johnston; H. D. Orr, 12/16 hp Sunbeam.

26 July — Sutton Coldfield & Mid-Warwicks AC, near Cropredy. Closed. FTD:

	Leslie Hands, 25 hp Talbot, 47·2s. 2nd, C. A. Bird, Coupe de *l'Auto* Sunbeam, 47s. 1st on formula: Leslie Hands.
Aug	Stanley AC, Hand Post Hill, Northaw. FTD: F. R. Goodwin, 20 hp Lancia, 59·2s. 1st on formula: F. R. Goodwin.
Aug (end)	Streatham & District MCC, South Harting. Two cycle-car classes. 1st in both, time and formula: A. Frazer-Nash, GN.
20 Sept	Manchester MC, near Buxton. Axe Edge? Closed. 1st on formula: Cecil Bianchi, 15 hp Crossley; 2nd, W. G. Tuck, 14 hp Humber.
27 Sept	Scottish AC, Cairn o'Mount. 1st in classes: W. Waldie, 25 hp Talbot; Edward Genna, 12/16 hp Sunbeam; M. F. Anderson, 27/80 hp Austro-Daimler.
1914	
Feb/ March	Cambridge University AC, Orwell Hill. FTD: J. W. Read, 25 hp 'Prince Henry'-type Vauxhall, 24s.
13 March	Essex MC, Kop. FTD: G. D. Pearce-Jones, 25 hp Vauxhall, 1m 16·6s. 1st on formula: G. D. Pearce-Jones. 1st, cyclecar class: W. G. McMinnies, Morgan, 1m 17s.
April	Stockport MCC, Greenway Hill. 1st in cyclecar class: J. F. Buckingham, 12 hp Buckingham.
April	Wolverhampton MCC, Style Kop. 1st in cyclecar class: J. F. Buckingham, 12 hp Buckingham.
Easter Monday	Westmorland MCC, Greyhound Hill, near Kendal. $\frac{5}{8}$-mile, mostly 1-in-8. 1st in cyclecar class: J. F. Buckingham, 12 hp Buckingham, 1m 4s (ca. 36 mph). This combination regularly met and beat a Grand Prix Morgan.
9 May	Sutton Coldfield & Mid-Warwicks AC, Hints Hill. 1st, cyclecar class: C. Ashton, 8 hp Morgan. 2nd, H. Thompson, 8 hp Buckingham, 47·5s.
16 May	Cardiff MC, Rhubina Hill. FTD: E. W. Lewis, 27/80 hp Austro-Daimler, 53·6s. 1st in other class: E. R. Insole, 16 hp Sunbeam, 59·8s. 1st on formula in classes: A. K. Neale, 14 hp Humber, 1m 17·2s; B. Davies, 12 hp Talbot, 1m 11·8s.
16 May	Hampshire AC, Stockbridge, on Stockbridge–King's Somborne road. Closed. FTD: N. S. Hinds, 25 hp Berliet saloon, 27·4s. 1st in other classes: H. Garnett, 38 hp Metallurgique, 32s; Miss Laura Starkey, 12/16 hp Sunbeam; N. S. Hinds, 8 hp Bugatti. 1st on formula: N. S. Hinds (Berliet saloon); R. A. Munn, 40/50 hp Rolls-Royce, 34·2s; J. G. Birch, 16 hp Darracq, 33·2s; H. Heath, 16/20 hp Benz, 41·4s.
23 May	North-Western Automobile Association, Boothdene, Oldham–Halifax road. 1st in light car class: G. F. Robson, 10 hp Singer, 1m 57·4s.
27 May	Dorset AC, Weymouth. ST. FTD: Leslie Hands, 25 hp Talbot, 35·4s. 1st in two classes: R. von Namen, 10 hp Bugatti.
6 June	Hillclimb at Doncaster. Club and course unknown. $\frac{1}{2}$ mile. 1st in cyclecar class: D. Ellis, Morgan, 40·2s.
13 June	Somerset AC and Bristol MCC, Weston-super-Mare. ST. FTD: Leslie Hands, 25 hp Talbot, 58·4s. 1st in classes: Leslie Hands (2 classes); E. Stokes, 15/20 hp Talbot; G. Kenshole, 12 hp Talbot; A. E. Ansell, 12/16 hp Sunbeam; 11·9 hp Arrol-Johnston; H. West, 25 hp 'Prince Henry'-type Vauxhall; F. G. Cox, Morgan.
13 June	Middlesex County AC, Hand Post. FTD: W. N. Vinson, 25 hp Talbot, 34·2s. 1st in class: D. H. Cohen, Bugatti.

24 June North Berkshire AC, White Horse Hill, Woolstone. FTD: Mrs Hippisley, 25 hp 'Prince Henry'-type Vauxhall.

27 June Nottingham AC, Clipstone. ST. Flying km: 1st, W. G. Higgin, 25 hp Vauxhall, 32·6s (3 events). Flying km handicap, light cars: 1st, J. Mather, 11 hp Lagonda. Standing mile handicap: 1st, Dr R. G. Hogarth, 10 hp Austin.

11 July Hampshire, Kent, Dorset and West Surrey ACs, South Harting. FTD: N. S. Hinds, 25 hp Berliet, 1m 42·8s. 1st on formula in classes: N. S. Hinds; H. R. White, 10/12 hp Bifort; H. Heath, 12/20 hp Benz; P. Jones, 'Prince Henry'-type Vauxhall. W. N. Vinson's 25 hp Talbot burst a tyre, charged the bank.

25 July Sheffield & District AC, Mirror Hill, near Woodhead. Closed. FTD: J. Hedge, 15/20 hp Talbot, 3m 9·6s. 1st in classes: H. Morten, 11·9 hp Arrol-Johnston; G. D. Flather, 12/16 hp Sunbeam.

27 July Sutton Coldfield & Mid-Warwicks AC, Style Kop. FTD: Leslie Hands, 20/30 hp Talbot, 57·2s. 1st in classes: B. Mortimer, 10 hp Calthorpe; F. Burgess, Calthorpe.

PART FIVE

1919-1925: The Flood

Each of the years 1910–14 had produced approximately the same number of recorded sprints. This figure of between thirty and forty was half that for 1907, but included (except in the case of 1910) a high proportion of good-quality, important meetings. This new-found consistency did not survive the war. In 1919, the first year of peace, people were preoccupied with the restoration of features of the national life more important than sprints. As far as the motor industry was concerned, the production of private cars for a car-starved populace had first priority, and before even this could get under way, most factories had to be re-equipped and their outlets reorganised. The Society of Motor Manufacturers and Traders declared itself against a resumption of sprints for 1919 and 1920 'almost unanimously'. Nevertheless, half-a-dozen sprints took place during the year, and considering that the war had ended only the previous November, this is proof of the strength of the desire to revive the sport. By 1920, far from having declined to nil, the figure was back to the pre-war annual average. Then the flood began, growing in volume until, in 1923 and 1924, more meetings were recorded than in the previous peak year of 1907.

The main reason for this resurgence of interest should be sought in the post-war boom in motoring for the masses: the 'new motoring' made possible by the mass-production of the comparatively inexpensive light car, born, as we have seen, before the war, and by the importation of larger (but still cheap) American cars built for the same market. More and more people could afford to run cars and so take an interest in all sides of motoring, including motor sport. Most would take part vicariously, reading of meetings or at best watching them; some would actually compete. Scores of new firms, most of them extremely small, sprang up to make cars and satisfy the demand; many of them, and their agents, took an interest in competition and fielded trade entries. The Cyclecar Club was renamed the Junior Car Club now that light cars began to displace cyclecars in popularity, and expanded mightily.

A second factor was that manufacturers and sportsmen were starved of all kinds of sport, as well as of private motoring. Peace was the signal for these fewer, but better-to-do people to unleash their pent-up motor sporting ambitions, and they started the ball rolling with their experience and enthusiasm. True, this was the age of sporting 'efficiency trials', involving untimed climbs of wicked 'observed sections' and catering mostly for the light car; but it was just as much the golden age of sprints as it was of the 'Land's End', the 'Exeter' and the 'Edinburgh' trials. Sprinting, together with the type of spectacle Brooklands had to offer, provided the better sport.

A combination of the expanding popularity of the light car, plus the growing appeal of motor sport of all kinds, produced the touring cyclecar, or light car's sporting derivatives. By the end of our period, a high proportion of makers listed a sports or semi-sports version of their standard bread-and-butter product. The pre-1914 successes of, for example, GN, Hillman, Singer and Calthorpe were mostly won by very special works racing cars. Now they had to cater for a far larger number of enthusiasts who wanted to race themselves. The 1920 Finance Act, which raised the tax on cars to a punitive £1 per rated horsepower, also enhanced the popularity of the small car; much to the chagrin of the large car manufacturers. But this latter section of the industry continued to produce large-engined sports models for their wealthy patrons, just as they had done before the war. Vauxhall, Sunbeam, Crossley, Straker-Squire all did this, while at least one firm, Bentley, made sports cars exclusively in these years.

In October 1919 the RAC and its affiliated clubs decided solemnly to exclude 'enemy-made' cars from competition. This was a close call for Bugatti, who, their factory being in Alsace, were 'enemy' during the war and 'friendly' as from 11 November 1918. As it was, if the RAC's object was to avoid supporting, however indirectly, the revival of German industry, this gesture was somewhat pointless. Only second-hand, pre-war German or Austrian cars would be affected, because 'enemy' motor cars did not invade British sport for several years, and when they did, the prejudice had abated, and the cars—such as the little Sascha Austro-Daimlers—were too attractive for such an ordinance to be enforceable.

The boom era opened very quietly on 14 June 1919, when the re-formed Middlesex County AC assembled at Hand Post. A 25 hp Vauxhall, driven by F. H. W. Church, made absolute fastest time in 50s, while in the light-car class, S. J. Prevost's Morris Cowley achieved 65s. This little occasion was almost 'lost' in the excitement presaging the first major pre-war meeting to be held a week later: the Junior Car Club's climb of South Harting.

This was a closed affair, with a capacity ceiling of 1,500 cc, but racing cars were eligible, the JCC was already a power in the land, and the manufacturers of light cars and cyclecars who already appreciated the value of competition turned out in force. Many people, both amateur and trade, joined the club so as to be able to compete.

However, lack of driving experience was painfully obvious in many drivers, and bad starts and premature gear-changes were numerous. In the 1,100 cc touring class, three GNs in a row were fastest, led by Captain Frazer-Nash's car, W. Wadham's 9·5 hp Standard, fourth on time, winning on formula. Among the 1,500 cc tourers, Lieut G. C. Stead's 10 hp AC set the best time, followed by Capt J. T. Wood's 10·8 hp four-cylinder GWK. The racing classes were won by Frazer-Nash (H. R. Godfrey in a similar car coming second), and by Godfrey in a 10 hp GN 'Vitesse', with George Bedford's 10 hp Hillman second. Bedford was the Hillman works driver, and his car was the first of the post-war generation of sporting light cars. Capt J. S. Coates's 10 hp Singer, fourth on time, won the first class on formula. His car had been built for the 1914 Light Car Tourist Trophy race planned for the Isle of Man but never held. Coates was third on speed in Godfrey's class, which Bedford won on formula. Some machines of interesting appearance were present, including ACs with racing bodies, a Chiribiri and an Eric-Campbell, but none of these achieved any success.

The second major meeting of 1919, on 23 July, was that of the Essex MC, which held its open and closed speed trials on the front at Westcliff. Owing perhaps to the organisers' lack of experience, this was not an exciting day for spectators. No announcements were made concerning the event in progress at any given moment, and in the handicaps cars were so paired that a fast machine generally ran against a slow one. It was also raining, which didn't help.

There were classes for 'unrestricted' (ie, racing) cars as well as tourers, but E. H. Lees's 30/98 hp Vauxhall set up fastest time of the day, averaging 60·1 mph. Two classes also went to Lees on time, as they did to Malcolm Campbell's 12 hp Talbot and S. B. Wilkes's Hillman Speed Model (as the production sports Hillman was known). W. D. Hawkes, later the mainstay of Montlhéry record breaking with Gwenda Stewart, went one, or rather two, better. He won two classes with his 10 hp GN and two more with his 27 hp Austro-Daimler. Frazer-Nash in a 10 hp GN, J. Taber with a DFP and Miss Ivy Cummings with a 30/98 hp Vauxhall won one event each, and Malcolm Campbell came first on handicap as well in both the classes he won on time. Otherwise, AV cyclecars, successors to the Carden of pre-war days, were singularly successful in this respect. Woolf Barnato, the future driver and financier of Bentleys, turned up with a 10 hp Calthorpe, Capt C. A. Wallace with a 1914 Grand Prix Piccard-Pictet, Lieut-Col Tate on a 1908 Grand Prix Mercedes, and no less a personage than Miss Yvonne Arnaud at the wheel of a 10 hp Eric-Campbell.

This meeting was notable for its assembly of names soon to be famous in motor sport; Campbell, Hawkes, Cummings and Barnato as well as the already well-known Frazer-Nash. Campbell had been a familiar figure at Brooklands before 1914, but not in sprints. The glamour of sprinting had returned in full measure; although many of the names were new.

The last two recorded meetings of the season were both held on 31 August. American cars, which had begun to pour into Britain at about the same time as the small-car boom started pre-war, took the first two places on time at the Southend & District AC's climb of Bottledown Hill between Little Burstead and Billericay. J. H. Burrows's Studebaker ascended in 40s, and T. A. Jones's eight-cylinder Knight in 41·6s, while Miss Ivy Cummings ran third in 42·4s in her 24 hp Brasier.

Meanwhile, the Bristol MCC were holding their speed trials on the sand at Weston-super-Mare. There were only two starters in the class for light cars and cyclecars, the fastest of which was T. Gilmore Ellis's 10 hp GN 'Vitesse', with 1m 25s for the mile. A great deal more was to be heard of Ellis.

As a close to the season, the Yorkshire, Manchester and Lancashire ACs intended to hold a joint open and closed climb of Pateley Bridge on 4 September, but it attracted so few entries that it was postponed until 1920, and so sprinting in 1919 ended with these meetings of 31 August.

*   *   *

By 1920 sprints were back to normal by pre-war standards, in terms of numbers and quality; with the difference that a lot of new courses would be coming into use.

This, however, was not the case with the Essex MC's open climb on 27 March. Nobody was told where it would be held until twenty-four hours before it was due to start, but the course turned out to be a familiar one—Kop—as was usually the case when secrecy was enforced to prevent illicit practising. Touring cars of up to and over 1,500 cc were eligible, and to accelerate the proceedings, competitors were dispatched while their precedessors were still on the hill: not really a good idea in these days of high speeds. Talbot supremacy was not yet broken, though it was not long to survive the factory's abandonment of sprinting. G. A. Vandervell's 25 hp machine, powered by the engine out of the ex-Lambert Brooklands car, made fastest time in 35·8s, Malcolm Campbell's 12 hp coming second with 51·2s. The latter, a pre-war motor, was the latest of Campbell's cars to bear the name 'Bluebird'; which suggests that it was a rather unusual 'touring' car. . . . W. D. Hawkes's 10 hp GN was third fastest of the day. Noel Macklin's 10 hp Eric-Campbell was quickest in the 1,500 cc class, with a time of 59·4s, but he was destined to become more famous when associated with the name Invicta. Major E. S. Lefrere's Bugatti was quite a long way behind with 1m 14·4s, but his was the heaviest of the 'light' cars. Capt L. H. Manders's 10 hp Mathis was slower still, in 1m 40·2s, and Campbell was allowed to put up the best formula performance of the day.

Little now happened until 15 May, when the Liverpool Motor Club chose a new course for its speed trials; a kilometre (standing and flying) at Storeton, four or five miles south of Birkenhead. This meeting attracted the astonishing total of over 300 entries, but motor-cycles were included, and some of the cars were duplicated as entries in different classes. The road was allegedly 'safe for any speed', which was just as well, for although it was on ground that could be closed, the spectators could not be controlled, and wandered all over it.

The little AV's were very fierce-looking, but not fast enough for A. Horrocks's 10 hp Morgan, which won two events on time. His time in the first (standing-start) event was 42·4s, with T. Gilmore Ellis's GN scoring on formula in both cases. The 1914 TT Sunbeam of L. V. Cozens did very well to win its class on formula as well as time, and in the latter result, it was followed by two 18 hp Essexes, dark American horses which were extremely fast; 'travelling prodigiously with a thunderous noise', to quote one reporter. This was very much Cozens's day. He went on to score four more formula wins and one more 'time plus formula' success.

However, formidable though his car must have appeared, it did not have the acceleration of the 30/98 hp Vauxhalls. On time, W. Watson's car won all the four events which Cozens took on formula, Cozens in two cases occupying third place behind a pair of the Vauxhalls. When Cozens won on time again, it was, as before, against an Essex, though this time driven by Watson. The instant success of the Essexes was attributed to special 'sprint' gearing, but their normal performance was excellent for their class, and it is revealing to note that they were unusual among American cars at this time in having overhead inlet valves. In one of his wins with the Vauxhall, Watson registered 33·2s for the standing kilometre, or 67·41 mph. R. Wilton's 90 hp chain-driven Mercedes, a very pre-war machine indeed, must have looked and sounded marvellous, but not surprisingly made no impression.

Mill Moor Road, Meltham, having for many years enjoyed gentle obscurity, was now suddenly promoted to the status of an 'open' course; though there were two closed events as well as two open ones when the Huddersfield AC met there on 5 June. H. F. Clay's 30/98 hp Vauxhall set up fastest time of the day with 1m 21·8s in one of the open events, and was followed by the 25 hp Talbot of E. R. Hall (another driver soon to be famous) with 1m 53·6s, though Clay won on formula. The other open contest went to Drysdale Kilburn's 18 hp Essex, in 1m 28·6s. Kilburn was also best on formula, and this was very much an 'American' meeting, for the two closed classes were won on time by J. H. Clay's Essex (1m 47·5s) and A. Dawson's 30 hp Hudson, which climbed in 1m 49·6s. Mr Dawson, who also won on formula, climbed but did not drive. His chauffeur, in cap and livery, performed this chore while his master sat in regal style beside him. E. Brook's 12/40 hp DFP and E. R. Hall's 25 hp Talbot were second on time in each case, but desperately far behind: Brook ascended in 2m 12·4s and Hall in 2m 0·6s. The formula winner in the first instance was C. L. Dawson, driving a 12 hp Talbot.

But, whatever pious resolutions had been made before war broke out, it seems that no lesson had yet been learned from the clashing of dates. It was on 5 June, too, that the Southend & District AC attacked a new course, Thundersley Church hill, near Hadleigh; but this event, with its two open and two closed classes for cars of up to and over 1,500 cc, was thought important enough to attract a number of the 'big names' and a very large entry of ordinary mortals, many of them new to the sport. The latter displayed their inexperience with bad starts; the spectators by swarming all over the road during the ascents. Frazer-Nash in his racing GN had an exciting moment with these spectators while making fastest time of the day (20·8s): 'The sensation of speed was heightened by a series of huge skids performed by this car, the while Nash wildly waved the spectators away from the top bend with one gyrating arm.' It must have been trying for a driver to be called upon to act as his own course marshal.

In this class, Malcolm Campbell's 12 hp Talbot was timed at 22·6s, and W. D. Hawkes's 10 hp Morgan at 24·4s. Other classes were carried off by Malcolm Campbell (in 23s), Noel Macklin's Eric-Campbell, J. H. Burrows's 25·4 hp American Chalmers, and Maitland Keddie's GN. The latter, whose time was 28·4s, also won his class on formula. As far as the first three categories were concerned, B. S. Marshall's 8 hp Mathis, F. W. Keddie's Morris Oxford and Marshall again were respectively best. This course was 400 yd long, and had an average gradient of 1-in-8.

The revival of Shelsley Walsh on 3 July did not attract the number entrants one might have expected, perhaps because an entry fee of no less than 20 guineas—at least £60 today—was demanded. However, the meeting drew some of the finest cars and drivers in Britain, so neither organisers nor spectators could feel thwarted, for everybody knew that a factory, agent or amateur driver who wanted to make his name in sprints *must* take in Shelsley.

C. A. Bird in a 1919 Indianapolis Sunbeam team-car made fastest time of the day, though his 58·6s was not so good as had been anticipated; lack of practice or of suitable gear ratios were thought responsible. On lack of experience, it was noted that many drivers were still changing gear too early. They had either never driven up Shelsley Walsh before, or had not done so for seven strife-torn years. G. A. Vandervell's 25 hp Talbot and G. D. Pearce-Jones's 30/98 hp Vauxhall ran Bird pretty close, in 60·8s and 62·2s. L. T. King's 20 hp Austin won the open event on formula; the first of a great many formula wins by this works combination, and in the closed contest Pearce-Jones improved his time to a winning 60·2s, followed by Vandervell, who also did better by recording 60·4s. J. A. Barber-Lomax's 30/98 hp, fourth on time in the 'open', won the closed event on formula.

The light car climb, last of the day, was interrupted by a terrific downpour which temporarily stopped proceedings, and turned the road into a quagmire. This did not deter Frazer-Nash, who went on to set up second fastest time of the day and, of course, win the event by registering 60·2s in his 10 hp GN. This single-seater was described as 'a tin whistle at the front and a queer sort of fish at the back'. Its progress up the hill, a fitting conclusion to the day, gave rise to a classic piece of reporter's prose:

> The crackle of the open exhaust of the little two-cylinder engine was plainly audible as the GN waited the word to go. Then followed a screaming rattle of acutely sharp explosions, altering in tempo, slowing and quickening as the driver negotiated the various bends or changed gear. The car unseen, the varying sound was dramatic. Each change in note suggested violent skidding, rushes up banking, and all kinds of disastrous imaginings. Yet the rapid increase of intensity made it evident that the car was climbing at a prodigious speed, and the feeling grew that it would be advisable to climb higher up the natural grandstand, formed by the banks at the S-bend, in order to be safe from this infuriated reptile. With an ear-splitting din, the shining torpedo rushed into view, the engine being cut out before the corner and cut in again as the car swung dizzily round, skidded a little on the straight, and disappeared like a flash round the second bend, with a volley of sound, to a dashing finish.

The GN had arrived at Shelsley. Although they were not to proliferate until after 1925, this description from *The Autocar*, with few modifications, could apply to hundreds of climbs made by the GN and GN-based specials which swarmed at Shelsley in those later years. The suggestion of wild power only just held in leash and sometimes momentarily escaping, of hairbreadth avoidances and driving which occupied all the road and some of the surrounding scenery applied to most climbs; either because drivers were inexperienced, or because their cars were driven to the limit of their road-holding. The sliding technique had not yet been superseded by the more economical methods brought to their finest pitch by Raymond Mays, and even when it was, few could hope to approach his virtuosity.

Before Mays arrived with his Bugattis, works GNs could dominate almost any sprint they entered. H. R. Godfrey attributes its success to five factors. The car held the road well. Gear changes on the dog clutch were extremely rapid, and ratios could be altered to suit any course exactly, thanks to the chain drive. The GN was very light in weight, and, finally, the works car 'Kim' possessed an engine of very advanced design. GNs generally had an advantage over other cyclecars in using a specially-designed engine rather than a proprietary motor-cycle unit, but 'Kim' was a different case again. Its two cylinders were set at 90°. The valves were large—48 mm in diameter—and were set, also at 90° to one another, in a bronze head with hemispherical combustion chambers. They were operated by forked rockers on collars below valve springs halfway down the valves, as on the modern HRD. Other GN engines had overhead camshafts as well, but in 'Kim' the parts were a good deal lighter. Most proprietary motor-cycle engines had side valves only, and in the few with ohv, the valves were set parallel to one another. 'Kim's' engine was built as early as 1913–14.

The superiority of the GN was so complete for a time that the inevitable body of legend began to grow up round them. Rivals noticed that the exhaust of works cars was smelling strongly of sulphur, and the rumour went round that they were using some potent form of gunpowder-based dope. In fact, the odour of fireworks emanated from the oil, not the petrol. GNs had discovered that an addition of sulphur was a sovereign specific against 'nipping-up' of the main crankshaft bearing.

Nobody could touch the combination of 'Kim' and Frazer-Nash at this period; G. Bird's 10 hp Calthorpe, second on time in his class at Shelsley Walsh, was no less than 26s slower, with C. C. Ash's 10 hp Hillman taking the formula award, and being third fastest.

GNs put up an equally sensational performance at the Westcliff speed trials run jointly by the Essex MC and the Southend & District AC on the 15th. Cars were run in pairs over the standing kilometre, and between them, H. R. Godfrey in 'Kim' and Gilmore Ellis in an 8 hp 'Vitesse' cleaned up six events on time, were second on time in eight, and won seven on formula. Their rivals were of no mean order. Two GNs, Ellis leading, beat Capt G. D. F. Keddie's 'Silver Hawk'; two GNs, Ellis first again, led in two more events; Ellis beat George Bedford's Brooklands Hillman; Ellis beat Woolf Barnato's 10 hp Calthorpe, with Bedford in third place. Godfrey took first place and Ellis second in two contests, Godfrey setting speeds of 60·43 and 52·57 mph while so doing; it was only Ellis on another GN who could call out his reserves like this. Ellis did almost as well to come second to Malcolm Campbell's 12 hp Talbot in the 3-litre class, with his 1,100 cc vehicle, at 51·5 mph, and to G. D. Pearce-Jones, who achieved 57·07 mph with his Vauxhall, among the 'unlimited tourers'. He took five of GNs formula wins, and Godfrey two.

The remainder of the laurels, such as they were, were divided up between B. S. Marshall, whose 8 hp Mathis collected seven formula awards, Miss Ivy Cummings, who won the Ladies' race in her Brooklands Gregoire, Campbell at 46·41 mph, and C. L. E. Geach, to whose 1919 Indianapolis Sunbeam went the 'unlimited' race. His speed of 61·12 mph was creditable, but compared rather sadly with Godfrey's 60·43 mph on less than a quarter of the cubic capacity. G. Foresti's old 75 hp Austro-Daimler was second in this class, 0·4s behind. The day was rounded off by a match between Geach and the fastest motor-cycle of the day, Harveyson's Indian. It resulted in a beautiful dead heat, at 73·58 mph for the standing kilometre.

It is significant that 'atmospheric' descriptions of sprints—accurate ones, leaving aside those generated in the overheated imaginings of the popular press—are not found before the early 1920s, when enthusiasm for this sport gripped the country as never before. Bald accounts, often limited to an angular table of results, had previously been the rule. The first attempt to convey to the motoring public the atmosphere of a seaside speed trial appeared now, in 1920; the first of a hillclimb, a year later. In the thirties, the press gloried in evoking the very special atmosphere of Shelsley Walsh, but this was at a time when it was the last venerated survivor of the old-time hillclimbs. No other course produced anything like the same sentiments.

Listen to *The Autocar*'s reporter at Westcliff on 15 July, sitting beside the competitor as he drives through the town, warms up in the paddock and burbles back down the return road, glowing in the awed respect radiated by the *canaille*:

> For several glorious hours the competitor, with pardonable pride, admired of all beholders, can drive a real racing car, complete with long asbestos-wound exhaust pipe. True, he may not win great honours in the tourney—may, indeed, be very far behind his rivals—but who among the crowd can remember which was the really successful car after a meeting, when once again, our competitor's car slowly promenades the town amid the now interested and envious crowd, a king among kings for just a few hours?
>
> There is a glamour about this racing which calls for certain details of deportment. It is the fashionable thing, for example, to drive very much on the brakes, with little dabs at the throttle to accentuate the exhaust noise and give the idea that the car is hard to handle. It is also desirable to have as passenger the prettiest girl available in her best—and most unsuitable—frock.

Closed it might be, but the results of the Sutton Coldfield & North Birmingham AC's meeting at Style Kop on 17 July read like those for an open event. In the light car class, H. R. Godfrey's GN registered 51s, followed by George Bedford's works Hillman with 55·2s and Noel Macklin's 'Silver Hawk' with 60·6s. Bedford won on formula. The same three gentlemen disposed of the unlimited class, in the same order; in 50·4s, 55·2s and 62·2s respectively. Bedford even won again on formula. There were only fourteen entries, and one wonders why the other eleven bothered. A small point of interest: the name of this club, after several transformations, could at last be abbreviated to the familiar SUNBAC, and will so be referred to henceforth.

This very full July ended with a bang: the JCC's climb of South Harting on the 24th; for which there were sixty-six entries. A special class for 'sports' cars, the first of its kind, was instituted to cater for the new breed of production car: enough firms were now cataloguing ing them for it to be said that the type had 'arrived'. They could not, in any case, be fairly included with either touring or racing cars. The class winners on time were Kaye Don's Tamplin cyclecar (1m 40·2s), S. Watson's Deemster being second with 1m 41·4s; W. J. H. Phillips's Deemster with 1m 38s, followed by Major Warren-Lambert's Warren-Lambert in 1m 40s; and Kaye Don again, with a time of 1m 27s in the monocar class. This was too good for a brace of AV's, the best of which managed 1m 34s. The formula winners in the first two classes were Watson and Phillips. T. Gilmore Ellis's GN collected the sports-car class in 1m 15·8s, beating Godfrey by 3s.

Among the racers, Frazer-Nash's 'Kim' was best in both classes, Godfrey's pre-war belt-drive GN 'Blue Bottle' following him into second place in each. 'Kim's' best time was 1m 4·6s; 'Blue Bottle's' 8s worse. One of the touring classes accidentally consisted entirely of GWKs. The winner in this case is worth recording, because D. H. Owen-Edmunds had only one leg. His time was 2m 11·8s. Perhaps his performance inspired the special 'all hand-control' GWKs which the company built for the disabled a little later? The fastest lady driver was Mrs Warren-Lambert who, with 1m 49·2s, well beat Mrs Frazer-Nash's GN. She won on formula, too.

The JCC officials examined every car with great care to be certain that each belonged in the class in which it had been entered. Such strictness was a new thing and called forth special comment, but it was more than ever necessary now that entries were increasingly complex and distinctions subtle.

A notable new course was used for the first time on 7 August, when the Bradford AC organised a match between itself and the Huddersfield and Halifax club on Holme Moss, near Holmfirth on the Holme-Woodhead road. The timed distance was $1\frac{1}{4}$ miles; its steepest gradient 1-in-8·77. It included five corners; a feature which was more important than the gradient these days. Good road-holding was, or should have been, more sought-after than sheer power. The open events went mainly to the experts, who could not afford to scorn a hill because it was new. Malcolm Campbell's Talbot made fastest time of the day in 1m 42·6s, and won its category on formula, beating E. H. Lees's Essex, which climbed in exactly 2m 0s. However, J. H. Clay's Essex took its class with 1m 59·4s, seeing off two Austin 'Twenties'. This might not sound too difficult a feat at first, but the Austin 'Twenty', especially in the hands of men like Felix Scriven, was a respectable opponent, and a 'Brooklands Sports Twenty' was catalogued in the following year. Finally, R. W. Pradier's Charron-Laycock, with a time of 2m 6·2s, led its class on time and formula.

It had been included in the RAC's Light Car Trials of 1914, but the first major car hillclimb on Sutton Bank, between Thirsk and Helmsley, fell on 21 August 1920, when the York & District Motor Club held its open meeting there. The course, in the Hambleden Hills, lay between Thirsk and Helmsley, and consisted of a measured nine-tenths of a mile. Its gradient was exceptionally severe, rising to 1-in-3·9, averaging 1-in-7 and including several bends. The time of H. F. Clay's Essex, in 1m 58·6s, was the best of the day, and those of the other class winners were slow in comparison. Felix Scriven's 11·9 hp Hampton climbed in 2m 13·2s in one event, beating a GN and a Morgan, and in 2m 16·8s in another, disposing this time of a Calthorpe and a GN. Clay, however, now went on to take another class, his time of 2m 3·8s being second fastest of the day, too good for a Chevrolet and for Scriven, placed second and third.

A week later, on 28 August, there took place the earliest recorded race meeting for cars on the sands at Southport, run by the Southport Motor Club. Motor-cycle races had already been held there, in June, and after 1925, when there was little else to occupy the sprint motorist, the Southport sand races were to become the major feature of the northern sprint season. They began as simple mile or kilometre speed trials, but by 1939 the highlight of the Southport year was a 100-mile race, lapping round markers, supported by other long-distance races down to 3 miles in length, all quite overshadowing the short, straight-line sprints. Up to seven meetings a year were eventually organised, but in the later years reports get very tedious indeed, for there were periods during which one, two or three men in the same cars won just about every event run. Their machines were extraordinarily fast, and they had perfected the esoteric techniques of circuit-racing on sand, so it was not unusual for one or two to share all the wins in all the numerous classes included in a meeting.

On this first occasion, H. O. D. Segrave's ex-Karl Joerns 1914

Grand Prix Opel made fastest time over the standing mile, in 51·4s, while George Bedford's Hillman won the 1,500 cc class in 63s. This was Segrave's earliest known sprint victory. He did not compete very often, as he disliked speed trials and hillclimbs. There was always a long wait before the fastest cars were released—indeed, they usually started last, so as to retain the interest of the spectators. The fun was all over in a couple of minutes, and one error of judgment was enough to spell defeat: there was no time to retrieve it.

Just as important to the historian was the Hampshire AC's hill-climb on 4 September, for it was probably the first to be held on Spread Eagle Hill at Melbury, 1½ miles south of Shaftesbury on the Blandford road. The timed seven-tenths of a mile with its worst gradient of 1-in-6 was loose and bumpy, but it was accounted a fast course. Stripped cars were allowed in the open classes, and one of these went to Kensington Moir's 20/25 hp Straker-Squire in 56·4s; an average speed of 45 mph. The next best time of the day was set by Malcolm Campbell's 12 hp Talbot, with 1m 1·6s, and the rest were nowhere, which must have been galling for one of them—G. D. Pearce-Jones. He muffed his first attempt with the 30/98 hp Vauxhall, but was then timed at 51·2s, better than anyone else, in an unofficial climb. The other open event went to Campbell, who improved his time to 1m 1·2s. Drysdale Kilburn's 18 hp Essex followed him home in 1m 4·2s, Campbell and Kilburn winning these two classes on formula. The closed contests represented a clean sweep for Campbell, on both time and formula. The Talbot put up a time of 58·8s in each one; a further improvement. This was much too good for either Major F. B. H. Carroll's Mathis, which took 1m 29·2s, or Campbell himself on another Talbot, a 20/30 hp, who clocked 1m 8·6s. A 20 hp Austin tied with the bigger Talbot on time, underlining its performance potential.

There were signs during the year that the sport had got under way again rather too precipitately for its own good. A higher proportion than was usual of projected events never took place, one of the major cancellations being the Waddington Fells meeting planned by the Lancashire AC and Manchester AC. The same clubs' Pateley Bridge event, postponed from 1919, never materialised either, and these failures were sadly typical of many this season.

* * *

Nineteen twenty-one was the year which brought the first major increase (as compared with 1910–20) in the number of sprints held; the first sign that they were going to multiply on a scale at first matching and then surpassing that of pre-1910 days.

This year, university and 'inter-varsity' events got properly under way for the first time since 1914. The 1921 'Inter-Varsity' hillclimb took place at Aston Clinton on 5 March, and was a contest remarkable for the first success of one Raymond Mays of Cambridge. He was driving his first love, the Speed Model Hillman christened 'Quicksilver' to match George Bedford's works 'Mercury'. This car, as modified by Mays with polished ports and drilled piston skirts, was capable of over 80 mph when fully developed. When new, it possessed the odd characteristic of being faster in second gear than in top: 60 and 56 mph respectively! Nonetheless, Mays won the light car event at Aston Clinton in 45·9s, also making fastest time of the day, with R. M. Hamilton's GN second best at 46·2s. The timed distance was only 750 yd, as against ¾ mile when the course was first used in 1904. Curious anomalies in times set up over the years on what was ostensibly the same course are often explained by the fact that the timed distance could vary greatly, purely according to the whim of the organisers.

Kop was climbed by the Essex MC on 12 April. As in 1920, the venue was kept secret until the last moment, but this manœuvre can hardly have deceived the experienced, and was probably window-dressing to placate the prejudiced. An open contest, it significantly included a class for four-cylinder, water-cooled cars, so that GNs should not make the bigger sports cars look silly in *every* event. It was won by H. O. D. Segrave's Brescia Bugatti in 39·8s, one second faster than George Bedford's Hillman. As it happened, GNs only won three of the other six events on time. H. R. Godfrey took two at 43s and 48·8s, followed home by E. B. Ware's Morgan in 46·6s and C. Finch's GN in 49·6s; while the racing-car class went to Frazer-Nash in 34·6s—fastest time of the day and a new hill record. G. A. Vandervell's 25/50 hp Talbot was second here in 35·6s.

Leon Cushman's 'trade' Bugatti took one class in 52·8s from R. Pradier's 10 hp Charron-Laycock, which recorded 59·2s, and G. A. Vandervell's Talbot won two at 35·4s and 40·2s from C. J. Joyce's 30/98 hp Vauxhall and Finch's GN. Joyce recorded 44·8s. Felix Scriven's Austin 20 hp Sports was third to Finch with 45·8s, and Pradier won his class on formula, as did Godfrey, Finch (twice), and Nash. The formula win in the Vandervell-Joyce contest went to A. H. Pass's 20 hp Austin.

Frazer-Nash's car was not the original 'Kim'. This car had carried him backwards through the fence on the Railway Straight at Brooklands during the 1920 August Bank Holiday meeting, and only its engine, and its driver, had survived the impact. The former was put into another chassis, and the ensemble christened, predictably, 'Kim II'.

A fortnight later, the York & District MC held the second of its open hillclimbs on Sutton Bank. Here Frazer-Nash made no mistake, 'Kim II' winning all four car classes up to and including the 'unlimited', and, of course, making fastest time of the day—1m 21·6s—in the process. Furthermore, T. Moore with another GN was second to Frazer-Nash on two of these occasions. The other second places went to Leon Cushman's Bugatti in 1m 45·6s and J. Gjers's 30/98 hp Vauxhall with 1m 33s. As had happened in the past when one or two makes of car asserted total supremacy in their class, and even outside it, much correspondence appeared in the press asking how standard were the entrants in classes for standard cars. The sprint 'special', in the sense of a standard chassis highly developed, was evolving once again.

On 7 May, Kop was assailed again, this time by the Oxford MC (which was nothing to do with the Oxford University MC). As before, GNs carried off most of the plate, Frazer-Nash's 'Kim II' winning the class that admitted racing cars in 38·8s—fastest time of the day—from Humphrey Cook's 30/98 hp Vauxhall, which recorded 47·2s. This meeting saw Cook's earliest recorded success with his first 'Rouge et Noir', which he ran in 1921 and 1922. It was, he tells the author, a pretty well standard vehicle mechanically: its extraordinary run of wins would appear—therefore—to speak volumes for the skill of the driver.

G. L. Hawkins and his GN, for their part, accounted for three classes. His best time of 51·2s was too good for F. E. Wootten's Morgan (1m 8·2s) on two occasions, and on the other for A. E. Keen's works Morris Cowley Sports, which climbed in 1m 3·2s. Keen's car, which reached a high stage of development before being finally outclassed, was pronounced over-geared, and should have done better still. Humphrey Cook succeeded in winning the last class, his 46·8s beating G. Harcourt Smith's 49·6s in another 30/98 hp Vauxhall, and relegating Hawkins to third place. The Vauxhalls, incidentally, were observed to make most of their ascents in third gear.

Two weeks later, the Southport MC ran a sand race meeting closed to four local clubs, in which sprints were won by H. Horrocks's

Morgan, E. C. Ecroyd's similar car, Lieut Banks's 30/98 hp Vauxhall, and T. Rimmer's 12 hp Vulcan. Rimmer beat the Vauxhall in his event, which seems odd, but this Vulcan, a local product, may have been powered by the efficient Howard sleeve-valve engine, and was certainly stripped for racing. The sands were very heavy indeed on this occasion, while the spectators did not make for better sport by contriving to break the telephone wires linking start and finish.

Two other fairly important meetings were run on the same day, one being the Coventry & Warwickshire MC's closed climb of Style Kop. This was interesting mainly for the success of a make of light car new to sprints—the Crouch. J. W. F. Crouch's car took one class from R. M. V. Sutton's Hillman by the wide margin of 41s to 61·6s, and in another was second to J. Rowley's 25 hp Talbot by only 2s—40·6s to 38·6s. J. Cocker's Crouch tied for second place in another class with Leon Cushman's Bugatti, clocking 39·4s against the 31·2s of George Bedford's Hillman. S. H. Newsome's 10 hp Calthorpe was third on two occasions, tying for that place with Sutton once, but the last class for cars was abandoned after Cocker was baulked by a non-competing car crossing the course and took to the grass to avoid a smash. Presumably the crowd was by then quite out of hand.

Frazer-Nash's GN won both of the car classes in the climb of Chatcombe Pitch near Cheltenham, open to the Western Centre of the ACU. The Auto-Cycle Union was an association of motor-cycle clubs, as the Motor Union had been for car clubs. In the 1920s, its regional centres ran many sprints, the actual organisation being left to the club in, or near, whose territory the course lay. As we have seen, it had become usual before the war for motor-cycle climbs to include a class for cyclecars and light cars, cyclecars in particular being considered as much motor-cycles as motor-cars, and the ACU meetings continued the tradition in post-war years. Also, of course, many motor-cyclists ran a small car as a second string. Some clubs that catered primarily for motorists were similarly mixed in membership.

In this meeting, Frazer-Nash's times, 34·4s and 35·2s, were too good for Major W. Oates's Lagonda racing car and, in the over-1,500 cc class, for Capt A. C. R. Waite's 20 hp works Austin. Their times were 46·8s and 41·4s respectively, Oates improving his time in the second event to 46s, but only gaining third place.

The Banbury Motor Club and the Oxford MC held a joint inter-club climb on Irondown Hill on the Deddington–Chipping Norton road on 28 May. Humphrey Cook's 30/98 hp Vauxhall 'Rouge et

Noir' took one car event in 37·6s, a 23/60 hp touring Vauxhall coming second with 38·6s and G. L. Hawkins's GN third in 44·2s. But Hawkins cleaned up the other three classes on both time and formula. His best time in these was 45s. Cook, too, won his class on formula, and poor Banbury had little chance against such drivers as these, who represented Oxford. The final result was Oxford City 24 points, Banbury 0. This reads like the result of an 'Inter-Varsity' event, with Oxford University taking Banbury's place. It was at an Irondown meeting in 1921, possibly this one, that Cook first met Raymond Mays, who was present with his Hillman.

Cook and Hawkins may have been tempted by this minor affair, but it did little otherwise to damage the Essex County & Southend AC's prospects at Thundersley Church the same day. This event with its eight open and closed car classes, each with sub-divisions, attracted over 600 entrants, taking into account duplication between classes. Just about every form of mechanical road transport short of traction engines was represented, from racing cars to landaulettes complete with flower-vases and chauffeurs, a removal van and a bus. Unkind things were said of the running of the event: it looks as though the club, consisting of two bodies recently combined into one, was trying to be a rather too ambitious, but for the record, the removal van (58·8s) was a good deal faster than the bus (1m 20s)!

On a more serious level, Leon Cushman's Bugatti won two classes, his times of 23s and 24 s beating the 28s and 26·8s of A. W. Brittain's Calthorpe and G. D. F. Keddie's 'Silver Hawk'. Maitland Keddie's 10/30 hp Alvis was third in the latter class with 32·6s, and won no fewer than four classes on formula.

This meeting marked the first sprint success of another make destined for world fame: Bentley. F. C. Clement's car took its class in 24·8s, defeating Malcolm Campbell's Talbot (26·6s), and there was a splendid array of Bentleys present—almost all the experimental cars—although Clement's was the only one to make its mark. In another event, Campbell, now driving a pre-war Grand Prix Peugeot, set up fastest time of the day with 19·8s. H. R. Godfrey's GN collected its class with 21·6s, beating a Deemster, and also won an event on formula. R. Pradier's Charron-Laycock made best formula performance of the day overall, and T. H. Short's Deemster and W. Jay's Morris Oxford each won two events on formula.

The Middlesex County AC assembled at Hand Post once again on 4 June. An aberration permissible among organisers of unimportant closed events was the use of rather strange capacity classifications: on this occasion, up to and over 2½ litres. Another member of that redoubtable sporting family, Miss G. A. F. Keddie, was fastest in the smaller class with her 10/30 hp Alvis, while P. F. Pratt's 30/98 hp Vauxhall took the honours among the larger.

At the same moment Frazer-Nash and Moore were endeavouring to uphold GN honours at Holme Moss, where the Bradford and Huddersfield ACs met for their open and closed event. Frazer-Nash ditched himself, but Moore duly won his class in 112·6s, beating W. J. H. Phillips's Deemster. George Bedford's Hillman just as inevitably took its class in 94·6s from R. J. Sully's works HE (120·2s); but this was a meeting distinguished by the large number of old racing cars present, and their resounding success.

H. O. D. Segrave's 1914 Tourist Trophy Sunbeam ascended in 93·2s, defeating Malcolm Campbell's Talbot which, with 101·4s, led Felix Scriven's 20 hp Austin (102·8s). Real sensation was provided by the 1908 'Four-Inch' Hutton, still belonging to Colonel E. Hoyle, and driven by C. H. Mitchell, for it climbed in 92s, thereby making fastest time of the day. It did astonishingly well to beat Humphrey Cook's formidable 'Rouge et Noir' by a margin of 5·4s. Less surprisingly, the Hutton won its event on formula as well. A 1913 Coupe de *l'Auto* Sunbeam belonging to E. S. Myers was also present, but did not make its mark. H. F. Clay at the wheel of another 30/98 hp Vauxhall won his closed class in 99s, with E. R. Hall's Talbot second in 102·6s. A. K. Dawson's Hillman (141·8s) and J. E. Dyson's Essex (127·8s) likewise won their closed classes.

The earliest attempt to capture the 'romantic' atmosphere of a hillclimb meeting appeared in *The Motor* during June. Called 'Sixty Seconds' Thrill' and signed 'McM.', it is worth quoting in full:

> 'Three, two, one, go!'
>
> The crouching black racer spurts up the dust from the white line, the note of the exhaust bellows with the triumph of freedom from the end of its great pipe and the machine shakes itself free from the dark wedge-shaped crowd that buried it. Now it is flying up the narrow white road, a low black object, the head of a trail of white dust and blue smoke.
>
> Two or three thrilling moments while the turns are taken, a gathering of still more speed, a change of gear, and the finishing flags.
>
> The driver pulls up and runs back to the timing box.
>
> 'Sixty seconds. Fastest time of the day', comes the laconic answer.
>
> The driver goes away happy—for that mad sixty seconds' spurt has crowned a month's hard work and a great deal of worry and expense of which the gaping crowd that cheered him on the corner had no idea.
>
> A peep behind the scenes discloses weeks of preparation, possibly terminating with several days spent in actually tuning up on the hill. The journey from headquarters to the climb may be 100 or 200 miles.

So sensitive are some drivers that they believe that even in this short run their careful preparations may be spoiled.

Sometimes a special gang of mechanics, complete with all the tools and spares necessary for a special car, may be brought down. The selection of gears is an important subject which is often worked out by the technical staff weeks before the event—such items as wheel slip, wind resistance, weight and the particular formula to be used all being calculated.

The day of the climb arrives. Last-minute adjustments bred from over-anxiety are common to most race drivers. Those who arrive late have to convert alleged tourists into racers, which means much stripping of mudguards, hoods, lamps, cushions, and other paraphernalia. Others pile their machines with lead and iron, scour the hotel for more passengers, for they are only running on formula. The weighing-in takes place. It is late. It is hot. And the drivers are inclined to lose their tempers whilst manœuvring in the narrow space.

All thoughts of lunch are abandoned. A sandwich or a chocolate and a drink snatched anywhere and anyhow are enough. The car's the thing. There is a jet to change or a valve to be adjusted, or maybe the ignition will stand a bit more tuning. Then there are the numbers to be fitted. All this requires thought and care and the time is short.

Eventually the car takes its place in a long string of low, tapered racers. They are a motley crowd. Here is a tiny aluminium single-seater and just behind it a big black racer with a huge exhaust pipe extending almost to its tail. Farther ahead are the touring cars, enjoying quite a day out from their ordinary sedate existence.

Every now and then from the end of the string there is a splutter and then the crescendo of a mighty exhaust rising to a deafening pitch as a racing engine is accelerated. That valve clearance is now correct, for there is no sign of a miss.

And the drivers! Some do the work themselves, and others direct their mechanics. Some in blue overalls, others in Burberrys or lounge suits, the latter soon showing signs of the attentions bestowed on the beloved bus.

A final survey of the hill now rapidly filling with people may be made. The turns require special attention. The crowd already obscures the approach of the worst bend and the surface is terribly loose. The weather looks threatening and the wind is blowing down the mountain. Horrid thoughts of wrongly selected gears and other adjustments which might have been made if only there had been more time.

But class one is starting, and once more it is——

'Three, two, one, go!'

The crowd clears away, and number one, a small car, sedately makes its way up the hill.

Four hours elapse. The climb is over. The excitement has passed and the results are known.

Winners and 'also rans' have to pack up and get home. Some have many miles to cover. They are later than they anticipated, and they have no lamps. Others are busy refitting hoods, screens and mudguards. They are lying under, over and inside their cars. Racing carburettors are being exchanged. Bags of tools, spare parts, wheels and other junk have to be packed up and put on board.

When all is ready, a hurried meal or a scamper home in the dusty wake of hundreds of others, all of whom have caught the speed craze and are bumping their way back with the accelerator pedal flattened out to the floorboards.

This little piece is of interest for several reasons. It shows that practising, on what was almost always a public road, could go on for several days prior to an event. It also proves that it was still customary to drive one's car to and from the course, even if it were a racer. Most cars were not yet so highly tuned or otherwise specialised that they could not be used on the roads. They were sometimes driven to and from meetings without any kind of road equipment, and with open exhausts, their crews alert for police traps. Yet, as we shall see, this practice had died out before the end of our period: the faster cars had grown too temperamental, and had progressed beyond use on the open road.

The description also shows that serious hillclimbing had become a science as well as an art; a full-time, all-absorbing occupation during the season. Lastly, the reference to competitors for formula awards is significant in view of spectators' complaints of boredom at so-called 'speed' hillclimbs; complaints distinctly audible in 1921 and due to grow in volume in 1922. The heavier the car's load the more likely it was to be successful, so the winners, very often the roomy, strong Austin 'Twenties', used to claw their way up a hill loaded to the gunwales with lead, pig iron and large passengers. Their paralytic progress appealed not at all to spectators out for blood, metaphorically if not literally. Nor, incidentally, did the constant reappearance of more or less slow touring cars in an endless succession of allegedly different classes. Four hours might elapse before a fast machine appeared.

In his memoirs, Raymond Mays filled in another part of the picture: the scene in the nearest country town, the 'base' for the annual hillclimb, turned upside-down for the day. Competitors reserved lock-up garages from year to year. The peaceful courtyards of the inns were transformed into bedlam as last-minute tuning and adjustments were seen to. The locals in general looked forward to the occasion as a 'big day', and swarmed round the competitors as they worked, seeking autographs. The evenings were the time for gay parties at which the drivers, who all knew each other well, let off steam in company with their friends and the pressmen who followed the progress of each great man's 'circus'.

On 18 June, the JCC assembled the 'circus' at South Harting and, as in 1920, all starters were carefully scrutineered. Many which were not genuine catalogued touring or sports cars were summarily 'promoted' to other classes. Frazer-Nash's GN won both the racing categories; one from two other GNs and one from W. M. W. Thomas's Aston Martin and Cushman's Bugatti. G. L. Hawkins's GN was the fastest sports car, beating the Aston Martin on time and formula. These two second places were the Aston Martin's first sprint successes. The first half of the new car's name referred to Aston Clinton, where Lionel Martin (whose surname formed the second half) was successful before the war with his Singer. Another, but ephemeral, newcomer was the Tamplin cyclecar. G. A. Tamplin's machine ascended in a time denting the GN record by snatching a touring class from Frazer-Nash himself, though the GN was best on formula, and the Tamplin then won a class devoted purely to Tamplins, Cardens and AV's. W. G. Hedge's 10/30 hp Alvis beat G. C. Stead's AC on time and formula, and although D. L. Underwood's AC dominated another class to the same extent, it was only against a gaggle of GWKs. The post-war, four-cylinder GWK was but a shadow of its pre-war self in terms of performance: a less lively, if more comfortable, car.

Two weeks later the Hampshire AC climbed Spread Eagle again. Two of the three open events went to Malcolm Campbell, his 15 hp Talbot, with 54·8s, beating Leon Cushman's Bugatti. His 25/50 hp Talbot, climbing in 46·4s, was too good for Humphrey Cook's Vauxhall, but Cushman's time was 57·2s, gaining him the formula award, and Cook's 49·8s. J. H. Clay's Essex was first on formula in the latter class. The third open event was Frazer-Nash's: the 48·4s of his GN compared with George Bedford's 57·6s on the Hillman. Lionel Martin's Aston Martin took this class on formula, and his car —'Bunny', on its first outing—was driven by Kensington Moir, a works driver who later drove for Straker-Squire. 'Bunny', the very narrow, staggered two-seater side-valve, fitted two years later with one of the sixteen-valve twin-ohc engines, was one of the first three Aston Martins made, and became the most famous ever built.

There were also three closed events at Spread Eagle, which were taken on time and formula by Maitland Keddie's 10/30 hp Alvis, D. Baxter's Essex and Sir C. Morrison-Bell's 30/98 hp Vauxhall, in 1m 28·8s, 1m 26s and 1m 6·8s respectively.

The Essex MC's Westcliff speed trials were now being recognised as one of the classics of the sprint season, and the meeting on 7 July upheld their reputation splendidly. The twenty events for cars included very modern categories for sports cars, and a very ancient one for steamers. As it was, only one entry, a Stanley, was received for the latter. The only real surprise of the meeting was provided by Capt A. G. Miller's 1914 Grand Prix Opel, which, transformed into an 'unlimited sports car', presumably by the addition of wings, only managed to beat a Sunbeam tourer and A. H. Pass's 20 hp Austin by 1·2s and 2s. Miller's time was 49·4s; the car was badly off form.

Otherwise all was normal. Leon Cushman's Bugatti carried off four classes, the best at 48s, beating W. O. Bentley's Bentley (55s), a Charron-Laycock and a 'Silver Hawk'. Frazer-Nash also won four, defeating, among others, Cushman and F. C. Clement's Bentley. His best time was 38·2s; theirs 44s and 41·8s. H. R. Godfrey took three classes, seeing off two other GNs in one, and Cushman in another by 44·8s to 47·8s. In a different respect W. F. Milward surpassed everybody, for his 10 hp Charron-Laycock won no fewer than seven firsts on formula. Three more went to Nash, and two each to R. Pradier's Charron-Laycock and H. W. Martin's GN. Mere mortals who only won one class each were W. J. H. Phillips on his 10 hp Deemster, his 57·2s beating a GN, E. Butler with a 29 hp Chandler (54·8s), H. W. Martin's GN, and F. C. Clement, whose Bentley on this occasion covered the kilometre in 42·4s. Cushman was second fastest here with 45s.

As usual, the greatest excitement of the day was occasioned by the contest for cars unrestricted in any direction. J. F. Duff's 35·2s in his enormous 90 hp FIAT was fastest time of the day; too much for Kensington Moir's dazzle-painted racing Straker-Squire and Frazer-Nash's 'Kim II', which pair recorded 36·8s and 39s. Duff went on to beat Bert le Vack's Indian in the fastest-car-versus-fastest-motor-cycle race which, by tradition, closed the day.

E. Swain's works 1914 Grand Prix Vauxhall, which set up fastest time of the day in 46·8s at the Hertfordshire AC's Aston Clinton climb on 16 July, might have done better still had it not left the road while trying to improve on this time. Humphrey Cook's 30/98 hp Vauxhall was second in Swain's class, clocking 48·4s, and A. J. Hancock's works 30/98 hp third. But this was notable, nonetheless, for works Vauxhalls had not appeared on a sprint course since 1913. George Bedford's Hillman won this class on formula, and another class on time in 51·8s to 53·2s when contending with Hancock's car. The latter's engine was nearly thrice the size of the Hillman's. Cook won his class too, registering 53·6s to Hancock's 55·4s, but Hancock won on formula. W. J. H. Phillips's Deemster took the shrimps' class with 1 m 19·6s, P. F. Child making a very belated second in his

Morgan, taking 2m 22·8s; so far behind that the Deemster won on formula as well.

The ACU's East Midland Centre held speed trials on the Clipstone Drive on 23 July, but they were a mere shadow of Welbeck's former glories. Both the standing and flying kilometres in the 1,100-cc car class were taken by W. L. Bemrose's GN, his time of 45·8s and 35·8s being too good for C. Clarke's Morgan. Raymond Mays in his Hillman made another clean sweep in the 1,500-cc contests, beating H. Brayshaw's 10/30 hp Alvis in the standing kilometre, with 45·4s against 50s and R. M. V. Sutton in another Hillman in 33·2s to 38s in the flying event.

The JCC's South-Western Centre hillclimb at Dean Hill, near Romsey, on 6 August is of interest because it was the first of a series held by this important club. E. Scholefield's Morgan won two classes, and made fastest time of the day, with 1m 25s and 1m 26·8s. The 10/30 hp Alvis of W. G. H. Hedges, with 1m 41s, beat A. R. Simmins's 10 hp AC (1m 46·6s), but took second place in the sports car class to W. R. Steele's GN, which climbed in 1m 33·8s. D. Underwood's AC, with 2m 2·2s, defeated the 11 hp Riley of S. H. Snell by nearly half a minute.

On the 26th, the Worcester Motor Club were christening a course which would become not only one of the most famous in Britain, but was to survive as a site for driving tests, if not sprints, until the present day; the private grounds of Madresfield Court, Earl Beauchamp's estate near Malvern. The Gloucester Drive was used, fastest time over the flying ½ mile at this open meeting being set by R. J. Sully's 14 hp HE in 28s. J. E. Ingman's Essex was second best, and H. F. S. Morgan's Morgan, made at nearby Malvern, won the 1,500-cc class in 31s. For the drivers of the faster cars, Madresfield could be a terrifying place. R. R. Jackson, who drove Morgans and Frazer-Nashes, recalls an absolutely straight course on which really high speeds could be attained, but one which was also a narrow, loosely-surfaced switchback. He once found himself approaching the finishing line with all four wheels in the air, locking his wheels in mid-flight to spin off into the trees at the finish.

The Leicestershire AC revived its celebrated Beacon Hill series on 3 September, Humphrey Cook's Vauxhall scoring in the event designed to find the fastest car of the day, his time of 48·4s, or 55 mph, beating Felix Scriven's Austin 'Twenty' (52·8s) and Lionel Martin's Aston Martin (1m 0·4s). Lionel Martin had already won two classes on speed and formula from Raymond Mays's Hillman, his times being 1m 11s and 1m 8·8s, and Mays's 1m 11·4s and 1m 11·6s. B. Hopps, an unknown, took a class from Humphrey Cook with another 30/98 hp Vauxhall, their times being 1m 1s and 1m 2·2s, and Felix Scriven was third with 1m 3·2s. A. W. Brittain's 10 hp Calthorpe won on formula, climbing in 1m 39·8s. The Du Pré Cup was contested, but no results were published.

Shelsley Walsh a week later was disappointing in terms of the number of entries, as had been the case in 1920: there were only thirty-three. The entry fee, though reduced to 15 guineas, was still a great deterrent, and so, perhaps, was the fact that each car was only allowed one run, and that no practising was permitted, even though the course was private. However, as in 1920, the quality of the entry was very fine indeed. As for the spectators, about 5,000 turned up, in 1,000 cars, and stayed, undaunted by an admission charge of 5s per gentleman and an extra shilling asked for a very poor programme. This was the first year in which spectators were charged entry to the course. Later, the ladies, too, had to pay, if only 2s.

The public certainly could not complain that they did not get their money's worth. The hill record fell no less than three times, broken by C. A. Bird's 1919 Indianapolis Sunbeam, M. C. Park's works 30/98 hp Vauxhall, and Frazer-Nash's GN. They climbed in 52·2s, 54·4s, and 54·8s, with Humphrey Cook's Vauxhall fourth fastest in the open event in 57s. All the stars were there: Leon Cushman, G. A. Vandervell, J. A. Barber-Lomax, Felix Scriven, Raymond Mays, J. H. Clay and the rest. Count Zborowski and H. G. Day, the Talbot works driver of earlier days and still with the STD combine, appeared with two of the new eight-cylinder Grand Prix Sunbeams, but they were slow, clocking 65·4s and 62·8s. So was a newcomer, A. C. Bertelli and his Enfield-Allday. A. C. R. Waite's works 20 hp Austin won the open contest on formula.

The closed event went on time to Vandervell's Talbot, Barber-Lomax being runner-up and formula winner in his 30/98 hp Vauxhall. The excellent times set up produced further excitement in the form of numerous near-accidents. Indeed, W. E. Kean's 30/98 hp Vauxhall got out of hand completely and rammed the bank. Many people said, as they were beginning to do of other courses, that the cars were now too fast for the hill. The road was too narrow, the bends too acute, and the pull-up (flanked by a pair of close-set gate-posts) too short. Improvements were to be made, but this and other courses would become safer still when the fashionable driving style changed; when it was realised that sliding a corner and taking up all the road was a time-wasting procedure and no true match for precise placing and timing.

During the year, *The Autocar* noted the great increase in the number of sprints being held and deplored the low standards of organisation and control which obtained at so many of them. Lack of experience in clubs new to speed events and after the hiatus of war was probably one reason, but the fact that officials were all voluntary and amateur was thought to have something to do with it. The perils inherent in the situation were pointed up by a mysterious 'fatal accident' in mid-season (which the author has been unable to trace), and sprints were already described, probably prematurely, as being 'in danger'.

* * *

As was now becoming customary, the Essex MC ran the first important meeting of the new season. In 1922 its open climb of Kop was held on 25 March, and there were eighteen classes, divided as usual according to type and capacity. Judging by the times recorded, this seems to be the first year in which a flying start of 50 yd was allowed. The two most exciting contests, both for 'any cars', with no capacity restriction, were won by Count Zborowski's Grand Prix Ballot and G. A. Vandervell's Indianapolis Sunbeam on time, in 26·8s and 27·2s respectively. The first of these times was fastest of the day, while Frazer-Nash's GN won both classes on formula. Second places in each on speed went to F. C. Clement's Bentley (31·2s) and Frazer-Nash (31·4s).

Somewhat less spectacular, but more splendid still, were Lionel Martin's performance with his Aston Martin—five class wins on time—and the *twelve* class wins on formula of W. F. Milward's Charron-Laycock. Kensington Moir's Aston Martin took another class on formula. Leon Cushman annexed four 'best times' with his Bugatti, and H. R. Godfrey two in his GN, while one each went to Milward, Humphrey Cook's 30/98 hp Vauxhall, Woolf Barnato's Hispano-Suiza, H. V. Barlow's Ansaldo (which also won on formula twice), and C. J. Nesbitt-Dufort's Talbot.

In addition to the Essex MC's Kop climb, the Scarborough & District MC's Staxton event was becoming quite an institution. This course lay 7 miles from Scarborough on the Great Driffield road; in 1922 the distance was $\frac{1}{2}$ mile, and very greasy it was on this 17 April, a three-wheeler overturning and unfortunately hitting a spectator. T. Moore's GN set up fastest time of the day, with 33s, while very little lay between the fastest of the other cars. Bramham's Bugatti registered 37s, beating Leon Cushman into second place in the class by 0·8s. H. Hodgson's 11·9 hp Hodgson, a new force in North Country sprints, was not far behind, with 39·6s. This was a car of conventional specification, powered by a four-cylinder Anzani side-valve engine, but of startling performance. Finally, the 30/98 hp Vauxhalls of Pilling and G. S. Boston (36s and 37s) followed Moore home in his class.

Five days later there took place what might be called the forerunner of the North-Country 'freak' hillclimb, of the sort which was to become practically the only kind of climb known in the north after 1925. Rosedale Abbey Bank differed in being a public road, if 'road' was the word to use, but it was so rough (as well as being steep) that cars were not always timed up it. When they were, the distance used was ½ mile, with a worst gradient of 1-in-4. The 1922 event, run by the Bradford Motor Cycle and Light Car Club, was interesting enough to attract Frazer-Nash, and it was he who put up the best performance.

This year the Essex County & Southend AC boasted no fewer than a thousand entries for its open and closed hillclimb, held on Laindon Two Church Hill, 5 miles from Billericay on the Gravesend road, on 27 May. This extraordinary entry only begins to make sense when we learn that there were twenty-three classes, each with four or five subdivisions. However, there may really have been a thousand entries, but as usual, three or four of them accounted for most of the events. Leon Cushman's Bugatti collected five, relegating, among others, Alvis, Charron-Laycock and Ansaldo to second place, while Major C. G. Coe's 30/98 hp Vauxhall took five more with a best time of 31·8s from Woolf Barnato's Hispano-Suiza, A. Howego's fast Armstrong-Siddeley, J. Snell's Haynes, and Parry Thomas's Leyland Eight. Two of these splendid Leylands were present. Maitland Keddie's 10/30 hp Alvis annexed three classes, beating a Bayliss-Thomas twice and a Morris Oxford once, as did Frazer-Nash, leading a Morgan, a Grégoire and, on the other glorious occasion, the Bugattis of Raymond Mays and Leon Cushman, which placed second and third. Frazer-Nash registered 28·6s. Two events went to Barnato's Hispano-Suiza (with a fastest time of 34·6s), and one each to Howego and Snell in 46·2s and 49·8s. Keddie was second to Howego.

Raymond Mays's Bugatti, for which he had forsaken the Hillman, was 'Cordon Rouge', and details of this car and of 'Cordon Bleu' are given later in this book, when an explanation of their success is called for.

Unlike the six days' and two days' reliability trials run by the Edinburgh & District MC (which were in any case mainly for motorcycles), the Royal Scottish Automobile Club's Scottish Six Days' Light Car Trial of 1922 included timed climbs—six of them—and a timed speed trial. Their purpose was to add to the rigours of the event; to sort out the best light cars on the market from the not-so-good. The trial was run between 5 and 10 June, and competitors were divided into classes by price: a logical arrangement with cars whose prospective purchasers were concerned mainly with economy. The occasion was considered important enough to attract a number of foreign drivers.

The Salmson of A. Bovier, the British concessionaire, was fastest in its class up Tummel Bridge, and in the 2 mile standing-start speed trial between Amulree and Aberfeldy. Fastest in the other classes at Tummel Bridge were a Stoneleigh, the GN of L. A. Cushman, Frazer-Nash's racing mechanic, and the 11 hp Rileys of V. G. Walsgrove (of whom we shall hear a great deal more) and Anderson. Walsgrove made fastest time of the day, in 4m 29·4s. He did the same in the speed trial, with 2m 49·8s, while the rest of the classes here went on time to a Stoneleigh, a GN and an Alvis.

We are only told the formula results for Cairn o'Mount, but we know that on the mile of Rest and be Thankful, Blackstock's Bugatti and Walsgrove's Riley made joint fastest time, A. E. Bull's Amilcar, C. M. Harvey's works Alvis and two 8/18 hp Talbots leading the other classes. On Little Gruinard, between Dundonnell and Gairloch, the leaders were two GN's, Bull's Amilcar, Walsgrove (his 59s again fastest of the day) and Harvey's Alvis. On the ½ mile of Glendoe, E. J. Herbert's Stoneleigh, Bull's Amilcar, G. T. Dean's 8/18 hp Talbot, Richard Lisle's works 11·9 hp Star and Anderson's Riley led, Dean being fastest of the day with 2m 28s. No times for Loch-na-Craig were given.

Walsgrove's was the most remarkable performance of the trial: he led on all the hills on both time and formula until a magneto failure forced him to retire. The overall formula leaders, taking all hills into account, were Herbert's Stoneleigh, H. Kennedy's Rob Roy, the 8/18 hp Talbot of H. G. Day, and Anderson's Riley.

On 10 June, back in England, Bottledown was the scene of a 'knockout' hillclimb, run by the Essex County & Southend AC. All cars were given a trial run, and handicapped on the result, and the class winners were Frazer-Nash's GN and Miss Keddie's Alvis, both of which climbed in 37s. The appearance of Frazer-Nash, or at least of a works car entered in his name, in an event of such minuscule importance as this shows that some firms thought sprints so vital that they must enter in every possible one.

At the other end of the spectrum were the Yorkshire AC's Saltburn speed trials, revived on the sands near Redcar for the first time since 1914. The date of 17 June was not a very clever one to have chosen, however, for five days later the Tourist Trophy was due to be revived as well, and Saltburn it was that suffered. Speeds were extremely high, but their validity was open to some doubt when judged by the strictest standards, for hand timing was used, as on that previous unfortunate occasion. This was particularly sad for Malcolm Campbell because before the meeting began, he made an attempt on the world's flying kilometre record which was, on the face of it, successful. His 350 hp twelve-cylinder Sunbeam clocked an average speed of 134·07 mph and a best speed of 138·08 mph. The record had stood at 121·57 mph ever since the 200 hp Darracq had performed here in 1908, but as it was, Campbell's run was not recognised. Perhaps it was some small consolation to him to make fastest time of the day in the flying kilometre competitions. His 17·6s was too good for L. V. Cozens in a six-cylinder Sunbeam, though in his own event Cozens beat W. B. Horn's racing Straker-Squire in 22·8s.

Horn took three of the standing kilometres; one from Major Coe's 30/98 hp Vauxhall and two from A. C. R. Waite's Austin 'Twenty', in 36·8s, 36·6s, and 36·8s again. Raymond Mays, his times 42s and 40·6s, won two of these races, but he was beaten on another occasion by Hodgson, who clocked 41·2s. Frazer-Nash was another double winner, at 38·8s and 36·8s, from an Amilcar and Mays. As well as the huge Sunbeam, Malcolm Campbell was driving a twin ohc 1,500 cc 'Sascha' Austro-Daimler at this meeting, and he, too, carried off two classes; in this case from Hodgson and a Morris Cowley. This little Austro-Daimler was the first 'enemy' motor-car to make itself felt in British sprints since the end of the war, and nobody excluded it. The final victory of note was when the veteran driver A. E. George, now at the wheel of a 30/98 hp Vauxhall, won one event against Major Coe's Vauxhall in 40·8s.

June 28–29 saw another revival, in the shape of the Welsh 'double' run by the South Wales AC. The demand for panel beaters after Caerphilly on the 28th was greater even than in pre-war events, for most of the drivers were new to the course, and their cars were faster than ever before. Rain made the surface trickier than usual, and some competitors appeared to progress up the hill by rebounding from one bank to the other. In a few cases this abandoned behaviour spoiled what could otherwise have been excellent times. It was Kensington Moir's day. He made fastest time with his Straker-Squire racing car, and won another class as well, making third best time, in a 1922 Tourist Trophy Aston Martin. He also won this class on formula. R. J. Sully's racing HE, without a differential, made the best formula performance of the day irrespective of class, while on time, other classes went to A. C. Bertelli's Enfield-Allday, Raymond Mays's Bugatti and A. E. Keen's Morris Cowley Sports. E. R. Insole's Bentley took two closed classes on formula.

The speed trials at Porthcawl on the following day were not a great success. It was difficult to follow the events, and the weather could not have been worse: a full gale was blowing, and the sands were well awash. In the open events, W. B. Horn's Straker-Squire made best time, his 51s beating Humphrey Cook's Vauxhall and Raymond Mays's Bugatti, which tied for second place, and H. W. Lewis's Austro-Daimler. J. S. Couldrey's 18 hp Essex led D. Shipwright's SPA, and in his class Sully beat two other HE's into second and third places. Keen won his class, and Raymond Mays his, leading Kensington Moir's Aston Martin and Lewis's Austro-Daimler. Miss Thomas's 8/18 hp Talbot unsportingly (and surprisingly) beat her mother's Amilcar, and R. B. Jones's 12 hp ABC was too good for a Tamplin. The closed events went to a Bugatti, E. R. Insole's Bentley, and Humphrey Cook's Vauxhall (which beat a Bentley and a 25/50 hp Talbot). Insole made the best formula performance in the closed classes.

SUNBAC's open and closed climb of Angel Bank took place on the next day, and attracted few big names: two successive days of racing in Wales were presumably enough for them. Angel Bank, a new course on the Ludlow–Bewdley road, consisted of a timed ½ mile of up to 1-in-9. The weather was terrible here as well, and further annoyance was caused by heavy traffic on the hill. Delays were such that each car could have only one run. A. C. R. Waite's Austin 'Twenty' made the fastest ascent of the day, in 47·8s. Morgans won two classes, H. F. S.'s car climbing in 50·4s and N. Norris's in 66·4s. Morris beat F. W. Barnes's Calthorpe, which took 70·4s, but this time was good enough to give Barnes another class against a second Calthorpe. C. A. Potts's GN annexed its class in 72·4s.

There was a bad clash between Angel Bank, an important meeting from its inception, and the JCC South-Western Centre's second attack on Dean Hill. It was still raining. The surface was very treacherous, and some of the wilder skids were quite involuntary. Four cars came to grief; two bursting tyres, one breaking a stub axle and one buckling a wheel. Mays's Bugatti, and Alvis, an AC, an 8/18 hp Talbot and a Riley each won their classes on time and formula, Mays adding the fastest time of the day to his bag.

Competitors at Dean Hill did not have very far to go if they wanted to take part in the Hampshire AC's open event at Spread Eagle on 1 July; the last of a remarkable concentration of important events crowded into four days. 'Kim II' with Frazer-Nash at the wheel took two classes in 49·6s and 51s, beating Malcolm Campbell's Austro-Daimler and Raymond Mays's Bugatti into second place. Campbell's time was 65·4s, and Mays's 53·8s. And then 'Kim II' beat Mays a second time. But it was not Frazer-Nash who did so, but his mechanic, L. A. Cushman—not to be confused with the other famous Bugatti driver. However, Frazer-Nash could do little against metal of the weight of Campbell's racing Sunbeam on a fast course, and Campbell clocked 41s to set a new hill record, compared with Frazer-Nash's 48·8s. One class each went to H. Paull's AV in 1m 50·4s, D. L. Underwood's AC in 71·8s (thrashing W. G. H. Hedges's Alvis by 12·6s), J. H. Clay's Bentley, which beat Underwood by 69·6s to 70·4s, and Major C. G. Coe's 30/98 hp Vauxhall. The Major led Humphrey Cook's 'Rouge et Noir' by only 1s; 55·4s to 56·4s, while Clay and Lionel Martin's Aston Martin each won two events on formula, and Hedges and Frazer-Nash one each.

There was not much of a breathing-space before all the 'circuses' had to rush off to Westcliff for the open speed trials, run jointly this year as a two-day event on 5–6 July by the Essex MC and Essex County & Southend AC. As it was, rain washed out the meeting and made miserable the valiant efforts of a fair-sized entry. The wins were shared more evenly than was often the case, no one winning more than three events. Only Leon Cushman managed the hat trick, in fact, defeating H. J. Lines's 15 hp Wolseley and Capt A. G. Miller's 10 hp Wolseley by 48s and 47s against 59·8s and 55·2s. He also saw off an 8/18 hp Talbot very easily. Raymond Mays's Bugatti took two classes, each with a time of 44s, beating Miss Ivy Cummings's Bugatti and Captain Miller's little Wolseley, which recorded 46s and 64s. H. R. Godfrey also took classes with his GN, in 41·6s and 42·6s, and Frazer-Nash one in 40·2s, beating G. L. Hawkins's GN by 2s.

One class each was taken by G. D. F. Keddie's Bentley, leading Ivy

Cummings by 0·6s in 43s, and the same gentleman's Leyland Eight, which seemed rather unfairly matched against Capt A. W. Brittain's 9 hp BSA, beat it by 16·8s. Ivy Cummings collected her first in a 12·8 hp Ansaldo, in 44·6s, while Major Coe's 30/98 hp Vauxhall was too fast for G. A. Vandervell's 25 hp Talbot, though only by a bare 0·2s. Coe's time was 42s. Kaye Don's AC, with 40·8s, led home M. Luther's 1,500 cc 'trade' Austro-Daimler by 40·8s to 43s, but Luther, the British concessionaire for the make, took his class in the same time from George Duller's Ansaldo, which managed 44·8s. Two Bentleys headed another class, F. C. Clement beating W. O. Bentley by 39·8s to 40·2s, and N. W. Martin's GN, in 58·8s, saw off an Eric-Longden. The monster of the meeting, Capt Miller's 200 hp Wolseley Viper, made fastest time of the day in 34·8s, but George Duller, now driving a 30/98 hp Vauxhall, was not far behind, with 38·2s. The Viper also won the customary match against the fastest motor-cycle, in the same time.

The Wolseleys, newcomers to sprints though not to Brooklands, were an interesting trio: all racing cars, in descending order of size. There was nothing Wolseley about the Viper, apart from the fact that this firm was responsible for putting it together: it consisted of an Hispano-Suiza aero engine, built by the company under licence, installed in a pre-war Napier chassis. Such a combination was fashionable at Brooklands at this time, but not many of these aero-engined monsters appeared on sprint courses: there was no room for them to wind themselves up.

At least three major meetings were held on 7 July: a really catastrophic example of lack of co-operation between the clubs. At Holme Moss, where the Bradford and Huddersfield AC's assembled, Frazer-Nash collected two classes on time with 'Kim II', in 93·6s and 96s, from T. Moore's 200-Mile Race GN and E. R. Hall's Bugatti, their times being a very sick 143·6s and a splendid 96·4s. J. Lumb's 8/18 hp Talbot and Frazer-Nash won these two events on formula, while J. S. Couldrey on an 18 hp Essex did extremely well to beat J. H. Clay's Bentley by 104·8s to 116·8s, and he also won on formula. H. F. Clay, running a 1914 Grand Prix Vauxhall against Malcolm Campbell's six-cylinder, 5-litre racing Sunbeam, was 6·2s slower, with a time of 88·6s. Clay, however, won on formula. Parry Thomas was third on speed with his Leyland, clocking 106·4s.

Another class went on time and formula to E. S. Myers's Ansaldo in 11·6s, but Campbell went on majestically to make fastest time of the day, and set up a new course record, with 80·8s. But again, H. E.

Clay's old Vauxhall was not far behind (91s), and he actually beat Frazer-Nash by just 0·8s. Excitement of another sort was provided by L. Briggs's Vauxhall, which charged a bank sideways and tore off two of its tyres.

Meanwhile the JCC's Northern Centre were holding their hill-climb on a new and exceptionally steep course at Saltersford Church, near Macclesfield. The gradient on its 1,200 yd rose to 1-in-4·4, and helped to account for several abject failures to complete the distance. Raymond Mays's Bugatti won the racing car class in 1m 29s, thus making best time of the day, while another went to C. M. Harvey's 10/30 hp works Alvis in 1m 44s. P. Platt's GN carried off two more events, his 1m 57·8s accounting for both. (In order to reduce the length and tedium of meetings, the multiplied dangers of many ascents, and the strain on cars and drivers, clubs were beginning to allow one run by a competitor to count for more than one class in cases where he could use the same car.)

Simultaneously, the Liverpool MC were reviving the Colwyn Bay speed trials. George Bedford's Hillman annexed one class in 40·4s, and came second to W. B. Horn's Straker-Squire in another, with 38·4s against 36s. The Sunbeam of F. A. P. Zacharias collected a third class in 47·2s.

On the 27th, the East Midland Centre of the ACU assembled at Welbeck for speed trials run by the Mansfield MC. The two light car events, said to be for amateurs and novices, went to R. S. Clifford's 11 hp Riley and A. Richards's 10/30 hp Alvis. Richards covered the flying ½ mile in 29s, but A. E. Keen with the Cowley Sports, strange to relate, was beaten into second place by Clifford, with 23·8s to the latter's 22·4s. What is even stranger is the fact that Mr Keen was there at all: he could hardly be described as a novice, and was most certainly not an amateur.

Soon afterwards the Duke of Portland excluded motorists from Welbeck Park. However, as had happened once before, long ago, the ban had been lifted by the time the next season came round.

Shelsley was run off on 29 July, and in 1921, only one run per driver was allowed, and practising was forbidden. Both regulations made for some sensational climbs. However, the course had been improved considerably. The undergrowth had been cut away, the tarmac surface had been concreted where it was likely to break up, the banks had been railed off at a distance of 6 ft from the course, and the gateway at the top had been widened.

As usual, the open event brought the best time of the day; 53·8s by

M. C. Park's 1922 Tourist Trophy Vauxhall. C. A. Bird's Indianapolis Sunbeam was getting a bit long in the tooth now, but was only 0·2s behind, in spite of a bank-battering ascent. Humphrey Cook climbed in 56·8s, W. B. Horn's Straker-Squire in 60s dead, and J. S. Couldrey's very fast Essex in 61s. Count Zborowski's eight-cylinder Ballot, misfiring, was rather out of it with 64·8s, while an Austin 'Twenty' driven by L. T. Kings took the formula award, and Miss D. Heath in a 14 hp Sunbeam took the Ladies' Prize, also given on formula. Ladies had done well at Shelsley before, but they had not previously competed in sufficient numbers to warrant the institution of a special award.

The open event for light cars resulted in a win for Kensington Moir's Aston Martin, which ascended in 57·2s, with A. Paul's 1,500 cc Austro-Daimler second in 60s, and Count Zborowski with an Aston Martin third in 61·8s. It is odd to see three of the greatest champions further down the list: Leon Cushman with 62s, Frazer-Nash, 64·2s and Mays, 78·6s. Frazer-Nash at least had plenty of excuse for a comparatively poor time, and even more cause for self-congratulation, because theoretically he should never have been able to finish the course at all. In the course of a skid, he burst a tyre and buckled another wheel, but just pressed on regardless. His time was a miracle of control and determination, although *The Autocar* doubted whether he should have continued: the burst tyre could have locked his steering, turned him over and plunged him into the crowd.

As it happened, Lionel Martin's Aston Martin was 'nowhere' on time in this event, but the car's climb was exceedingly interesting to watch, as a pioneer example of the 'new style'. Abjuring long, spectacular slides, it lost no time and was always under perfect control. The closed climb went to Humphrey Cook in 64·6s, J. H. Clay's Bentley being runner-up with 66·8s, while L. T. Kings registered 89·8s at the wheel of a fascinating little newcomer: the Austin 'Seven'. This was its first-ever competition appearance.

A week later, but far away, a portent appeared. A. Francis, driving a sports Beardmore, won every one of the four classes in the Scottish Western Motor Club's speed trials, with a time of 37⅞s. Like the Picts of long ago, the Beardmores were about to start working their way down from the North, sweeping all before them as they did so. . . .

On the 23rd there took place an extremely important fixture, the so-called Southsea 'Speed Carnival'; part of a true charity carnival being run by the corporation under the patronage of the Duke of

York. These speed trials were held on the eastern end of the Southsea promenade, over a standing mile and flying kilometre between the Eastney end of the then-new concrete road and the Canoe Lake. The publicity was good enough to secure an excellent entry of 117 cars, and the course was so well policed that even some competitors found themselves summarily removed from it. Both the standing-mile handicaps were won by J. F. Slaughter's 8/18 hp Talbot. One of the mile scratch events went to Lionel Martin's Aston Martin at 52·17 mph, Martin also winning it on formula, while another resulted in an extraordinary dead-heat between three cars, all covering the course at 48·91 mph. There were R. Sahl's 10 hp Calthorpe, the Hon Victor Bruce's AC, and Raymond Mays's Bugatti, Sahl taking this event on formula. Mays did particularly well, considering that his engine cut out on the course. He was still using the original Bugatti petrol pipes and jets, which did not deliver fuel fast enough to feed an engine turning over at 6,000 rpm. In the mile for racing cars, J. A. Joyce's works AC triumphed at 69·5 mph, his time of 51·8s being best of the day for the distance. Frazer-Nash and Kensington Moir, the latter driving an Aston Martin and winning on formula, tied for second place with 67·16 mph.

Exciting though the 'miles' were, it was the flying kilometres for racing cars that produced the truly heavy metal. One class went to M. C. Park's TT Vauxhall at 64·28 mph, which was too good for F. C. Clement's Bentley (62·14 mph) and Frazer-Nash (61·12 mph). However, Frazer-Nash won another 'kilometre' easily, his 63·19 mph outclassing an Eric-Longden light car and a Tamplin. The 'unrestricted' kilometre race brought out the Brooklands monsters, and resulted in a win for Count Zborowski's 300 hp 'Chitty I', with 73·1 mph. His 30·6s was the fastest time of the day for the kilometre. E. A. D. Eldridge's 180 hp Isotta-Maybach was second at 69·47 mph, and A. Barlow's 84 hp Benz third. His speed was 68·62 mph. Park's Vauxhall, also taking part, won on formula.

These were merely the leaders; the less successful among this menagerie of strayed Brooklands beasts including Capt A. G. Miller's Wolseley Viper, the 15 hp Wolseley, and Parry Thomas's Leyland. The speeds indicate that the flying start to the kilometre, and the pull-up available at the other end, were far too short to allow drivers to fully unleash their cars, for at Brooklands, some were capable of almost double the speeds they recorded at Southsea.

The JCC, still pursuing its policy of discouraging freaks belonging in classes other than those for which they were sometimes entered, ran its South Harting climb on 9 September. The Bugatti of Raymond Mays made fastest time of the day with 59·8s, Leon Cushman coming second in the class in 1m 5s and Frazer-Nash third in 1m 9·2s, but Frazer-Nash's was the most creditable ascent, for his excellent time was set up while there was a blockage in the main jet of his carburetter. W. G. H. Hedges with his 10/30 hp Alvis made the finest performance among the other competitors, for one of the two classes he won on time was taken from none other than Leon Cushman in the Bugatti, by 1m 22·8s to 1m 24·6s. Hedges was in fact up against two Bugattis in his class, and it is interesting to the student of technique to note that when he beat an Albert and an AC in the other event, his time was very much slower. Hedges also took a third place, going faster still with 1m 20·4s, behind Mays (1m 4·2s) and the GN of G. L. Hawkins (1m 15·6s). Other, single classes were taken by Frazer-Nash against W. D. Hawkes's Morgan—1m 2·2s to 1m 2·4s—by A. R. Linsley's Bugatti—which with 1m 25·4s beat two Alvises, the best recording 1m 33·6s—and by W. H. Holmes's Morgan, in 1m 28·8s. This last class was won by J. F. Slaughter's 8/18 hp Talbot on formula.

The Eastbourne & District Motor Cycle Club chose the same day to christen another new speed trial course; ½ mile of Eastbourne's King Edward Parade between the Grand Hotel and Beachy Head. There were light car and cyclecar classes, won by Kaye Don's AC and Capt F. C. Peaty's Bleriot Whippet, the latter in 29·6s; but most of the interest lay in demonstrations by Brooklands cars which were not part of the competition at all. Eldridge's Isotta-Maybach, able to let itself go more freely than at Southsea, covered the distance in 22·4s, at 88·22 mph. Parry Thomas's Leyland and Captain Miller's Wolseley Viper were also performing, having once more wandered from Brooklands.

It seems strange to read that, at a time when you had only to announce that you were running a sprint—any sprint (like that of the St Austell gentleman noted in the appendix to this Part under 1921)—to attract a small avalanche of entries, the Hertfordshire County AC's open climb of Aston Clinton should have had to be postponed because of lack of interest. There were only thirty-seven entries even when the meeting was eventually held, on 16 September. However, a fair proportion of the champions put in an appearance.

M. C. Park with his TT Vauxhall won the unrestricted event, his 48s being fastest time of the day. F. C. Clement and Humphrey Cook on their customary mounts tied for second place 0·6s behind, but this was really Park's day, for he took two other classes, one from the same two gentlemen in 48·6s, against 49·6s for Clement and 49·8s for Cook, and one from Clement again (49s to 49·4s) with Raymond Mays in third place. Mays won a class with the Bugatti in 49·8s, beating the 52·2s of Kensington Moir's TT Aston Martin. The Austro-Daimler of C. J. Paul came in third with 59·6s, while G. L. Hawkins's GN very easily beat a brace of French EHPs in 1m 8·6s, and also took the class on formula. Three other classes went to Lionel Martin in this respect.

It did seem that, driving techniques apart, modern cars were becoming too fast for Aston Clinton, for they were heard to cut out before the corners. During one run, Kensington Moir experienced a very nasty moment when both of his rear tyres burst and were torn off. Urgent evasive action, in the form of a series of broadside slides, saved him from running into the spectators, or, should we say, saved the spectators from being run into by Kensington Moir.

SUNBAC attacked Angel Bank a week later. The two car classes both went to the Morgan of N. Norris in 37·4s, and he was best on formula as well. The second places belonged to a newcomer, D. M. K. Marendaz in his Marseal light car (42·4s) and to George Bedford's Hillman, which climbed in 42·8s.

Capt Marendaz tells an amusing story which seems to show that skullduggery in sprints was not the exclusive prerogative of the competitor. While taking part in a hillclimb at Margam Park during the 1920s, he was surprised (his being much the fastest car present) to find that the times the timekeepers allowed him never gave him anything better than a third place in a class. Before his last run, and while ostensibly indulging in a warming-up run at a suitable distance from the officials, he stopped to instal a friend under the tannoau cover of his car. The friend was armed with a stopwatch. At the conclusion of the run the marshals gave his time as 31s; whereupon Marendaz's friend emerged like the Demon King from his place of concealment, holding up a watch which had recorded 24s. After a great deal of argument Marendaz was allowed another run, during which he made fastest time of the day and won first place in all his classes!

This year the Great Wakering speed trials of the Essex County & Southend AC, held on 7 October, were both open and closed. The plan had originally been to hold them on, of all places, a stretch of the main London–Southend road at Ilford, but for reasons which are not difficult to imagine the idea was abandoned and the competitors repaired to the private road used previously. The experiment of including open classes was not a success, for there were only fifteen entries for the whole event. One would have thought that so few cars would be easy to handle, but the organisation disintegrated so completely that cars returning to the start after their runs were sent back down the course while later numbers were still on their way up.

Leon Cushman with a Bugatti won two of the open touring classes from Maitland Keddie in an unspecified motor-car, perhaps an Alvis, but was beaten in another by D. M. K. Marendez's Marseal. Cushman's winning time for his two classes was 32·8s against Keddie's 42·4s, and Marendaz won in 31·8s to Cushman's 33·4s. Major C. G. Coe's Vauxhall completely outclassed H. Hutchinson's Alpine Steyr by 28s to 37s, and also won one of the open sports-car classes against the Hon Victor Bruce's AC, timed at 28·4s to 34s. Marendaz beat Bruce in two classes by 30·6s to 34s, and the categories for any type of car went to S. F. Edge's work AC three times: once against Capt Peaty's Bleriot 'Whippet' by 25·8s to 29·2s, and twice against Cushman by 27·4s to 28·4s.

October 13 saw the revival, in a quiet way, of a course that had been very famous indeed to a past generation of racing men—Bexhill. The Kent & Sussex LCC ran open and closed speed trials over 650 yd of the West Parade, and Leon Cushman's Bugatti clocked 27·2s, thereby making fastest time of the day. D. M. K. Marendaz's Marseal was second fastest, with 28s. S. H. Constable's Morgan won two classes and R. J. Cramp's AC one, in 32·5s. There were unhappily few entries, so many classes were simple walkovers.

The resuscitation of Bexhill reflected the most typical trend of this period; a very great increase in the number of speed trials, usually held on new courses. In pre-war days, hillclimbs had been much more popular. In the last three years before the war, one sprint in six would be a speed trial. In 1920, by contrast, there were ten speed trials to twenty-one hillclimbs; in 1921, thirteen to thirty-eight; and in 1922, no fewer than twenty-one to forty-four. The growing inadequacy, and danger, of hillclimb courses on public roads and the comparative ease of finding a piece of road for a speed trial were the reasons for this trend. The number of hillclimbs held during any post-war year never even approached the massive total of over sixty recorded for 1907. Speed trial courses were safer for the faster cars of 1922 because they were wide and straight, and because, being mostly on promenades and beaches, they could be closed to the public.

The year had not been noticeably more crowded than 1921, but there were already rumblings to the effect that the RAC, alarmed by the speeds now being achieved and by the increase in phenomenal avoidances and actual crashes, proposed to grant open permits only to 'established' events. It would have been hard, and invidious, to choose between established and non-established competitions, and in the end, as we shall see, the club decided on a far more drastic method of control.

* * *

Nothing could keep a crowd off a course that was a public road if they insisted on wandering over it as a car ascended, but efficient organisation and marshalling, and the choice of a course that was as safe as possible, could limit the dangers to some extent. The RAC could watch over standards in open events, because a permit was essential and would not be granted unless the course were safe and the meeting properly run. RAC rules to govern all types of meeting had been in existence since 1900, but so long as no permit was in practice required for closed events, the rules could not be enforced. As we have seen, the RAC had already tried to impose its authority on closed meetings, and had failed due to the opposition of the provincial clubs.

The problem was now acute, not so much because of any great increase in the numbers of events held, but because speeds were so much higher, and the 'new motoring' had inflated the numbers of spectators. Poor organisation at closed events was now a potentially lethal factor. It was also, as always, extremely aggravating to the trade. Strange and widely-varying rules might be applied and disputes adjudicated by inexperienced officials with little real authority, and there was no appeal from their decisions to the recognised authority of the RAC stewards. Those concerns which believed in the commercial value of sprint successes, especially the smaller ones which gambled a lot of their money on them, saw their livelihoods affected.

These considerations impelled the RAC to announce, in February 1923, that in future all closed events would require permits. Competitors taking part in those without permits would be subject to the same pains and penalties suffered for participating in unrecognised open meetings: exclusion from future, recognised events. At the same time, an addition was made to the rules, aimed at discouraging trade participation in closed events. The trade had taken part in closed contests by the simple expedient of enclosing a subscription to the organising club with their entry fee. Any closed event they wanted to support thus became, to all intents and purposes, open. The presence of really fast cars and star works drivers drew the same crowds that attended open events; yet the dangers were multiplied: the standards of organisation were uncontrolled, and the course was subject to no approval by experienced authorities.

The new rule laid down that new members could only take part in a closed event if they had joined before the regulations were published. No firm could therefore be sure of the suitability of their cars to the conditions of an event until they had paid to enter it.

The howl that went up from a number of the provincial clubs was predictably loud. Some clubs, it is true, had applied for RAC permits for closed events and ran them under RAC rules when they were under no compulsion to do so, presumably in order to attract trade entries, but as in an earlier generation, others resented outside control of what they still regarded, somewhat illogically, as private meetings. Especially did they dislike the fact that competitors could now appeal over their heads to the RAC stewards. They were anxious that the trade should be encouraged to take part in their closed events, for the sake of their incomes and reputations, but they were unwilling to accept the controls which, in modern conditions, must follow from this. The fact that the RAC simultaneously aggravated its offence by trying to discourage trade entries infuriated the affiliated clubs still more.

In the end, the RAC made a concession, altering their new rule. New members intending to take part in an event could join a club up to three weeks before entries closed. This merely meant that the trade would have to organise themselves well in advance and send in their entries early, thereby helping the organisers; it cannot have had much limiting effect on their numbers. In fact, the RAC could afford some concessions, because although the trade had not been driven away from closed events, the latter would now, under the jurisdiction of the parent club, be able to cope with them more safely and efficiently. Neither was the concession a sign of weakness. In 1905 the RAC had been faced with the possibility, and in 1907 with the actuality, of a rival motoring organisation round which clubs offended with its policy could rally. In those years, too, there were great dangers inherent in splitting the motor movement. By 1923 none of these inhibitions remained: the RAC was much more powerful, and its prestige was higher still. After the February decrees, its control of competitions was unassailable.

The new rules were published just in time to help control the fullest season the sport had ever known. The number of recorded events increased by 10 per cent over 1922, and surpassed the earlier peak year of 1907 for the first time. There were twenty-eight speed trials recorded in 1923, as against forty-three hillclimbs.

Aston Clinton, it was said, was safer this year for being lined with iron railings in time for the 'Inter-Varsity' climb on 3 March. The spectators undoubtedly felt safer, but the reactions of the drivers are not recorded. The gentleman who made fastest time of the day, R. F. Summers with a 30/98 hp Vauxhall, made a spectacular climb in 45·5s, but one imagines that the exuberance of the drivers, generally more marked at university events than elsewhere, was somewhat damped. J. Lucas-Scudamore, in a Ballot, was second best in this class with 45·9s, while H. S. Eaton's GN with 1922 200-Mile Race ohc engine, collected the other class in 48·8s, beating an ABC and a Hillman, which clocked 53·9s and 57·9s.

Spectators were very much in the picture at Kop when the Essex MC met there for their open and closed event on 24 March. The antics of an exhibitionist in a Cubitt would have been funny in other circumstances, but according to *The Autocar*, he:

> delayed his change down until the car came to rest and commenced to run backwards. The driver then applied the handbrake so forcibly that he could not for some minutes release the ratchet. Finally he moved off triumphantly, only to reappear and descend the hill behind the competitors at such a speed that he could not pull up and nearly rammed Cushman's Bugatti in the stern. In avoiding the Bugatti, the Cubitt steersman cannoned into the bank and almost overturned.

Humphrey Cook, in registering 29·8s and fastest time of the day, averaged over 70 mph for the distance. He was just 0·2s better than L. C. G. M. Le Champion's Isotta-Maybach, which must have been a handful. Cook also took two other classes, one from Ivy Cummings in 36·6s to 37·8s, Miss Cummings driving the 1913 chain-driven Indianapolis Bugatti 'Black Bess', and one from F. C. Clement's Bentley by 29·8s to 33·6s. Leon Cushman collected four open classes, two from P. L. Densham in another Bugatti in 44s to 52s, and two from Frazer-Nash in 33s to 34s. Raymond Mays beat Du Cane's Bugatti, 40·2s to 43·4s, and A. H. Pass's sports Sunbeam 40·2s to 55s. One class went to J. F. Duff's Bentley, which beat Major H. W. Hall's Bentley by 39·6s to 48·6s, and one to Frazer-Nash, who was better than Eaton in another GN by 34s to 49s. Mays and Cushman each won four of the closed classes, and Cook another three.

This year, on 2 April, the Scarborough & District MC forsook Staxton for Octon Bank, 3 miles to the south. This 7-furlong course sounds fast, being straight and averaging only 1-in-12 for ½ mile, but the change was not auspicious: spectators swarmed on the road so thickly and persistently that competitors at first refused to start, and now we know only that N. T. Beardsell on a Hodgson won the 1,500-cc class in 32·4s, and that Ivy Cummings was there with 'Black Bess', Raymond Mays with (oddly enough) a Hillman once more, and E. R. Hall with a Marseal.

The 21st found the North-West London Motor Club tackling Waterworks Hill, which was certainly near to, and might have been identical to, Hand Post. The event is interesting only for the participation of Capt G. E. T. Eyston, whose Aston Martin took second place in one class to G. L. Hawkins's GN, recording 30·8s to the GN's 24·6s. Hawkins won another class with the same time, and was second in a third category to Ivy Cummings's 'Black Bess', which set up fastest time of the day in 22·6s. Hawkins registered 25s here.

Some time in April, but before the 28th, the Glasgow Motor Club climbed Dalgrain Brae near Sorn, a hill with a maximum gradient of 1-in-5. A. Francis's 12·8 hp Beardmore won the unlimited class on time and ascended faster than anyone else that day in 37s. David Carlaw's Austin 'Twenty' was next best on time, with 44·2s, with R. B. Tennant's Austro-Daimler winning on formula in this class, Francis coming second, and Tennant taking two other classes on both time and formula. One, in 59s, was from G. Evans's Austin 'Seven', which recorded 79·6s. This seems to be the 'Seven's' first sprint place. Tennant's other time-and-formula win was from D. S. Baddeley's ABC; on this occasion in 46·4s to 58s.

Humphrey Cook made best time of the day when the South Midland Centre of the ACU gathered at Kop on 28 April, his 1922 Tourist Trophy Vauxhall beating Mays's Bugatti by 27·8s to 31·8s. Ivy Cummings in 'Black Bess' registered 33·6s, but GN's were unbeatable in two other open classes. G. L. Hawkins and H. S. Eaton tied for first place in one with 36·4s, and in the other Eaton beat Mays by 34·2s to 34·8s: a fine performance.

While recording a Cook victory, it is apt to mention that the TT Vauxhall which he used in 1923–24 was the only one sold by the factory to a private individual. It developed 129 bhp at 4,400 rpm, and was christened 'Rouge et Noir' like its predecessor, which Cook now retired.

The JCC's Northern Centre hillclimb at Saltersford on the same day is of interest principally for the first appearance of the name B. H. Davenport, linked with GN, at the top of a class. Other class winners were P. M. Hills's Bugatti (twice; beating Davenport once and T. Simister's Alvis on another occasion), and N. Turner's ABC. Hills's best time, and fastest of the day, was 1m 30·6s.

A fortnight later, the Hertfordshire County AC held its open meeting on Aston Clinton. F. B. Halford's Aston Martin 'Bunny', making a noise 'like tearing calico', beat Raymond Mays's and Cushman's Bugattis into second and third place in their racing class, 'Bunny' ascending in 59·6s and Mays in 52·8s. However, Humphrey Cook it was who made fastest time of the day on the TT Vauxhall, in 46·4s. That was too good for F. C. Clement and his Bentley, though the latter was fast enough to record 49·2s while having a fit of temperament. Mays was third in this class with 49·6s, but the sensation of the day was the performance of E. Swain on what was allegedly a 23/60 hp, ie a very touring, Vauxhall. He won a racing class in 48·2s against two TT Vauxhalls, those of M. C. Park and Cook, which took 48·4s and 48·6s respectively, In a touring-car class, in the same car, he again beat Humphrey Cook (now with a 30/98 hp Vauxhall, perhaps 'Lady of the Lake'), by 50·4s to 56·4s, and won on formula. Lionel Martin with an Aston Martin took one touring class in 64·4s from the Bugattis of Leon Cushman (68·4s) and P. L. Densham, but then Cushman went on to win another class in 70s from Densham and Martin.

The Essex County & Southend AC's open and closed climb of Laindon was run off on 26 May, and here, as elsewhere, one time was allowed to count for more than one class, so endless repetition of climbs by the same car was avoided. There was also a dramatic decline in the number of entries: a mere thirty this year. Obviously each car was now counted as one entry, irrespective of the number of classes in which it was entered. In another respect, the organisation fell down: there was no finishing banner.

Parry Thomas on the Leyland, not knowing where to brake, shot past the timing box to the T-junction and rounded the bend on two wheels before stopping. *En route*, he had clouted two motor-cycles and run over a policeman's foot, fortunately without damaging its owner. The Leyland, a Brooklands monster, was not the most suitable motor-car for hillclimbs, and although Parry Thomas won his class, beating Raymond Mays by 32s to 34s, it was J. A. Joyce's racing AC that made fastest time of the day in 30s, leading H. S. Eaton's GN in his class by 2s. Leon Cushman, too, was faster than

Thomas, his 31s being good enough to give him no fewer than six classes. He did not have much opposition. P. L. Densham in another Bugatti took a class in 42·4s, as did W. M. Broomhall's 40/50 hp Rolls-Royce with 39·4s. W. G. Brownlow's AC beat G. D. F. Keddie's 11 hp Riley in 43·8s to 45·4s, but Keddie won three other classes with a best time of 45·2s.

The Skegness speed trials returned to the calendar with a two-day open and closed meeting on 31 May–1 June, at the beginning of Skegness Carnival Week. Although it included such excitements as a handicap race between an aeroplane and the fastest car, it was not a great success. The lack of experience of the organisers (the Skegness municipal authorities), and bad weather contributed to its downfall.

Cars were dispatched in pairs in heats and finals over a standing kilometre between the Seacroft Hotel and Gibraltar Point, but on the first day, when the touring-car events were run off, no times were forthcoming: the telephone broke down. It was known that J. A. Joyce's AC beat F. B. Halford's Aston Martin 'Bunny', that Lionel Martin beat Leon Cushman, and that C. H. Pettit's Morgan saw off R. M. Wright's 8/18 hp Talbot. The timing was better organised on the next day, but almost everything else was worse: the sands were wet, and there were fewer competitors and fewer spectators. Humphrey Cook's TT Vauxhall beat Halford in 36s to 38·8s to make fastest time of the day, equal to 62·13 mph, and also won two other classes: one from Cushman in 36·8s and another from Halford. Cushman collected a class with 48·2s, and so did Lionel Martin, who beat F. E. Cox's Hodgson.

Although the surface of Holme Moss and its five bad bends had been doctored, the joint open meeting of the Bradford and Huddersfield clubs on 9 June did not look particularly safe, owing to the spectators who blocked the course, parting before each car as it ascended. In these circumstances, the Hon Victor Bruce's AC burst a tyre. Sounding faintly surprised, a reporter commented that 'happily no accident occurred'. Fastest times in the open classes were made by Humphrey Cook's TT Vauxhall in 1m 22·8s, E. R. Hall's Aston Martin 'Bunny' coming second in 1m 24·8s. Cook took one of the other open classes in 1m 23·4s, as did Hall in 1m 28·4s, and with this meeting Beardmores had invaded England at last. Cyril Paul's car won its class, with 1m 39s. Cook, H. F. Clay with a 30/98 hp Vauxhall and A. Tinker on a GN each collected a class restricted to amateur drivers, in 1m 26·8s, 1m 27s and 1m 48·4s respectively.

A week later, still more speed trials were run off on the West Parade at Bexhill, this time by the Kent AC. Ivy Cummings again won the unlimited racing class with 'Black Bess', in 1m 27·2s, while the trade Bugatti of B. S. Marshall was fastest in the 1,600-cc class with 30·6s, and L. A. Cushman, at the wheel of a GN, led the 1,100-cc cars with a time of 39s.

It was highly unfortunate that Bexhill should coincide not only with the Saltburn meeting (as we shall see), but also with an even more important fixture, the revival of the famous Blackpool Speed Trials. Run by the Blackpool & Fylde Motor Club over a standing ½ mile of the Queen's Drive, North Shore, this was an open event. Cars were dispatched in pairs and in addition to the normal capacity classes, they were differentiated by price: a curious throwback reminiscent of the first series of races at Blackpool. The object was no doubt to endow the groups of starters with some variety; and also, perhaps, to put the small yet expensive Bugattis at a disadvantage in some events.

Leon Cushman's Bugatti won three classes, with a best time of 34·4s, as did F. B. Halford. His Aston Martin, covering the course in 31s, beat Cushman, F. C. Clement's Bentley, and J. A. Joyce's AC into second place in three of the racing classes. The best Joyce could do, in fact, was 32·6s. However, W. Watson's TT Vauxhall made fastest time of the day, his 30·8s being too good for W. B. Horn's Straker-Squire (31s), Clement (32s) and Halford (32s). N. T. Beardsell's Hodgson won a race in 35·8s from T. Moore's Horstman, 0·2s behind, and other classes went to the GNs of C. Williams, H. S. Eaton and P. Platt, the Bugatti of P. M. Hills, and W. H. Boston's Bentley, which recorded 39·6s.

Saltburn, meanwhile, was suffering from lack of entries, which was unfortunate, as the sands were in fine condition and there were eight open as well as three restricted events. Some very close and fierce duels took place, even so.

In the open standing-start races, Raymond Mays's Bugatti, running on alchohol fuel, twice beat Hodgson, in 38·6s to 39s and 36·8s to 38·2s, while L. Ropner's 30/98 hp Vauxhall disposed of another Vauxhall in 39s. But then Hodgson, his car going better with every new run, beat both the Vauxhalls in the first 500 yd, although his engine was little more than one-third the size of both his opponents. Mays then defeated George Bedford, at the wheel of a 1½-litre Hillman built for the 1922 TT, going ahead fairly easily in 35·8s to 40·2s. The Hillman had only three gears, however, which put it at a dis-

N

advantage. Humphrey Cook also beat Bedford with his TT Vauxhall, but by the narrower margin of 37·2s against 40s.

However, the Hillman seemed to be a bit faster than the Hodgson, given a fair run, for in one flying-start event Bedford led Hodgson by 25·2s to 26·8s. Cook took another from Ropner by 21·4s to 23·2s, but he lost a match with L. C. G. M. Le Champion's Isotta-Maybach which, in the best of three runs, covered the distance in 20·2s. This speed of 110·74 mph was fastest of the day, comparing with Cook's best of 107·55 mph, or 20·8s. Hodgson took two closed standing-start classes, and Ropner one, Hodgson not being pressed. His nearest rival was a standard 14 hp Sunbeam that recorded 51·2s, but Ropner, being up against Cook, was impelled to make his best time of the day, beating Cook by 37·4s to 41·4s.

This year the normal order of the Caerphilly-Porthcawl meetings was reversed: the speed trials on the Rest Bay sands were held on 28 June and the Mountain Road hillclimb on the 29th. Both brought surprises; though Malcolm Campbell's fastest time of the day at Porthcawl with a six-cylinder racing Sunbeam was not one of them.

Campbell covered the distance in 47·4s, Humphrey Cook's Vauxhall coming second in 51·4s and F.B. Halford's Aston Martin 'Bunny' third with 54·6s. Cook beat Kensington Moir's Bentley by 50·4s to 62·2s, but R. J. Sully's formidable HE found itself pipped by A. K. Neale's pre-war 14 hp Humber in 1m 12·4s to 1m 16s. H. D. Coates's Ansaldo, with 60s dead, beat not only Cyril Paul's Beardmore (64·4s) but also A. E. Keen's phenomenal Morris, which took 5 seconds longer still. It came as something of a surprise, too, to see A. J. Sgonina's very fast GN lead A. E. Rollason's 9 hp Ariel home by only 6s, in 1m 16s. J. A. Joyce's AC won a class from F. B. Halford, their times being 56·4s and 57s. F. J. Boshier-Jones's Gwynne Eight was too fast for J. Thomas's 8/18 hp Humber, in 1m 12·2s against 1m 24s, but two of the closed classes went to 8/18 hp Humbers (Miss D. Vaughan and Miss G. Thomas), and one each to a Hillman, an HE, a 30/98 hp Vauxhall and a 20 hp Austin.

Enormous crowds of spectators lined the Mountain Road at Caerphilly the next day, including 'an unbelievable number of small boys', who did nothing to promote the heroic efforts of the police to clear the course. They at least had their money's worth, seeing the unfortunate Cook ram the bank and bend his Vauxhall. Earlier, Kensington Moir's Bentley had beaten him for fastest time of the day, with 1m 1s against 1m 11·4s, but this class was the only one to be won on time. The rest were judged on formula, though times were given, and it was a very remarkable thing for Cook, or indeed any Vauxhall driver, to be beaten by a 3-litre Bentley in a hillclimb, but it had happened now.

J. A. Malins, who competed to good effect in the Welsh 'double' in 1923 and 1924 with a Sports Morris Cowley, recalls that Malcolm Campbell, having spoiled a first run by spinning on the last bend, was allowed a second attempt. It was quite usual for 'VIPs' to be favoured in this way, and curiously, there is no record of the practice causing resentment among the other drivers.

There was again a pretty narrow margin between Sgonina's GN (1m 11·2s) and A. E. Rollason's Ariel (1m 19s), while Neale's museum-piece drove home its superiority over Sully's HE by climbing in 1m 29·6s to 1m 33·2s. W. T. Charles's 8 hp Rover, which must have been one of the least suitable cars ever to take part in a speed hillclimb, did extraordinarily well to beat one of the nippy 10 hp flat-twin BSAs, in 2m 23·2s to 2m 42·2s, while F. B. Halford, with 1m 7·2s, led a class from G. E. T. Eyston and Lionel Martin with other Aston Martins. A. E. Keen's Morris beat two HE's, of which Sully's was the better. Keen was timed at 1m 8·2s and Sully at 1m 16s, and Lionel Martin was fastest in one class, his 1m 21·6s beating R. C. R. Pomeroy's 1m 28·2s in another HE. But his main achievement was on formula, for in this respect he put up the best overall performance of the day. Closed classes were won on time by an 8/18 hp Humber (J. Thomas), a Hillman, J. A. Malins's Morris Sports, and a Gwynne, and that was the Welsh 'twin' event over for another year.

The success of the Humbers at these meetings was the last and isolated fling of a make which had once been much feared in sprints and circuit racing. The tiny 8/18 hp Humber was a fast car for its type, but by this time the *marque* looked incongruous in a speed event. *The Autocar* commented: 'To see these little cars streaking up the hill on second all the way and skidding on the corners was a great sight, and if the Humber engineers were present, they must have been amazed at the going and probably horror-stricken at such handling of what is essentially a small car of refinement.' But the importance of formula awards at Caerphilly probably accounted for the appearance of the Ariel, BSA and Rover as well as Humber light cars.

On 5 July the Essex County & Southend AC, in conjunction with the Essex MC, were to have held their usual speed trials at Westcliff, but the event did not take place. Postponed to 8 September, when they were supposed to be run at Great Wakering, they were again put off to October, but were never heard of again. The reason given was that no suitable road was available, but we are not told why the club had lost Westcliff, though the previous season's fiasco at Great Wakering could account for the denial to them of that course.

However, all went well at the Hampshire AC's Spread Eagle climb on 7 July, now 'one of the accepted classic events of the year', according to *The Autocar*. In the open events Frazer-Nash beat J. A. Joyce's AC by 44·4s to 46·6s, though Joyce won on formula, while Humphrey Cook twice beat Frazer-Nash, 43s to 45·2s and 43·6s to 44s. The Aston Martins of G. E. T. Eyston and F. B. Halford took each class on formula, yet Parry Thomas's Leyland could do no better than follow Frazer-Nash in the second ascent, climbing in 44·8s. W. G. H. Hedges's Alvis collected two of the closed class wins, with a best time of 77s, and in one instance he beat Malcolm Campbell's Itala, which recorded 77·6s. W. G. Barlow's Bentley with 54·6s saw off C. M. Harvey's Alvis of half the capacity (57·2s), but Major C. G. Coe's 30/98 hp Vauxhall beat Barlow by 50·2s to 52·8s in another class.

It may have been this year when Humphrey Cook realised just how dangerous a course Spread Eagle could be. He 'had a go' with the new works Aston Martin 'Razor Blade', which on this occasion had no brakes at all. The marshals at the top of the hill would wave people across the road in between runs, but could not, of course, do other than advise. One farmer with his cart was still retiring down the road beyond the finish when Cook crossed the line. He was quite unable to stop before reaching the cart, but managed to take to the grass verge and pull up alongside.

Back to the south coast, where yet another famous revival took place on 14 July, when the Brighton & Hove Motor Club held speed trials over a standing ¼ mile of the Madeira Drive. These were on a modest scale compared with the 1905 event, and were restricted to cars of less than 1,500 cc, but a fair entry was attracted to fill the six car classes. The JCC, the Surbiton Motor Club and the Kent AC were invited to participate, and class winners included Frazer-Nash, Leon Cushman, and Joyce with his AC. Second places in these runs were taken by a GN, an AC, and Frazer-Nash himself, while Joyce's time (not quoted) was fastest of the day and gave him the 1,500 cc class. B. E. Lewis's Frazer Nash twice defeated Vernon Balls's Amilcar in a notable performance.

Unfortunately SUNBAC was holding its Angel Bank meeting on

the same day. There, each car was allowed two ascents; the first for all classes on time and the second for all classes on formula, and apart from the usual capacity classes, there was one exclusively for Fords. Raymond Mays made very easily the best time of the day with 27·8s, beating Marendaz's Marseal and a Crouch in one class, and then proceeding to defeat A. E. Keen's Morris Cowley (by now a very special single-seater) in two more classes. Keen's time was 34·8s, but Mays rounded off what was very nearly a clean sweep by collecting three classes on formula. H. F. S. Morgan's Morgan was left with a lonely class win on time, in 37·8s.

South Harting two weeks later, on the 28th, drew surprisingly few of the best drivers. It could be that trade entries were discouraged by the JCC's reversion to the old practice of indicating relative times only, by means of a differential. Certainly even the 1,500-cc racing cars were now too fast for this hill—it was noticed that they were cutting out on the bends—but if the organisers' action helped placate public opinion, it probably antagonised the competitors.

Leon Cushman was there, his Bugatti beating A. Noble's Deemster by 3s, and so was Frazer-Nash, but he was relegated to second place in his class by E. R. Hall's Bugatti, with a margin of 0·4s. C. M. Harvey's Alvis won two classes, but no other drivers of the front rank were present. The meeting is of interest mainly for the appearance of Frazer-Nash's first four-cylinder car, equipped with an 8·7 hp Ruby engine and called after its creator. A word of caution is called for here, because reporters of sprint events tended to become confused for a year or two, referring to twin- or four-cylinder cars as either 'Frazer Nashes' or 'GNs' indiscriminately. It does not follow that the first had four or the second two cylinders. Indeed, GN put four-cylinder engines, into some of their products at the end of the company's career.

Frazer-Nash drove a 'Frazer Nash' at South Harting, as did J. A. Hall, and Hall was the luckier, taking two classes, one from a GN by 3·2s and the other from the Salmson of O. Wilson Jones by the even healthier margin of 5·4s. In the classes which C. M. Harvey won, Hall was second in one by 12s and Cushman in the other by 1·6s. The other Hall, E. R., with his Bugatti, beat Frazer-Nash and also Harvey by 1s. A. A. Pollard's Alvis led A. R. Linsley's Bugatti by 0·8s, and, surprisingly, the Tamplin of F. A. Houghton defeated D. Chinery's Gwynne by no less than 7·2s. Wins by cyclecars other than GNs and Morgans were pretty rare now, the small 'four' becoming too fast for them.

At the other end of the island, meanwhile, the Scottish Western MC were holding their speed trials, and Beardmores swept the board at Inchinnan, Cyril Paul taking two classes in 30$\frac{5}{16}$s and 28$\frac{1}{2}$s from A. Francis on a similar car, who registered 30$\frac{7}{8}$s and 31$\frac{1}{8}$s. These were very easily the fastest times made that day. Two classes also went to R. B. Tennant's Austro-Daimler, which beat D. S. Melvin's Singer in each. Their times were 38$\frac{1}{4}$s and 37$\frac{5}{8}$s (Tennant) and 43$\frac{1}{16}$s and 42$\frac{5}{16}$s (Melvin). W. H. Stevenson's Sunbeam led J. Ross's Ford by 34$\frac{1}{8}$s to 35$\frac{13}{16}$s. The curious timing, by sixteenths of a second in the published lists, was very seldom used in sprints. Apart from this, the meeting was notable only for the impressive turn of speed shown by the Ford, which was faster than the slightly smaller, twin ohc racing Austro-Daimler.

The Edinburgh & District MC was due to hold an open climb on Whitbridge Hill near Tummel Bridge on 11 August, but motor-cycle police stopped it. The competitors moved off to Trinafour, but the law pursued them there and forestalled them once again. It was rumoured that shooting tenants on adjoining estates had taken exception to their plans, but curiously enough, two other clubs who held a joint event on the same day far to the south had also had police trouble.

The Epsom MC and the Wallington MC had intended to use Epsom Downs for a speed trial, but the police had forbidden it. The clubs had to make do with a hillclimb consisting of a timed $\frac{1}{2}$ mile, rising to 1-in-8, of a very rough lane near Ewell, between Chipstead and Coulsdon. It was impossible to extend the cars fully, but in collecting one of its two class wins, Kaye Don's Deemster covered the distance in exactly $\frac{1}{2}$ minute, which sounds quite alarming enough, even granted a flying start. G. C. Griffiths's Deemster also won a class, but Ivy Cummings's cars—a Bugatti and a 200-Mile Race Frazer Nash—appropriated two. Her times were 32·8s and 37·8s.

The Kent AC, who ran a climb on Sharnden Hill near Mayfield on 18 August, had intended to confine all Bugattis to a class of their own, but this idea was dropped. It is not hard to imagine why, for some of the finest Bugatti drivers were members of the trade, and would not care to waste their money and effort only against other cars of the same make where victory would be quite valueless. Yet they would attract money and fine publicity to the club and its event and they must not be antagonised. It is of, course, impossible to generalise, for other clubs had resorted to similar desperate measures against GNs without having lamely to recant.

This year's Southsea speed trials, held a week later, were not quite so spectacular an affair as in 1922. They were organised by the South-Western Centre of the JCC instead of by the corporation, and were hence confined to cars of under 1,500 cc. Four other clubs were allowed to take part, but the restriction remained. Gwynnes had a good day, L. Horn's winning two classes, one at 42·25 mph from a pair of 8/18 hp Talbots, and D. Chinery's car beating A. Simmins's special 8/18 hp Talbot at 42·65 mph. J. A. Hall's Frazer Nash led home a GN and another Frazer Nash at 49·32 mph, while Raymond Mays won two events, in each case from other Bugattis. The first was a touring-car race, won at 44·01 mph, and the other was taken at 50·42 mph. In a sports car class, W. G. H. Hedges's Alvis did very well to beat an Aston Martin and a Frazer Nash with 54·22 mph, and in her class, Miss W. M. Pink's Aston Martin defeated a Bugatti and an Alvis at 50·99 mph.

Naturally the racing classes provided most of the excitement. J. A. Joyce's Brooklands Hour-Record AC was there, and its 70·04 mph was just too good for G. E. T. Eyston's Aston Martin (69·9 mph) and Ivy Cummings's four-cylinder 1,500-cc Frazer Nash (69·77 mph). G. Morgan's Morgan, with 61·43 mph, beat two 'Frazer Nashes', including Ivy Cummings's two-cylinder 1,100-cc car, which completed the distance at 59·21 mph.

Back to the beaches on 1 September when, on Birkdale sands, H. V. Hughes's Morgan won three events in the Southport MC's meeting from another Morgan, a Hillman and a Bayliss-Thomas. One of these events was a 10-mile race, the earliest recorded continuous long-distance sand race in Britain. These were to become common where the sands were wide enough to provide a long, narrow 'circuit'. The Morgan of J. M. Bullough also won its sprint, and Bentleys won three others, driven in two cases by F. O'Rourke. More Bentleys were second in each case.

Concurrently, the Slough & District Motor Cycle & Light Car Club were climbing the unspeakable Alms Hill. A course almost, if not quite, in the 'freak' class, it had not been attempted by cars since 1913. Competitors were timed over a ¼ mile, and the times were published, H. E. Hewens's Morris Cowley clambering up in 38s, and E. N. A. Remington's GN in 45·2s. The Oxford MC was to repeat the experiment three weeks later, while in the north the Yorkshire AC planned to hold a climb on Pateley Bridge, also on 1 September, but, not for the first time, an event on this course was cancelled for lack of entries.

A week later came Shelsley. Originally, the idea had been to use the usual classification—open and closed, unlimited and light cars—but this year, for the first time, results were given by capacity classes. No doubt the club wanted to attract more entries, by giving the slower cars a chance of making their mark.

Raymond Mays took his class with a time of 52·6s, thus also making fastest time of the day, but he was allowed an extra run in which to have a go at the hill record, standing to the credit of C. A. Bird's big racing Sunbeam since 1921. He broke it, with a time of 51·9s, on $1\frac{1}{2}$ litres of Bugatti. Frazer-Nash was second in Mays's class with 54·8s, and Hodgson third in 56·8s. A. C. R. Waite's Austin 'Seven', a two-seater sports car, won its class in 75·4s, and so did Cyril Paul's 2-litre ohc Beardmore. The latter's 56·6s was much too fast for R. J. Sully's HE (60·8s) and Oates's Ansaldo (64·2s). M. C. Park with his 1922 TT Vauxhall climbed in 52·8s, a time for his class win which was better than Malcolm Campbell's $4\frac{1}{2}$-litre racing Sunbeam could achieve when it took another class (54·8s). R. F. Summers's 30/98 hp Vauxhall and W. B. Horn's Straker-Squire were second and third to Campbell, Summers clocking 58·2s; Horn was 0·2s slower. The Ladies' Class (its first appearance as a separate entity) went to Miss Roper's AC in 71·4s on time and to Miss W. M. Pink's Aston Martin on formula.

On the 17th the Lancashire AC ran speed trials over a flying kilometre in connection with the Morecambe Carnival, on the sands between Lancaster and Bare. Again, there were few entries, and of these, H. F. Clay's 30/98 hp Vauxhall was fastest, recording 24·6s, or 90·93 mph. The Ford of E. Bradshaw caused consternation by defeating a Horstman and three Bentleys with a time of 28·8s.

The Essex MC's second open and closed meeting of the year on Kop was run off on 6 October, but because it was so late in the season, the many classes only attracted nine entries. The spectators, too, were thin on the ground, and Cyril Paul and his Beardmore raked in no fewer than six classes on time and eight on formula, though F. C. Clement's Bentley, which took four classes on time and one on formula, made fastest time of the day in 29·2s. Paul was second best with 31s, and Raymond Mays won three classes on time, one on formula; Vernon Balls's Amilcar took two on time and two on formula. A. G. Gripper's Bentley and R. C. Mann's Eric-Longden repeated the Amilcar's performance, while A. H. Dalton's Bugatti scored one time win and two formula wins, as did W. Dickie's Ansaldo. C. List's Amilcar took one time and one formula win, so in other words, all the lucky entrants took home at least two awards.

The season closed on 20 October with the Essex County & Southend AC's open and closed climb of Thundersley. Fastest time of the day went to Cyril Paul's Beardmore, R. F. Oates's Ansaldo being second best. The Hon V. A. Bruce's AC took a third open class, and Maitland Keddie's Alvis was judged to have made the best overall performance on formula; while the fastest car in the closed classes was F. A. Jones's Paige-Jewett.

Not before time, it was announced at the end of the season that the RAC, as the central organising body of motor sport, was to help in preventing clashes between important events; and so 1923—so far as sprinting was concerned—came to an end.

Nineteen twenty-four, the last year of the golden age of sprints, opened conventionally with the usual dark warnings from *The Autocar*. Spectators at sprints were becoming more and more numerous; where there was no strong police force present the dangers were multiplying in proportion. The legal position of an organiser could well be extremely fraught in the case of an accident involving onlookers, but *The Autocar* did not strengthen its arguments by stating that the numbers of sprints on public roads had diminished. In fact, 1923 had shown an increase over 1922, and later on, having checked its figures, *The Autocar* admitted as much. As for 1924, a truly colossal number of sprint meetings was planned—well over one hundred—but many never took place and others, no doubt, went unreported for lack of editorial space. Even so, the recorded total was appreciably higher than in the previous year, standing at over eighty.

The first, as usual, was the Essex MC's open and closed climb of Kop on 29 March. In an attempt to give them variety, classes according to price as well as capacity were arranged, in the antique mode. An interesting complexity of class divisions was, indeed, a feature of many of the sprints to be held that year.

C. J. Joyce, Gordon England and F. H. B. Samuelson all won classes open to any type of car, all driving Austin 'Sevens', with England setting the best time at 43s. Other classes open to racing cars went to Ivy Cummings's Frazer Nash in 34·2s, E. R. Hall's Aston Martin 'Razor Blade' in 32·6s, Cyril Paul's Beardmore in 32·8s, R. C. Morgan's Aston in 67·8s and, in the category for 'any cars' of unlimited capacity, to Humphrey Cook's Vauxhall, which climbed in 29s. Cook won three classes in all. The formula awards in the last three divisions specified were won by C. M. Harvey's Alvis

(35·8s), R. F. Oates's Ansaldo (35·4s), and J. A. Joyce's AC (32·4s). This very special ohc AC of Joyce's developed 70 bhp on Discol fuel.

The open and closed events for sports cars went to C. J. Joyce, D. M. K. Marendaz's Marseal (76·4s), B. S. Marshall's Bugatti (two classes), I. Ashcroft's Darracq (47·2s), R. F. Summers's 30/98 hp Vauxhall, E. L. Smith-Masters's Marseal, and R. G. Mundy's Ansaldo. Mundy's time was 63·8s. P. L. Densham and his Bugatti won two of the open touring classes with a fastest time of 46·8s, and also two of the closed classes. Other 'touring' wins were scored by E. J. Anderson's GN, Mundy's Ansaldo, and W. Edmunds's Wolseley.

On 26 April the York & District MC again attacked Sutton Bank, finding its surface soaked and streaming. E. R. Hall's Aston Martin won all the classes, and its best time of 1m 18·6s was fastest of the day. Second places were taken by M. B. Lax's Bugatti with 41·4s, Frazer-Nash with 1m 31s, H. F. Clay's 30/98 hp Vauxhall with 1m 29·4s, and T. Moore's Horstman, which took 1m 31·8s. It is only fair to record that both Frazer-Nash's GN and Paul's Beardmore, which climbed in 1m 33·6s, were off form.

The 'Inter-Varsity' hillclimb had been postponed from 8 March to 3 May, and it was run at Kop by the Oxford University Motor Club, which allowed each entrant two ascents, the faster one to count. R. F. Summers's 30/98 hp Vauxhall won one of the two classes with a time of 36·9s, which gave him fastest time of the day. He beat B. E. Lewis's Frazer Nash, which, however, took the other class in 37·5s from two Alvises. The better of these managed 40·65s. Lewis's Frazer Nash had a water-cooled 1,100-cc engine, which sounds like the French Ruby 8·7 hp four-cylinder unit, making his second place and then his class win most meritorious.

A week after this Kop climb, SUNBAC climbed Angel Bank, this being a closed meeting held in teeming rain. Once more, each competitor was given two runs, the best to count for all classes. Raymond Mays, driving an Austin 'Seven' for once, defeated D. W. Beck's 'Seven' by 40·2s to 43·4s, while H. F. S. Morgan's Morgan beat a similar car in 30·4s. Mays, reverting to his familiar Bugatti, climbed in 31·8s to take a class from B. S. Marshall's Bugatti, which was 4s slower, and at the same time took second place to Cyril Paul's Beardmore in another class, Paul registering 29·8s to set fastest time of the day. This ascent was also quick enough to give him a class victory over H. F. S. Morgan's car, daringly entered alongside him.

Between 12 and 17 May, the RAC ran a Small Car Trial, mostly in

Wales, which was very similar to that organised two years earlier by the Scottish AC. Its aim was to encourage the all-round efficiency of the breed. It drew entries from the trade rather than private owners, and classification was by price. The trial, based on Llandrindod Wells, lasted six days, and was extremely testing. Hills so difficult that some cars failed on them altogether were used, *and* timed. There were eleven such ascents, as in the 1914 Trial; three on Bwlch-y-Groes, three on Gibbet Hill, two on Senni Hill, two on Panne Hill and one on Birdlip over the border in England. A speed trial at Brooklands, consisting of a short acceleration test followed by a flying mile, concluded the proceedings.

D. Chinery's Gwynne won the premier award for general merit, for it was one of the faster cars, and drank less petrol than any of them. It made fastest time of the day on only one hill, however, that being the first ascent over the 2 miles of Bwlch-y-Groes, climbed in 4m 36·4s. Tatlow's Lea-Francis was the star performer so far as sheer speed was concerned and was fastest on seven ascents: twice on Gibbet, with a best time of 1m 43·2s, twice on Senni (3m 33s), twice on Panne (4m 11·4s) and once on Bwlch-y-Groes (4m 10·6s). The Palladium accounted for the other three: Gibbet once (1m 46s), Bwlch-y-Groes once (4m 12·2s), and Birdlip (2m 29·2s). This Palladium also proved itself the fastest car on the level, achieving 59·21 mph at Brooklands. Its nearest rivals, the Lea-Francis and an AC, covered the flying mile at 55·55 mph.

On the last day of the trial, the Hertfordshire County AC were running their open climb of Aston Clinton, and drawing most of the finest drivers. Dario Resta in the new 2-litre Grand Prix Sunbeam set a new hill record of 44·6s. Humphrey Cook came nearest to him, with 47·8s, and won another class in 48·6s from E. R. Hall's Aston Martin 'Bunny', but only by 0·2s. Still, Hall was not fast enough to beat Mays, who took his class in 46·6s against 49·4s. Ivy Cummings in turn defeated Mays, but her Frazer Nash was running against his Austin 'Seven' this time, and not against the Bugatti. Her time was 53·6s; his 56·4s. G. S. Boston's Horstman won two of the sports-car classes from R. M. V. Sutton's Alvis, by 52·8s and 52s against 57·8s and 58·4s. A. R. Linsley's Bugatti and Miss W. M. Pink's Aston Marton won the touring-car classes on time. The timed distance most commonly used at this period was 1,400 yd.

One of Humphrey Cook's most vivid memories of Aston Clinton is of the courage of the timekeeper at the finish. He lay with his timing tape in what appeared to the driver bearing down on him to be a suicidal position; on the very verge of the grass, and almost in the road.

It may have been at this Aston Clinton meeting that Vauxhalls tested the new low-pressure tyres, with disastrous and understandably unpublicised results. While cornering, the 'guinea-pig' car tore two of them clean off.

The ACU's speed trials at Welbeck on 24 May were, in retrospect, a melancholy occasion, for they were the last for cars to be recorded on this famous course, by now the oldest in Britain. It is known that R. Blake's Morgan won the 1,500-cc class at 76 mph, but the distance is unknown, and deductions are dangerous.

Rain, again, made for a treacherous surface at South Harting a week later, when the Surbiton MC and the Ealing MC held a joint meeting there, and wild skids were common. R. C. Morgan's ex-Eyston 200 Mile Race Aston Martin lost a tyre and wrote itself off against the bank, but on a happier note Dario Resta's Grand Prix Sunbeam was again in evidence, not unexpectedly winning the three classes it entered. Its best time, and fastest of the day, was 25·8s. Humphrey Cook came nearest to this, with 29·2s, while R. F. Oats in his Ansaldo was inspired to make a climb in 29·8s. He had already collected three classes himself, one of them from two Bugattis, with a best time of 31s, while Leon Cushman took a class in 36·6s. But Ivy Cummings won two: one in her 1,500-cc Frazer Nash in 29·8s from J. A. Joyce's AC (32s), and one from J. P. Dingle's Austin 'Seven' when using her 1,100-cc car. Her time on the latter occasion was 31·4s, against Dingle's 34·8s. By way of an experiment, a 30/98 hp Vauxhall bearing a blackboard on which times were inscribed ascended between runs. Unfortunately, nobody could make out what was written on it. Perhaps the combination of car and locale was too much for the driver's self-control.

Simultaneously, the Midland Car Club (no relation of the Midland Automobile Club) was holding speed trials in the grounds of the Government (Shell) Filling Factory at Rotherwas, near Hereford, in conjunction with the Wye Valley MC & LCC. The course was a nightmare: a flying $\frac{1}{2}$ mile with a narrow, steeply-cambered, rutted and wet surface across which spectators continually made risky excursions. After several contestants had experienced very close calls, the meeting had to be stopped. Morgans had made the best times, H. F. S. Morgan's car recording 25·6s, in spite of making the wildest skids of any, and G. H. Goodall's 26·2s. C. M. Harvey's 'new racing Alvis' and G. S. Boston's Horston both covered the distance in 27s dead.

This year the Blackpool open speed trials, held on 12 June, were run by the York MC in conjunction with the Blackpool Corporation's Carnival. The timed distance was a standing kilometre and the sixty competitors included many of the most famous names in the land. The organisation was excellent, and there was much excitement.

H. F. Clay's 1914 Grand Prix Vauxhall did extraordinarily well to defeat Cyril Paul's Beardmore and Joyce's AC, although the margin was narrow: 36·8s against 37s set by both the others. Clay, indeed, had thereby established joint fastest time of the day with Paul, who also won a class in 36·8s against G. Blackstock's Bugatti, which clocked 37s again. This class, too, saw fantastically close finishes: Joyce, Leon Cushman and R. F. Oates's Ansaldo all tying for third place. Paul took a second class, this time from Cushman, by 37s to 37·4s, while Raymond Mays and E. R. Hall, the latter in 'Bunny', dead-heated for first place in their class, and L. T. Kings with his Austin 'Seven' won his in 43·4s from T. Moore's Frazer Nash (44s).

Not only the racing classes held excitement, for among the sports cars G. J. Jackson's 16/40 hp Sports Sunbeam, in production form a slightly hotted-up version of a very sedate tourer, led home two Bentleys. Jackson, with 44·8s, was 1s faster than the best Bentley. T. Moore, in Frazer Nash and Horstman, took classes from an Austin 'Seven' and another Horstman, while Oates's Ansaldo won one. Leon Cushman won two of the touring classes with his Bugatti, and 30/98 hp Vauxhalls collected two more.

The Skegness races were better run this year, and the weather was fine, both of which made for a successful meeting on 18–19 June. The timed distance was shortened to a standing ½ mile, and the main interest was provided by a rather unequal duel between Malcolm Campbell's twelve-cylinder 350 hp Land Speed Record Sunbeam and Parry Thomas's Leyland-Thomas. Campbell won, setting a new course record of 29·2s, but Thomas's time was not given. Leon Cushman did very well indeed, winning four classes in all. His times of 42·2s and 41·4s in touring car events beat two Aston Martins in one case and a 30/98 hp Vauxhall and a Bentley in the other, and his two racing-car class successes were scored against J. A. Joyce's AC and Oats's Ansaldo in one instance, and against Humphrey Cook's TT Vauxhall and Paul's Beardmore in the other. His times were 34·8s and 34s. For his part, Raymond Mays gathered in three wins. One was a handicap, won in 37s from Cook, and the others were in 36·8s and 41s from Oats and an Aston Martin. L. T. Kings's Austin

'Seven' won the other handicap race in 42s, leading Mays's and A. R. Linsley's Bugattis. Kings also took home an award for a class win against two other Austins, in 41s. Linsley himself beat Cushman on one occasion, and Joyce, with 36s, took a racing class from Cushman and Ivy Cummings's Frazer Nash. C. M. Harvey's works Alvis was there, but was not going well.

Many of the same 'circus' moved north for the Yorkshire AC's open speed trials at Saltburn two days later. The highlight of the standing kilometre events was the battle between E. A. D. Eldridge's 300 hp FIAT and Malcolm Campbell's 350 hp Sunbeam; both of which were Land Speed Record attempt machines. The FIAT, slightly larger with its 21,714 cc, was too fast for the Sunbeam, winning at 76·09 mph. The Sunbeam's cubic capacity was a mere 18,322 cc and its time 31·2s. The contest was renewed over the flying kilometre, this time with the opposite result, Campbell's 145·26 mph, or 15·4s, outdoing the FIAT'S 139·81 mph. Parry Thomas's Leyland-Thomas, much smaller with only 7,266 cc, achieved 125·67 mph. In so doing Thomas cut his face on the timing thread at the finish, which rode up over his car's streamlined nose without breaking.

After this, the rest of the open classes understandably seemed rather tame. Cyril Paul and Humphrey Cook each took one racing-car class over the standing kilometre, the Beardmore beating C. M. Harvey's Alvis by 61·12 mph to 54·56 mph, and Cook winning at exactly the same speed as Paul. Raymond Mays won two of the sports car classes, at a best speed of 57·36 mph, and M. C. Park's works 30/98 hp Vauxhall collected another at 57·65 mph. In the flying kilometres for racing cars, E. R. Hall's Aston Martin, with 92·44 mph, beat Paul and Harvey, who tied for second place with 85·38 mph. Cook won his race at 101·68 mph.

It was highly unfortunate for the Kent AC that they should break in a new speed trial course, the front at Herne Bay, on the same day as Saltburn. This meeting, open to three other clubs, was run over a ½ mile of the front. However, the organisers were not too unlucky in the quality of their entry. Leon Cushman was there, winning no fewer than five classes at a fastest speed of 73·17 mph. So was Ivy Cummings with her 1,100-cc Frazer Nash, which took a class at 65·93 mph from Gordon England's Austin 'Seven', which achieved 57·69 mph. Count Zborowski should really have been able to give the crowd their money's worth with his 12,742-cc 'Chitty-Bang-Bang', but it needed more room in which to wind itself up, and lost its class to Cushman, covering the distance at 70·31 mph. Still, its performance must have been worth watching, on a course which was both bumpy and overrun by spectators. Two classes went to A. R. Linsley's touring Bugatti, at a best speed of 53·89 mph, and two to G. C. Boulding's Amilcar. He beat E. A. Wiffen's Austin 'Seven' into second place in each, with a speed of 43·27 mph, compared with Wiffen's 41·28 mph. Nevertheless, this speed was good enough to give Wiffen a class of his own. Bugattis took home two other class awards.

The 28th found the Hampshire AC making their annual assault upon Spread Eagle. This, as it turned out, was an historic occasion, for the course record was broken no less than seven times. The fact that Mays was there to win three open and three closed classes with 'Cordon Rouge' and 'Cordon Bleu' had something to do with it, for he made 'open' ascents in 39·4s, 38·6s and 39·2s, beating, respectively, Joyce's AC (40s), Malcolm Campbell's Ballot (42·8s) and (tying for second place with 40·4s) Campbell's racing Sunbeam and Joyce's AC once again. However, Campbell in the Sunbeam won the event run to determine the fastest car of the day, in 39·8s. Ivy Cummings's 1,100-cc Frazer Nash led home Gordon England's Austin 'Seven' by 48·45s to 54·8s.

Mays's three wins in the closed classes were from B. S. Marshall's Bugatti (twice), Marshall making a fastest climb of 51·2s, and Major Coe's 30/98 hp Vauxhall, which ascended in 50s. Miss W. M. Pink's touring Aston Martin took two classes, with a best time of 63·8s, beating Campbell's Star (70s) and a Bugatti. An 8/18 hp Talbot won one category, but in another A. R. Simmins's Talbot, now much modified and called a Simmins-Talbot, was beaten by J. A. Hall's Frazer Nash by 57s to 59·6s. Strange though it sounds, Mays's day earned him so many awards that he was asked to return some of the silverware, so that it could be given to those placed second. It seems that while the aristocracy might be allowed extra runs, they had their obligations as well as their privileges.

This year again, small or medium-sized cars outshone their large brethren at Shelsley Walsh. The reputation of Beardmore reached its zenith when, on 12 July, Cyril Paul's car, much drilled and lightened, made fastest time of the day and set up a new course record (50·5s) as well as taking the 2,500-cc class. Mays's 'Cordon Rouge' was a very close second with 50·82s, and won the 1,500-cc class, while E. R. Hall's Aston Martin 'Bunny' climbed in 50·82s, Humphrey Cook's Vauxhall in 52·8s (leading the 'unlimited' cars) and Joyce's AC in 53·2s. L. T. Kings's Brooklands Austin 'Seven' carried off the 1,100-cc class, and Miss W. M. Pink's Aston Martin did extremely well, leading the Ladies' Class on formula and taking three firsts on formula in the open classes. Her time was 79·4s. Fastest overall among the ladies was Mrs O. Stewart-Menzies's 30 hp racing Peugeot (an ex-Grand Prix car perhaps?) which climbed in 66s.

There were several other interesting, if fairly slow cars taking part, such as Goodwin's very unlikely-sounding 14 hp Bean racer, which nevertheless clocked 58·8s, and J. H. Clay's 20/70 hp Sports Crossley, which managed a time of 70s. On this, his first recorded appearance at Shelsley Walsh, Basil Davenport and his 'Frazer Nash' did no more than give rise to the comment that he 'wobbled somewhat alarmingly'. It was also said that: 'his driving was noticeable for a curious way he had of holding the steering wheel with both hands on the top of the rim, which seems to cause him to wrench the wheel round at the corners and so produce skidding'.

The remarkable times set at this meeting involved some spectacular incidents, for more than one car lost a tyre, or tyres, or ran up the bank, and Harvey's Alvis was especially frightening: it burst a tyre and crumpled a wheel, yet finished its run. 'Kim II', now driven by J. A. Hall, actually leapt over spectators' heads when it left the road.

On the 18th and 19th came the Welsh 'double' of the South Wales AC. It was noticeable, at Porthcawl on the 18th, how many cars now came to a meeting on trailers or in vans. They were altogether too fierce, fragile or simply illegal to be driven on the road. As the end of the golden age of sprints drew near, so did its cars grow less and less like normal vehicles. The sands at Porthcawl were firm, but full of puddles, and there was, in fact, talk of abandoning the venue and holding the meeting at Pendine in future. Success in the open classes was evenly distributed. One class went to J. A. Joyce's AC, which with 49·6s for the standing mile made fastest time of the day, beating Harvey's Alvis (55·8s) and F. N. Morgan's FIAT (64·8s). A. E. Keen's Morris 'Sports', at the limit of its development, was now being outclassed, and Paul's Beardmore led it home by 53·6s to 61·8s. H. K. Neale's Sunbeam, with 72s, beat R. J. Sully's HE (76·2s), and Humphrey Cook's Vauxhall was too good for Kensington Moir's Straker-Squire by 50·6s to 54·2s. Cook and Joyce shared first place in another class with 50·2s, leading Moir (52·8s) and Paul (53s); while O. Wilson Jones's single-seater racing Salmson, with 63s, defeated

H. Hudson's Austin 'Seven' and a Gwynne, the Austin recording 72·8s. A. J. Sgonina's GN won the last open scratch event with a time of 81·4s, and Cook beat Paul in a handicap. In the closed classes, Hudson's Austin beat a flock of 8/18 hp Humbers and a Gwynne, the best of the Humbers clocking 84·8s.

At Caerphilly the next day, a surface even looser than usual added to the hill's horrors. Several tyres burst, and some other things broke as well, including Raymond Mays's two Bugattis. They were now so highly tuned that they were likely to disintegrate at the slightest provocation, and one snapped an axle shaft and lost a wheel while travelling at 50 mph. The other ruined its gearbox on the starting-line, but before the rot was complete Mays had managed to win one open class in 63·2s from Joyce's AC (65s), Harvey's Alvis (72·6s) and two 1,500-cc twin ohc Darracqs. Paul's Beardmore beat Oates's Ansaldo by 63·2s to 68·8s, and Sully's HE led Neale's Sunbeam, both touring cars, by 90·4s to 94s, thus having his revenge. Sgonina's GN and Wilson Jones's Salmson each collected one class, as at Porthcawl, Sgnonina climbing in 72·8s and Wilson Jones in 70s. In some of the most exciting racing of the day, Kensington Moir's 1922 TT Straker-Squire beat M. C. Park's Vauxhall by 61·4s to 64·8s. Considering that Park's car was a '30/98', not a TT machine, and that this was his first ascent of the hill, his time was excellent. Moir also beat Cook, on his TT Vauxhall, by 63s against 64·4s.

At South Harting on the 26th, the JCC again gave only relative times. Mays in 'Cordon Bleu' was best, with E. R. Hall's 'Bunny' 2·4s slower. Joyce's AC was third fastest of the 1,500-cc racing cars, 2·6s after Hall. Among the 1,100-cc racers, J. A. Hall in 'Kim II', described variously as a GN and a Frazer Nash, beat B. E. Lewis's Frazer Nash by 1s, with Basil Davenport's GN 4s behind. H. Heath's twin ohc 1,500-cc Darracq, classified as a sports car and doubtless wearing wings to prove it, defeated B. H. Austin's Bugatti by 0·6s, but Austin led Miss W. M. Pink's Aston Martin by 3·2s. Miss Pink, in her turn, won two classes, beating other Aston Martins and a Horstman.

On 16 August the Sheffield & Hallamshire MC & CC organised what it called a hillclimb on the 1-in-20 gradient of the Ringlinglowe Road near Sheffield. Miss Mitchell's 24/90 hp Straker-Squire won its class in the miraculous time of 29·8s for the standing ½ mile—miraculous because in the course of her run she was baulked by a spectator, spun, hit another car and then struck a motor-cycle. J. A. Joyce collected two classes, his AC winning comfortably in 26·8s from two Morgans, and in 28s from the Straker-Squire (29·4s) and a 1,500-cc Austro-Daimler (30·2s). Another win went to R. A. Blake's Morgan, which beat Miss C. P. R. Turner's Bugatti by 30s to 36·4s.

The Brighton & Hove MC & LCC ran its second speed trial of the season on the Madeira Drive on 6 September. Four other clubs were invited, the course was lengthened to a standing ½ mile, and the crowds were prodigious. J. A. Joyce's AC covered the course in 28s, making best time of the day. He took three classes, beating B. E. Lewis's Frazer Nash twice and Oates's Ansaldo once. Lewis's fastest run was in 32·2s, and Oates's took 31·2s. Lewis, however, won another class in 32·6s, as did Ivy Cummings's 1,100-cc GN, which easily beat that of Lewis Humphries (36·8s). Among the sports cars, A. R. Simmins's Simmins-Talbot beat Chinery's Gwynne Eight by 43·6s to 45·6s, and Oates, with 32·4s, defeated the Hon G. Cunliffe's 1,500-GN, which managed 38·4s. In his turn, Cunliffe led a Bugatti home by 37·8s to 40·8s, and a touring class went to G. C. Boulding's Amilcar, which saw off Chinery by 47·8s to 48·4s. It seems that the club, growing more ambitious, had over-estimated its own, or the police force's, ability to control the spectators, for they were all over the road. Whatever the reason, no more speed trials were held at Brighton until 1932, when they were revived on the grand scale of 1905, and have continued to this day.

Up in the north, the Holme Moss meeting of the Bradford AC and Huddersfield AC had been postponed from May to 27 September. A handicap was instituted so as to encourage amateur entries for this open meeting, and the organisers were rewarded with a record entry and fine weather. Mays damaged 'Cordon Bleu', but then broke the course record in Humphrey Cook's TT Vauxhall, winning two classes from Cook himself in 1m 15s and 1m 15·6s against the latter's best time of 1m 18·8s. On its first run in Mays's hands the Vauxhall had burst into flames, but thereafter behaved perfectly. Cyril Paul's Beardmore saw off Oates's Ansaldo with 1m 21·6s against 1m 24·6s, and E. R. Hall's Aston Martin beat T. Moore's Horstman by 0·4s in 1m 20·8s. Basil Davenport's car, described as a Frazer Nash, also defeated Moore in another class to win by 1m 27s to 1m 30·4s, and the amateur events went to a Talbot, a Straker-Squire and G. S. Boston's Horstman, which beat Davenport's car by 1m 25·8s to 1m 26·4s.

Mays's experience with 'Cordon Bleu' was terrifying. Near the finish he took his foot off the throttle but it had jammed wide open. Neither ignition switch worked, and he dared not declutch or go into neutral for fear of bursting his engine. Consequently, the car tore off on to the verge, bucketing over the grass and half-throwing Mays out of his seat. He managed to jerk the wheel hard over, climbing the steep bank in an effort to avoid the spectators, and in doing so the Bugatti almost overturned but finally came to rest right side up. In spite of his care, the engine had suffered in this traumatic moment, and this was to be Mays's last outing with his Bugattis. After being repaired, 'Cordon Bleu' was sold to Francis Giveen, a driver of whom, tragically, we shall hear more later.

At the end of this last 'Bugatti' season, Raymond Mays described his hill-climbing technique in an article in *The Motor*. He emphasised how it had become a highly specialised science in which, he considered, road holding was of the greatest importance. Second only came the best possible power-to-weight ratio. By now he had increased the standard Brescia Bugatti's maximum engine revolutions to 6,000 rpm, and with the help of minute attention to correct gearing, held the 1,500-cc class records for Angel Bank, Aston Clinton, Spread Eagle, Caerphilly, Holme Moss, South Harting and Shelsley Walsh. The unlimited course record was his on Spread Eagle, Angel Bank and Holme Moss.

According to Mays, a good start was half the battle won. 'Clean' cylinder heads and valve guides were absolutely essential, for over-lubrication was a cause of chronic misfiring, and he would warm up on old plugs, and put in new ones just before the 'off'. Two seconds before he left the line, he would let the clutch in at three-quarters of maximum engine revolutions, and hold the car on the handbrake. The instant the flag fell, he would give the Bugatti full throttle, drop the clutch and away it would go. Bottom gear was good for about 50 mph, and he would go through the gears from there, changing down well before the corners so that he would have both hands on the wheel to correct a possible time-wasting slide.

In retrospect, it seems fitting that at the end of the last full season of the age of sprints, when the art had probably been brought to its highest pitch of perfection, its foremost exponent should thus epitomise its finest points. It is fair to say that, leaving aside special techniques for individual hills, the basic principles had by now been established. Certainly Mays, writing another article in the same vein nine years and many victories later, had found no cause to change his views.

Right up to the end, the old, old complaints were being aired. *The Autocar* discussed competitors' problems in its Boxing Day issue.

The factories dominated the country's courses completely. Timing, carried out with apparatus varying both in type and accuracy, still caused much argument and ill-feeling, as did the prevailing variety in club formulae, the many definitions of touring, sports and racing car, and of what was and what was not 'standard'. Weighing-in was still subject to abuse at events where there was opportunity for the weight to be altered after the check. This was known to happen at Kop, for example, yet the offenders were never disqualified. Finally entry fees, at £2 or £3 per head, were still too high.

There had been, however, one new development, which was full of menace. In October, a spectator was awarded damages against a competitor for harm received in an accident. The defendant's claim that the plaintiff had accepted the risk by attending the meeting was not allowed.

* * *

Other signs and portents of a disquieting kind began to appear early in the New Year of 1925, for police had placed bans on public road speed events in three counties: Worcestershire, Warwickshire and Staffordshire. Public and official displeasure had often manifested itself before, but it had been sporadic and very restricted in the area it affected. Protests from local residents and local authorities on this scale were new. Practising, much more than the meetings themselves, was the cause, for it was much more prolonged, and was uncontrolled—indeed furtive, for most clubs forbade it.

The Southport Motor Club did not need to worry, however. They used the beach. The year 1925 was to be their most active season to date, and began as early as it conceivably could. A surprising number of hardy gentlemen gathered on the sands on New Year's Day, in the midst of a bitter gale with which was mingled the driven sand and spray. H. S. Maw, attired, as if in contempt of the elements, in a bowler hat, took a class from R. H. Upton's very fast Crouch in his 11·9 hp Star, while another Star, that of C. G. Cathie, annexed two classes, one from Upton's Crouch and another from an Alvis. Upton, however, won three: from Maw, T. Simister's Alvis and A. Buckley's Morgan. Buckley took one class from G. P. Williams's Gwynne, but Williams won from a Morgan in his turn. Finally, R. de Larrinaga's 30/98 hp Vauxhall defeated Cathie and Maw, taking their two classes.

Most of the clubs were not so hardy, although Oxford and Cambridge met on 28 February at Aston Clinton; and that, as it transpired, was the last time this historic course was used. The classes went to E. S. Berry's Alvis in 47·47s, with R. Millais's AC second in 48·15s, and to G. B. Legge's 30/98 hp Vauxhall, which climbed in 43·5s. M. M. Chalmers's Beardmore and J. Heaton's 2-litre Bugatti tied for second place with 45·6s each, and that was that.

Then, on 21 March, the Southport MC were out again, G. Jackson's straight-eight Grand Prix Sunbeam winning three classes from the 'Frazer Nash' of Basil Davenport and the GN of C. J. P. Dodson. However, Dodson took one class from Jackson, and Davenport one from J. Bullough's Morgan. Bullough in his turn collected two classes, while the 10-mile race went to Jackson, followed home by the Hon Victor Bruce's AC.

A week later, on 28 March, the Essex MC held their opening meeting on Kop, and perhaps irked by accusations of laxity, the organisers scrutineered the entries with more than usual care, upgrading several into 'faster' classes. H. O. D. Segrave's 2-litre Grand Prix Sunbeam took two classes and fastest time of the day, with 28·8s. The second places went to Francis Giveen's Bugatti ('Cordon Bleu') in 31·2s, and to Oates's Ansaldo and Major C. G. Coe's Alfa Romeo, which dead-heated with 33·2s. Major Coe, in his turn, won two classes, beating B. S. Marshall's Bugatti by 33s to 40·8s and E. L. Meeson's 30/98 hp Vauxhall in 33·2s to 36s. S. J. Bassett's Austin 'Seven' carried off a class in 54·2s, as did Vernon Balls with his Amilcar in 43s, beating W. E. Humphries's time with a similar car of 48·2s. Then, H. S. Eaton's Gwynne led Balls by 38s to 43s, and Frazer-Nash in one of his own cars beat Giveen by 30·6s to 31·2s, and J. A. Joyce's AC very easily disposed of P. L. Densham's Bugatti in 30s, having a margin of 12·4s over the French car.

Leon Cushman won two classes, in a best time of 42·4s, beating C. M. Harvey's Alvis in one by 46·4s to 52·6s. B. S. Marshall did the same, making a fastest ascent in 42s, and this was much too good for A. E. Mayner's 2-litre Mercedes, which managed only 54·4s. Anthony's Senechal took one class in 71·6s, and W. E. Humphries two, beating a Senechal by 10s in a time of 46·6s. Rounding off the meeting, R. M. V. Sutton's Alvis, with 42·6s, saw off H. Aldington's Frazer Nash which clocked 44·2s.

After Shelsley Walsh, the Essex Motor Club's open meetings at Kop were regarded, with good reason, as being the finest of the year's sporting occasions. All the most magnificent motor-cars and drivers were to be seen there, all driving on the limit, all exerting themselves to the extreme to win on this very fast course. Spectators thronged there in their thousands, massing in solid clumps on the steep banks bordering the road. As at other venues, they took scant notice of the pleas of marshals. They chose dangerous places to sit—on the outside of the corners—because these afforded the best visibility, and they persistently crossed the road when they should not have done so. The police had no more authority to keep them off the road than had the marshals, though their uniforms helped, and at Kop there were not enough police, nor enough marshals, to manage such a crowd. Spectators not only wandered in the road: when they felt like going home, they walked down it while competitors were coming up. They knew their rights: no wretched jack-in-office with an armband was going to tell them where or when to walk. In a letter written to the motoring press after the event, Viscount Curzon, later Earl Howe, complained of the lack of crowd control and warned of its consequences.

At Kop this day a motor-cycle entrant had already crashed, just missing several people and injuring himself, when Francis Giveen, on another ascent, lost control of his Bugatti and charged the bank, mounting it, hitting a spectator and breaking the unfortunate man's leg.

R. R. Jackson saw it all, a few yards away from where he was sitting as, on this occasion, a spectator. The injured spectator, exercising his rights to the full, had refused to move farther back up the bank out of harm's way when asked. This was on a course at which, on the crest of the hill, cars not infrequently took off completely, covering most of the last twenty yards in mid-air.

With this accident, the RAC steward stopped the meeting. This was not an astonishing decision; there had been accidents before, and meetings had also been abandoned before. But it was a great pity, for the crowd and the competitors, as well as for the unfortunate driver and victim—but then, there would be other hillclimbs to watch and to compete in. Why, there was even a Bill before Parliament which, if made law, would stop such a situation arising ever again, for it would permit the closing of public roads for racing just as was already possible in Northern Ireland and in the Isle of Man. Herein lay the truly bitter irony of what was about to happen.

The Bill had come before Parliament just a little too late. The Competitions Committee of the RAC met at once, and on 2 April their decision was made public: 'Owing to the apparently insuperable difficulties that have been experienced in controlling the spectators in places to which the public have the right of access . . . all permits for speed contests on the open highway' would be cancelled, and in future withheld. Permits would still be given for speed events on promenades and beaches, and would be issued for speed events on private roads only if adequate arrangements were made for protecting both the course and the public. The Auto-Cycle Union and the Royal Scottish Automobile Club followed the RAC's lead, and nothing more was ever to be heard of the Bill to allow the closing of public roads for racing.

The controllers of British motor sport had had enough. The accident at Kop had merely been the spark which had caused the ban. The atmosphere had become so tense, nervousness in high quarters had increased so much, that the next incident—whenever and wherever it might occur—would be enough to precipitate the crisis. The fact that the life-saving Bill was actually under consideration at the time did not stem it. Better that the RAC should act before the government did so. The legal impossibility of exercising strict control over spectators; the fact that more and more of them were flocking to see sprint meetings; the growing number of crashes and near-accidents; the rising hostility of large sections of the public—all were considerations which, becoming more urgent with every season, had mounted irresistibly.

But for the brief and unregarded wails of a few irreconcilables, the RAC's decision went unquestioned in most quarters. The general reaction was one of understanding, and resignation to the inevitable. The fault was mostly that of a foolish, inconsiderate minority of spectators, who had been with us since the sport began. In any case, now that the RAC controlled closed as well as open events—and had not a single rival—such decisions could be completely effective. There was no danger of a repetition of the 1907 débâcle. But at this point it is interesting to note that the only positively-recorded fatality in the history of sprinting up to 1939 took place on 'closed' land (or rather sand), after the ban on the public road had been instituted. This is another choice piece for the collector of ironies.

Now, it is generally supposed that this Kop meeting was the last public-road sprint, but in fact the joint ruling of the RAC and ACU came too late to affect two others, both of which were run on 4 April. The melancholy distinction of being the last of their kind to be successfully run belong to the speed trials of the Western Centre of the ACU, run on ½ mile of macadam on the Whitecross Road, leading out of Hereford towards Hay-on-Wye, and to the West of England MC's trials on the Brentnor Straight, near Tavistock, over a flying ½ mile.

At Whitecross, F. Taylor's Bugatti clocked fastest time of the day in 25·8s, while on the Brentnor course J. A. Joyce's AC made fastest time, its 19·8s sufficing to win two classes, one from H. Dobbs's Morgan and Walsgrove's Riley, both returning 23·8s. The other was won from the colossal 10½-litre Peugeot of A. E. S. Walters (21·4s). The Hon Victor Bruce's AC took a class in 26·8s from an Alvis that clocked 31·6s, while Dobbs beat the Frazer Nash of R. T. Grogan by 1s in a time of 25·6s. Finally, M. Didham's Gwynne led W. A. Stewart's AC by 31·8s to 33·6s.

For reasons not stated, the York & District MC went ahead with its climb of Sutton Bank, scheduled for 10 April and proceedings did, indeed, begin in direct defiance of the RAC, ACU et al. But spectators obstructed the course so completely and persistently that the meeting was abandoned at an early stage. So ended an era.

APPENDIX OF OTHER EVENTS

(ST = speed trial; all others hillclimbs. FTD = fastest time of the day)

1919	
19 July	Sutton Coldfield & Mid-Warwicks AC, Style Kop. FTD: Leslie Hands, 25 hp Talbot, 54·4s. 1st in classes: H. R. Godfrey, GN, 75·2s; H. Underwood, 10 hp Calthorpe, 92·6s.
1920	
9 April	Scarborough & District MC, Staxton Hill, Scarborough–Driffield. ¾ mile, max 1-in-5. 1st in class: D. Pickering, 10 hp Eric-Campbell.
9 April	Warrington MC, Keckwick Hill. FTD (light car class): S. Parker, AV.
28 May	Luton & South Bedfordshire AC, Kop. 1st in classes: Noel Macklin, Eric-Campbell, 50s; Gripper, 25 hp Talbot, 1m 1·6s.
5 June	Middlesex County AC, Hand Post. 1st in classes: S. J. Prevost, Morris Cowley; H. C. Burn, 25 hp Talbot; Mrs V. A. Bruce, 10 hp Mathis.
July	Basingstoke MC. Course unknown. FTD: Baxter, AV.
3 Aug	North Berkshire AC. Course unknown. FTD: Sir Mortimer Singer, 40/50 hp Rolls-Royce, 76·8s. 1st on formula: J. R. Hargreaves, 19 hp Oakland.
8 Aug	ACU East Midlands Centre, Chatsworth Park. ST. ½ mile. FTD: F. W. James, Morgan, 40·8s.
26 Aug	Pembrokeshire AC, Arnold's Hill. Closed. 1st on formula in classes: H. J. P. Thomas, 10 hp Stellite, 86s; F. D. Phillips, 12 hp Rover, 92s.
4 Sept	Cardiff & District MC, Rhubina Hill. FTD: C. Sgonina, Humber, 41·6s. This car was said to have achieved 104 mph at Brooklands.
11 Sept	Coventry & Warwicks MC, Style Kop. FTD: George Bedford, Hillman, 44s.
11 Sept	Luton & South Beds AC, Putteridge Park? ST. 1st in class: G. D. F. Keddie, Silver Hawk, 39s.
9 Oct	Southend & District AC, Great Wakering, near Shoeburyness. ST.

½ mile. Closed. 1st in classes: G. D. F. Keddie, Silver Hawk, 47·2 mph (4 events); Duncan Campbell, 10 hp Hillman; J. H. Burrows, 25 hp Chalmers; A. E. Mayner, 20 hp Maxwell.

9 Oct Luton & South Beds AC, Putteridge Park. ST. ¼ mile. FTD: G. A. Vandervell, 25 hp Talbot, 13s. 1st in class: A. Frazer-Nash, GN, 13·6s.

23 Oct Stockport MC. Course unknown. ST. FTD (light car class): G. L. Mason, Calthorpe, 35s.

30 Oct Mansfield & District MC & LCC, Welbeck. ST. ½ mile. FTD (light car class): C. Atkey, Charron-Laycock, 38·8s.

October Brighton & Hove MC, Windmill Hill, Horndean. FTD (light car class): W. Welford, Morgan, 37s.

October Edinburgh & District MC. Course unknown. FTD: Ford.

October Ealing & District MCC, Pebble Combe. FTD: A. Frazer-Nash, GN, 23·6s.

13 Nov Cambridge University AC, West Harling Common, near Thetford. ST. 1 km. 1st in class: J. Goodenough, 30/98 hp Vauxhall, 67·9s.

1921

20 March Stockport & District MC. Axe Edge. FTD (light car class): W. J. H. Phillips, Deemster, 2m 25s.

21 March Wallington & District MC, Bore Hill, Dorking. On Dorking–Coldharbour road. FTD: Leon Cushman, Bugatti.

28 March Scarborough & District MC, Staxton. 1st in classes: F. W. James, Morgan, 1m 27s; W. J. H. Phillips, Deemster, 1m 40s.

16 April Surrey MC & LCC, Newlands Corner. ½ mile. FTD (light car class): E. R. C. Scholefield, Morgan, 40·4s.

24 April Manchester MC, Rushup Edge. ½ mile. FTD (light car class): P. Platt, GN.

30 April Glasgow Western MCC, Garshake Hill. FTD (light car class): C. Duncan, Morgan, 28·7 mph; 2nd, E. Gearing, Deemster, 25·5 mph. 1st on formula: C. Duncan.

1 May Cambridge & County MC. Course unknown. ST. FTD (light car class): K. Sanderson, Morgan, 33s.

1 May Inter-Varsity event, West Harling Common. ST. FTD (unofficial): R. M. Knowles, 30/98 hp Vauxhall, 33·4s. 1st in class: Raymond Mays, Hillman, 36·6s.

7 May JCC Northern Branch, Axe Edge. FTD: W. F. Milward, Charron–Laycock, 1m 47s. 1st in classes: R. C. Murray, Calthorpe, 2m 19·2s; W. A. Connell, Morris Oxford, 2m 42s; C. R. Mills, Morgan, 2m 10·2s; G. L. Mason, Calthorpe, 1m 49s.

7 May Luton & South Bedfordshire AC, Haynes Park. ½ mile, max 1-in-8. 1st in light car classes: H. R. Godfrey, GN, 29s.

11 May Luton & South Beds AC, Putteridge Park. ST. FTD: P. Childs, Morgan, 15·8s.

28 May ACU Yorkshire Centre, Otley Chevin. 1 km. 1st in light car classes: R. E. Hutton, GN, 1m 12·2s; T. Moore, GN, 1m 17·6s.

May Surbiton & District MCC, Bore Hill, Dorking. FTD: A. Frazer-Nash, GN, 37·2s. 1st in classes: A. Frazer-Nash, 37·2s; C. Finch, GN, 1m 0·2s.

4 June Wellingborough, Rushden & District MC, Castle Abbey. ST. 1 km. FTD (light car class): C. H. Pettitt, Morgan, 62s.

4 June Oxford MC, Kop. 1st in classes (all 4): H. R. Godfrey, GN, 42·8s.

5 June Stockport & District MC, Rushup Edge. FTD: Leon Cushman, Bugatti, 39s.

12 June Luton & South Beds AC, Putteridge Park. ST. FTD: Humphrey Cook, 30/98 hp Vauxhall 'Rouge et Noir', 13·6s. 1st in class: Humphrey Cook, 13·6s. 1st in class: Humphrey Cook, 30/98 hp Vauxhall 'Lady of the Lake', 14·4s.

18 June North-West London MCC, Kop. 1st in car classes: H. E. K. Sawtell, Morgan, 70s; W. Cooper, Morris Sports, 53·8s; 12/16 hp Sunbeam, 47s.

June 'A St Austell motorist's private hillclimb', Greymare Hill, Bodmin–Liskeard road. ½ mile. 80 entries. 1st in classes: B. H. Ryder, 25 hp Talbot, 1m 38·8s; M. Marshall, ABC, 1m 30·4s.

2 July SUNBAC, Penkridge Bank, near Rugeley. FTD: R. J. Sully, HE, 59·4s. 1st in classes: F. W. Barnes, Calthorpe, 62·6s; S. H. Newsome, Calthorpe, 67·2s; W. A. Hudson, New Hudson, 80s.

9 July South Wales MCC, Catsash Hill near Newport. ½ mile. FTD (light car class): W. Davies, Morgan, 42·4s.

23 July North Berkshire AC, Sparsholt Firs Hill. FTD: Mrs Hippisley, 30/98 hp Vauxhall, 47s.

6 Aug Cardiff MCC, Porthcawl. ST. FTD (light car class): L. Davies, Morgan.

21 Aug ACU, Western Centre, Kingsdown Hill, near Bath. ½ mile. 1st in classes: A. Frazer-Nash, GN.

26 Aug York & District MC, Garrowby. FTD: Felix Scriven, 20 hp Austin, 62s. 1st in classes: H. Hodgson, Morris Cowley; W. K. Bramham, Bugatti; Raymond Mays, Hillman, 74·8s.

1 Sept Cambridge & County MC, Cambridge. Course unknown. 1st in classes: H. Dix, Morris Cowley, 28s; K. Sanderson, Morgan, 29·4s.

9 Sept Norfolk MC & LCC, West Harling Common. ST. FTD, standing and flying km: A. H. Walker, 6 hp Peugeot Quadrilette, 49 mph (flying km).

1 Oct Oxford MC, Aston Clinton. FTD: Humphrey Cook, Vauxhall, 48·8s. 1st in classes: H. R. Godfrey, GN, 59s; H. F. Barge, GN, 1m 29·6s.

8 Oct SUNBAC, Penkridge Bank. FTD: George Bedford, Hillman, 46·6s.

8 Oct Essex County & Southend AC, Great Wakering. ST. 1st in classes: N. W. Martin, GN; Maitland Keddie, 10/30 hp Alvis, 25·2s; J. H. Burrows, Chalmers; Miss Keddie, Morris Oxford and Silver Hawk; A. G. Whiting, Calthorpe.

9 Oct Oxford MC, Akeman Street, Chesterton, near Bicester. ST. 1 km. FTD: Humphrey Cook, Vauxhall, 52s. 1st in classes: G. L. Hawkins, GN (3 classes); R. Weston-Stevens, Talbot; 20/30 hp Talbot.

1922

9 April Rugby MC, Edge Hill. 1st in car classes: George Bedford, Hillman.

23 April Essex MC, Bottledown. Closed.

29 April Oxford MC and ACU South Midland Centre, Kop. 900 yd. FTD: H. R. Godfrey, GN, 38·8s. 1st in class: Humphrey Cook, Vauxhall, 41·2s.

29 April York & District MC and ACU Yorkshire Centre, Sutton Bank. 1st in classes: H. Hellewell, 10·5 hp Horstman, 1m 58·8s; Felix Scriven, 20 hp Austin, 1m 47·6s; Hodgson, Hodgson (2 classes), 1m 31s.

6 May Liverpool MC, Pen-y-Ball, Holywell. ¾ mile av 1-in-6. 1st in classes: J. O. Walker, Calthorpe, 1m 11·6s; W. Watson, Essex, 47·2s; W. B. Horn, Straker-Squire, 45·4s.

7 May Redditch & District MCC. Course unknown. ST. Tie for 1st in light car class: J. Cave, GN; F. Barnes, Hillman.

7 May Sheffield & Hallamshire MC, The Highway, Ringlinglowe, near

Sheffield. ST. $\frac{1}{2}$ mile. 1st in classes: W. F. Milward, Charron-Laycock, 44·8s.

27 May — Kent & Sussex Light Car Club, Balkum's Hill, near Goudhurst. $\frac{3}{4}$ mile, av 1-in-12. FTD: Lewis Humphries, GN, 1m 0·2s. 1st in classes: E. W. Foster, GN, 1m 17s; H. E. Barham, 30/98 hp Vauxhall, 1m 1·4s; W. Gadd, Salmson, 1m 7s; W. H. Oates, Lagonda, 1m 9·6s.

3 June — Middlesex County AC, Hand Post. FTD: A. C. Toller, 30 hp Lancia. 1st in classes: P. F. Pratt, 30/98 hp Vauxhall; J. Ogilvie, 12 hp ABC; R. F. Moss, Warren-Lambert.

3 June — Oxford MC and Oxford University MC, Akeman Street. ST. FTD: A. E. Keen, Morris Cowley Sports, 57·67 mph. 1st in class: Raymond Mays, Bugatti, 54·83 mph.

3 June — Barrow & District MC. Course unknown. ST. 1st in class. H. Wakefield, Bugatti.

3 June — Norfolk MC, Ringland Hill, Norwich. FTD: Maitland Keddie, Alvis.

10 June — Barrow & District MC, Eskmeals, Cumberland. ST. $\frac{1}{2}$ mile. 1st in car classes: H. Wakefield, Bugatti, 40·82s.

21 June — York & District MC, Garrowby. 1st in class: H. Hodgson, Hodgson, 62·4s.

22 June — Worcester & District MC, Madresfield. ST. FTD: Raymond Mays, Bugatti, 25·6s.

1 July — Surbiton & District MC and Ealing & District MC, Kop. FTD: W. H. Oates, Lagonda.

7 July — Leicestershire AC, Beacon Hill. FTD: F. C. Clement, Bentley, 52·1s. 1st in class: Leon Cushman, Bugatti 53s.

10 July — Colne & District MC. Course unknown. FTD: A. Frazer-Nash, GN, 43·6s.

22 July — JCC Yorkshire Centre, Pateley Bridge. 1st in classes: T. Moore, GN, 1m 47s; E. R. Hall, Bugatti, 1m 26·6s.

5 Aug — Kent & Sussex LCC, Kidd's Hill. 1,320 yd. FTD: G. L. Hawkins, GN, 1m 1·8s. 1st in classes: L. Humphries, GN, 1m 15s; H. S. Moore, Amilcar, 1m 54·6s; J. L. Deverall, Albert, 2m 44·8s.

12 Aug — Sheffield & Hallamshire MC, The Highway, Ringlinglowe. ST. 1st in classes: E. R. Hall, Bugatti, 35·2s; H. Hodgson, Hodgson, 36·8s.

21 Aug — ACU Western Centre, Chatcombe Pitch. FTD: Raymond Mays, Bugatti, 32·4s.

2 Sept — Coventry & Warwicks MC, Why Not Hill, near West Haddon. 800 yd approx. 1st in classes: George Bedford, Hillman, 36·4s; J. Rowley, 20 hp Austin, 35·2s.

9 Sept — Central Cornwall MC, Greymare Hill. FTD: M. Tretheway, Morgan, 1m 0·6s; 2nd, Capt R. G. Cookson, 1914 T.T. Straker-Squire, 1m 8s. A contest for fully-laden motor coaches included.

16 Sept — Organisers?, Weston-super-Mare. ST. FTD: Horstman.

22 Sept — Scarborough & District MC, Marine Drive, Scarborough. ST. Closed. $\frac{1}{2}$ mile. FTD: W. B. Horn, Straker-Squire, 27·8s. 1st in classes: A. Methley, HE, 28s; H. Hodgson, Hodgson, 28·6s; H. F. Clay, 30/98 hp Vauxhall, 28·4s; A. W. Robinson, Berliet, 28s; E. R. Hall, Bugatti, 29·8s.

23 Sept — RSAC, Cairn o'Mount. 2 miles. FTD: R. B. Tennant, 30/98 hp Vauxhall, 3m 26s. 1st in classes: T. S. Stout, Mathis; J. W. Scott, Bugatti; W. H. Stevenson, 24 hp Sunbeam; T. C. Smith, 8/18 hp Talbot; A. Milne, 14 hp Sunbeam; David Carlaw, 20 hp Austin.

29 Sept — Wallington & District MC & LCC, Betchworth Park, Dorking. ST. FTD: Kaye Don, AC, 27·6s. 1st in class: H. Humphries, GN, 30·4s.

30 Sept Southport MC, Southport. ST. 1st in classes: D. M. K. Marendaz, Marseal; M. B. Lax, Hodgson; H. F. Clay, 30/98 hp Vauxhall.

30 Sept Worcester & District MCC and Worcestershire MC, Angel Bank. FTD: G. S. Boston, 30/98 hp Vauxhall. 1st in class: C. Williams, GN.

7 Oct ACU South Midland Centre, Kop. 1st in classes: G. L. Hawkins, GN; Raymond Mays, Bugatti.

20 Oct Essex County & Southend AC, Laindon. FTD: F. C. Pearl, Silver Hawk.

20 Oct Blackpool & Fylde MC, Stricker's Lane, Garstang. FTD: R. Edge, Bentley, 26s. 1st in class: Mrs M. Parkinson, ABC, 36s.

October Wolverhampton MCC, Why Not Hill. 1st in classes: Raymond Mays, Bugatti, 55·3 mph; C. M. Harvey, Alvis, 31 mph; C. H. Pettitt, Morgan.

1923

2 April Neath & District MC, Margam Park. ST. 1st in classes: GN, 39·5s; Morris Cowley, 36s.

7 April ACU Western Centre, Chatcombe Pitch. FTD: H. F. S. Morgan, Morgan, 32·6s.

14 April Kent AC, Balkum's Hill. 1st in class: R. J. Cramp, AC.

14 April ACU Wessex Centre, Avonmouth-Shirehampton road. ST. $\frac{1}{2}$ mile. FTD: A. J. Sgonina, GN, 33s.

14 April Disabled Drivers' MC. Littelbury Hill, near Saffron Walden. 700 yd. Versus team of able-bodied drivers. FTD: N. Black, GN, 30·4s. 1st in classes: N. Black; F. Payze, Derby; A. Walsgrove, Riley; R. J. Lockyer, GN; C. Finch, GN.

21 April SUNBAC, Angel Bank. Closed. FTD: Raymond Mays, Bugatti, 35·2s. 1st in classes: Raymond Mays.

28 April York & District MC, Sutton Bank. Closed. FTD: H. F. Clay, 30/98 hp Vauxhall, 1m 17s. 1st in classes: A. Frazer-Nash, GN, 1m 19·4s; G. S. Boston, Austro-Daimler, 1m 26·2s; T. Moore, GN, 1m 30·4s.

28 April Scottish Western MC, Dalgrain Brae. FTD: A. Francis, Beardmore, 36·8s. 1st in classes: L. Lancaster, Bugatti, 44·6s; J. B. Fenwick, GN.

5 May Southport MC, Southport. ST. 1 km. Closed. 1st in classes: D. M. K. Marendaz, Marseal; E. R. Hall, Marendaz; G. Porter, Bentley.

5 May Exeter MC & LCC, Tiverton. 1st in class: C. G. Briggs, 30/98 hp Vauxhall.

12 May Neath & District MC, Margam Park. ST. 1st in classes: C. Sgonina, GN, 34s.

21 May Eastbourne & District MC, Sanatorium Hill. FTD: G. L. Hawkins, GN.

24 May Norfolk MC & LCC, Ringland Hill, Norwich. FTD: V. G. Walsgrove, Riley. 1st in class: W. Hurrell, Gwynne.

26 May Middlesex County AC, Hand Post. $\frac{3}{5}$ mile, max 1-in-10. 1st in class: R. F. Moss, Warren-Lambert.

Whit Monday Carmarthen & District MC & LCC, Pendine. ST. 1st in classes: A. J. Sgonina, GN.

2 June Oxford MC and Oxford University MC, Akeman Street. ST. 1st in classes: G. L. Hawkins, GN, 60·2s (standing mile); G. L. Hawkins, 30·8s, A. E. Keen, Morris Cowley 'Sports', 26·8s (flying km).

9 June Mid-Buckinghamshire MCC, Akeman Street. ST. 1 km. 1st in classes: G. L. Hawkins, GN; Ivy Cummings, Bugatti 'Black Bess'.

20 June York & District MC, Garrowby. FTD: Cyril Paul, Beardmore, 58·4s. 1st in classes: D. Walker, Hodgson, 63·4s; T. Moore, GN, 66·2s; T. Moore, Horstman, 60·2s.

23 June Liverpool MC, Waterloo Sands. ST. 1 mile. 1st in classes: W. B. Horn, Straker-Squire, 51s; Lloyd, Straker-Squire, 61·4s; G. S. Boston, Horstman, 59·8s.

23 June JCC Northern Centre, Pateley Bridge. FTD: E. R. Hall, Bugatti, 1m 25s. 1st in classes: T. Moore, GN, 1m 38·4s; H. Sunderland, GN, 2m 4s.

23 June JCC South-Western Centre, Dean Hill. FTD: W. G. H. Hedges, Alvis. 1st in classes: A. R. Simmins, 8/18 hp Talbot; A. Bovier, Salmson; A. S. Burnett, 8/18 hp Talbot; A. Reading, Wolseley.

27 June Wallington MC, near Bletchingley. FTD: Leon Cushman, Bugatti, 27·6s. 1st in classes: C. A. Hardy-Mason, sports ABC, 33·4s; C. A. Hardy-Mason, touring ABC, 49·6s; L. Humphries, GN, 35·2s; G. C. Griffiths, Deemster, 40s.

28 June ACU East South Wales Centre, Catsash Hill. FTD: A. E. Keen, Morris Cowley Sports, 34s. 1st in class: F. J. Boshier-Jones, Gwynne, 40·6s.

30 June Slough & District MC & LCC, Kop. Joint FTD: 2 Morris Cowleys, 50s.

7 July Eastbourne & District MC, King Edward's Parade. ST. 914 yd. FTD: Kaye Don, Deemster, 33·8s. 1st in classes: H. Lucas, AC, 41·8s; G. L. Hawkins, GN, 40·2s; R. Spikins, Salmson, 52·8s; D. Chinery, Gwynne, 48·2s.

7 July Southport MC, Southport. ST. 1 km. Closed. 1st in classes: M. B. Lax, Hodgson; H. Hodgson, Hodgson; W. B. Horn, Straker-Squire; G. Porter, Bentley.

12 July Worcester & District MC and Worcestershire MC, Madresfield. ST. FTD: Humphrey Cook, 30/98 hp Vauxhall, 34·2s. 1st in classes: Raymond Mays, Bugatti, 37·6s; F. J. Boshier-Jones, Gwynne, 41·8s.

14 July Liverpool MC, Colwyn Bay. ST. ½ mile. FTD: W. Watson, 30/98 hp Vauxhall, 22·8s. 1st in classes: G. Cowley, Morgan, 30·8s; W. H. Boston, Bentley, 29·4s; E. R. Hall, Bugatti, 26·2s; A. Francis, Beardmore, 26·4s; N. T. Beardsell, Hodgson, 26s.

21 July North Berkshire AC, Litcombe Bassett. FTD: L. A. Barrett, AC.

4 Aug ACU West Wales Centre, Pendine. ST. 1st in classes: A. J. Sgonina, GN.

4 Aug Southport MC, Southport. ST. 1st in classes: M. Parkinson, ABC; G. Porter, T. T. Bentley; C. J. P. Dodson, Alvis; C. J. P. Dodson, Bugatti. Course kept clear by patrolling motor-cycle combinations.

16 Aug Norfolk MC & LCC, West Harling Common. ST. Closed. FTD: A. E. Keen, Morris Cowley 'Sports'. 1st in classes: C. M. Harvey, Alvis; W. G. Hurrell, Gwynne.

18 Aug Sheffield & Hallamshire MC & LCC, The Highway, Ringlinglowe. ST. FTD: C. M. Harvey, Alvis, 33·2s. 1st in classes: H. G. Sissons, ABC, 39·4s; J. Mitchell, 8/18 hp Talbot, 42·8s.

18 Aug ACU Wessex Centre, Brean Sands, near Burnham. ST. ½ mile. 1st in classes: A. J. Sgonina, GN, 31·6s; A. B. Cox, Ansaldo, 32·6s; E. A. Cannock, G. P. Morgan, 38·2s.

18 Aug Kent AC, Sharnden Hill, near Mayfield. FTD: C. M. Harvey, Alvis, 33·8s. 1st in classes: L. Cushman, Bugatti, 40·4s; D. M. K. Marendaz, Marseal, 47·2s; J. P. Dingle, Riley, 38·8s; R. Humphries, GN, 51·2s.

1 Sept York & District MC, Garrowby. 1st in classes: T. Moore, Horstman, 56·4s; H. F. Clay, 30·98 hp Vauxhall, 55s; T. Moore, GN.

1 Sept Oxford MC, Kop. Closed. 1st in classes: A. E. Keen, Morris Cowley 'Sports', 31·6s.

1 Sept	Wye Valley MC & LCC, Ross-on-Wye. 1st: L. Weston, Hillman, 36s.
8 Sept	Ealing & District MCC and Surbiton MC, Kop. FTD: L. C. G. M. Le Champion, Isotta-Maybach, 26·83s. 1st in class: G. N. Norris, Morgan, 29·65s.
15 Sept	Luton & South Beds AC, Luton Hoo Park. ST. 1st in classes: C. Paul, GN, 24·8s; I. Bradley, GN, 24·6s; H. H. Brayshaw, Alvis, 22·4s.
22 Sept	Kent AC, Bexhill. ST. $\frac{1}{2}$ mile approx. FTD: Ivy Cummings, Bugatti 'Black Bess', 28s. 1st in classes: Mrs George Duller, Amilcar, 40·6s; S. H. Constable, Morgan, 40s; H. P. Lucas, Wolseley, 39·6s; J. K. Buchanan, Horstman, 32·8s; G. Norris, Morgan, 29s.
22 Sept	North-Eastern Automobile Association, Legs Cross, 7 miles from Darlington. FTD: L. Ropner, 30/98 hp Vauxhall, 28·6s.
22 Sept	Oxford MC, Alms Hill. FTD: A. E. Keen, Morris Cowley 'Sports', 17·6s. 2nd and 3rd places also taken by Morris 'Sports'.
1924	
30 March	Scottish Western MC, Dalgrain Brae. FTD: A. Francis, Beardmore.
5 April	ACU Western Centre, Chatcombe Pitch. FTD: B. E. Lewis, 2-cyl 'Frazer Nash', 28·8s.
12 April	JCC Northern Centre. Saltersford Church. FTD: E. R. Hall, Aston Martin, 1m 9·8s. 1st in classes: Basil Davenport, GN, 1m 27·2s (3 classes): T. A. N. Leadbetter, 12/50 hp Alvis, 1m 41s; S. T. Gardner, 8/10 hp Mathis, 2m 39s.
12 April	Disabled Drivers MC, Saffron Walden. Versus team of able-bodied drivers. 1st in classes: Leon Cushman, Bugatti, 29·6s; C. M. Harvey, Alvis, 36·4s; A. Payze, Derby, 46·2s; S. A. Wenmouth, Derby, 35·2s; Gordon England, Austin 'Seven', 36·8s; E. Smith, Bugatti, 39·8s.
19 April	Blackpool & Fylde MC, Hest Bank Sands. ST. 1st in classes: C. Hayes, Bugatti; G. Porter, Bentley; B. Parkinson, Bayliss-Thomas; R. Edge, Bentley; J. Ledson, Vauxhall; E. H. Altmon, Austin.
21 April	Neath & District MC, Margam Park. ST. 1st in all classes: A. J. Sgonina, GN, 32·1s.
21 April	Scarborough & District MC, Staxton. FTD: Cyril Paul, Beardmore, 22·2s. 1st in class: E. R. Hall, Aston Martin, 22·6s.
21 April	Chester & District MC, Llangar Hill, near Mostyn. 816 yd. FTD: Basil Davenport, GN, 41·8s. 1st in classes: T. Simister, Alvis, 42s; D. W. Beck, Austin 'Seven', 43s.
26 April	Southport MC, Southport. ST. 1st in classes: T. Simister, Alvis; J. M. Bullough, Morgan.
14 May	Inverness & District MC, Druids Temple Hill. $\frac{1}{2}$ mile. 1st in classes: H. Cox, Beardmore, $40\frac{1}{16}$s; Lt Farquhar, Eric-Campbell, $54\frac{5}{8}$s.
15 May	Norfolk MC, Ringland Hill. Norwich. 1st in classes: W. Hurrell, Gwynne, 29·52s; L. P. de Cohen, Alvis, 30·78s; L. W. Carey, Lagonda, 33·6s.
17 May	Kent & Sussex LCC, Kidd's Hill. FTD: Leon Cushman, Bugatti, 52·4s. 1st in classes: J. A. Hall, Frazer Nash; D. E. Calder, Horstman; H. E. Woods, 8/18 hp Humber.
24 May	Ipswich & District MC, Shrubland Park. ST. $\frac{1}{3}$ mile. Closed. 1st in classes: F. C. H. Katon, Marseal, 29·16s; F. H. Olorenshaw, Singer, 35·12s.
24 May	Slough & District MC and ABC Car Club, Alms Hill. FTD: E. N. A. Remington, GN, 34·2s.
25 May	Brighton & Hove MC & LCC, Brighton. ST. 1st in classes: G. N. Norris, Morgan, 16·4s; Leon Cushman, Bugatti, 22·4s; S. H. Constable, Morgan, 23·4s; F. G. Cole, Gwynne, 30·2s.

29 May	Northamptshire MCC, Chinkwell Lane, Upper Harlstone. 770 yd. FTD: C. M. Harvey, Alvis, 29·2s.
31 May	Middlesex County AC, Hand Post. Closed. FTD: P. F. Pratt, 30/98 hp Vauxhall, 35·6s.
9 June	Eastbourne & District MC, Sanatorium Hill. FTD: K. Rolfe, GN, 45·4s. 1st in classes: O. Wilson-Jones, Salmson, 47·2s; S. H. Constable, Morgan, 59s; C. C. Russell, AC; J. C. Boulding, Amilcar, 86·8s.
14 June	JCC South-Western Centre, Dean Hill. 1,540 yd. 1st in classes: L. R. Oldmeadows, Bugatti; C. J. Randall, Talbot; A. Y. Jackson, Alvis; A. R. Simmins, Talbot; J. A. Hall, Frazer Nash; A. Frazer Nash, 'Kim II'; W. G. H. Hedges, Alvis.
14 June	Colwyn Bay MC, St George's Hill, Abergele. $\frac{1}{2}$ mile, av 1-in-9. 1st in classes: K. A. B. Wilson, Morgan, 48·4s; Basil Davenport, Frazer Nash, 48·8s; G. S. Boston, Horstman, 46s.
15 June	Bradford MC & LCC, 'Yorkshire moors'. FTD: G. Hepworth, Alvis, 25·18s.
21 June	RSAC, Cairn o'Mount. FTD: J. D. Orr, 30/98 hp Vauxhall, 3m 19s. 1st in classes: C. H. Hamilton, ABC, 5m 20s; R. H. Carlaw, 20 hp Austin, 4m 5s.
26 June	Bridlington & District MC, Kingsgate Road. ST. 1st in classes: Miss M. Mitchell, Straker-Squire, $25\frac{7}{16}$; Miss C. P. R. Turner, Bugatti, $26\frac{7}{8}$s. A class for tradesmen's vans included.
28 June	Slough & District MC & LCC, Butwell Hill, near Henley. $\frac{1}{2}$ mile, av 1-in-10. 1st in classes: H. E. Hewens, Morris 'Sports', 44·8s; E. N. A. Remington, GN; H. E. Hewens, Alvis.
28 June	Essex County & Southend AC, Bottledown. 420 yd, av 1-in-9. Closed. FTD: D. Taylor, Sunbeam 'Sports'. 1st on handicap: D. Taylor.
5 July	Liverpool MC, Colwyn Bay. ST. 1st in classes: D. W. Beck, Austin 'Seven', 27·6s; J. A. Joyce, AC, 22s; G. S. Boston, Horstman, 26·2s; A. Braid, Austin 'Seven', 29·2s; M. C. Park, 30/98 hp Vauxhall, 24·2s; N. T. Beardsell, Aston Martin, 31s; G. Hitchon, Bentley, 28·4s; G. S. Boston, Bentley.
5 July	Kettering & District MC. Braybrook Hill. 704 yd. FTD: P. Wilmot, Alvis, 26·5s; 2nd, J. Goodfellow, Alvis, 29·14s.
6 July	Newton Abbot & District MC & LCC, Mainhead Road, Starcross. $\frac{1}{2}$ mile. 1st in classes: J. B. Roofer, 12/50 hp Alvis, 32·4s; F. L. Angell, 10 hp Singer, 35s.
10 July	Worcestershire MC, Madresfield. ST. FTD: J. D. Benjafield, Bentley, 37s. 1st in classes: H. Beart, Morgan; D. W. Beck, Austin 'Seven', 45·4s; B. E. Lewis, Frazer Nash, 40s; H. C. Lones, Morgan, 38·8s; M. Wilmot, GN, 44·2s; G. S. Boston, Horstman, 40s; C. M. Harvey, Alvis (6 classes), 38·4s.
12 July	North Berkshire AC, Blowing Stone Hill. 1st on formula: Mrs Hippisley, Vauxhall.
13 July	Rochdale & District MC, Chessenden Bar Road, near Edenfield. ST. 1st in classes: T. A. N. Leadbetter, 12/50 hp Alvis, 36s.
19 July	Kent & Sussex LCC, Bexhill. ST. 700 yd. FTD: Leon Cushman, Bugatti, 28s. 1st in class: Miss Ivy Cummings, Frazer Nash, 28·6s.
24 July	Norfolk MC, West Harling Heath. ST. 1 km. 1st in classes: F. C. H. Katon, Marseal, 28·34s; S. J. Bassett, Austin 'Seven', 40·07s.
26 July	Southport MC, Southport. ST. 1st in classes: G. Porter, T. T. Bentley,

	102·8 mph; T. Simister, Alvis; J. M. Bullough, Morgan; Morgan; Crouch.
27 July	Brighton & Hove MC & LCC, 'a private road near Lewes'. ST. ¼ mile. FTD: J. A. Hall, 1,500 cc Frazer Nash, 16·6s. 1st in classes: J. A. Hall, 1,100 cc Frazer Nash, 26·4s; H. S. Eaton, Aston Martin, 23·2s; G. C. Boulding, Amilcar, 25·8s.
9 Aug	Stalybridge & District MC, Carrbrook Road, Millbrook, Stalybridge. ⅓ mile. FTD: G. Porter, Bentley, 56·46 mph.
16 Aug	Bury St Edmunds & District MC & LCC. Course unknown. FTD: F. C. H. Katon, Marseal, 24·4s.
16 Aug	ACU Wessex Centre, Kingsdown Hill. FTD: G. H. Goodall, Morgan, 24s. 1st in classes: R. R. Jackson, Morgan, 26s; A. J. Sgonina, GN, 27s; W. J. Bowley, Alvis, 32s; F. R. Carter, Austin 'Seven', 30·6s.
August (end)	Bradford MC & LCC, 'Yorkshire moors'. 1st on handicap: Miss Mitchell, 24/90 hp Straker-Squire.
23 Aug	Southport MC, Southport. ST. 1st in classes: J. M. Bullough, Morgan; D. M. K. Marendaz, Marseal; G. S. Boston, Horstman; G. J. Jackson, sports Sunbeam; G. Pemberton, 30/98 hp Vauxhall.
31 Aug	Rochdale & District MC, Chessenden Bar Road. ST. 1st in classes: T. A. N. Leadbetter, Alvis; G. K. Gilchrist, Palladium, 48·8s; G. Porter, Bentley, 42·4s.
21 Sept	Eastbourne MC. ST. FTD: D. M. K. Marendaz, Marseal.
27 Sept	Liverpool MC, Wallasey Sands. ST. 1st in classes: G. S. Boston, Horstman.
27 Sept	Southport MC, Southport. ST. 1st in classes: R. H. Upton, Crouch; A. Moss, Morgan; G. J. Jackson, Sunbeam; G. Porter, Bentley; J. M. Bullough, Morgan.
Sept	Pembrokeshire County LCC, Arnold's Hill. 1st in classes: D. M. K. Marendaz, Marseal.
11 Oct	JCC Northern Centre, Saltersford Church. FTD: Raymond Mays, AC, 1m 0·4s. 1st in classes: Basil Davenport, GN, 1m 2·4s; T. A. N. Leadbetter, Alvis, 1m 33·4s.
11 Oct	Kent & Sussex LCC, Bexhill. ST. 1st in classes: J. A. Joyce, AC, 23·2s; G. C. Boulding, Amilcar, 33·6s; D. M. K. Marendaz, Marseal, 34s; R. Humphries, GN, 37·8s; The Hon G. Cunliffe, Aston Martin, 42·2s; Ivy Cummings, Frazer Nash, 27·4s.
18 Oct	Essex MC, Kop. FTD: J. A. Joyce, AC, 26·8s. 2nd, Raymond Mays, T.T. Vauxhall, 28·8s. 1st in classes: Beans won 3 classes for touring cars.
26 Oct	Littlehampton & District MC, Ford Road, near Arundel. ST. FTD: Wolff Barnato, Hispano-Suiza, 23s. 1st in classes: Ivy Cummings, Frazer Nash, 23·8s; J. S. Lee, Alvis, 30·2s.
October	North-West London MC and North London MCC. Course unknown. 1st in car classes: A. Mansell, KRC, 38·8s; A. Pollard, Aston Martin, 24s.
Nov	Stalybridge & District MC, Stalybridge. ST. 1st in classes: T. A. N. Leadbetter, Alvis, 27·75s.

Epilogue 1925-1939

It might be thought that sprints on courses which could be closed to the public would increase greatly in numbers and variety after April 1925, but such was not the case, only a small national growth being noticed. In 1924 there had been twenty-three, and in 1926—the first full season of the new régime—there were thirty-four, including eleven meetings held on seven new courses. At least six 'closable' new courses had been brought into use in 1924, the last boom year, so regarded either absolutely or relatively, the increase was not spectacular. There were thirty-four sprints held in 1927 as well, but only eight were on this year's six new courses. In 1928 there was a further heavy decline to seventeen sprints, none of which were on new courses. Two of the nineteen events of 1929 were on new courses, while rock-bottom was reached in 1930, with only sixteen recorded sprints and just one new course.

The national clubs' veto was the most grievous blow struck at sprints, but there were two others which hastened their decay after 1925. They both fell almost exactly a year later. Complaints over the noise and crowds that accompanied sand races had been growing, and in March 1926 the Board of Trade, which controlled the foreshore through its Harbours and Fisheries Department, announced that it was ready to consider withholding permission for future sand races, and stepped in to stop meetings planned for Bracklesham Bay, near Selsey Bill. The RDC of Rye, in Sussex, had already asked for the prohibition of some proposed sand speed trials at Camber, and nothing more was heard of either of them. Sand racing did not die completely before 1939, and flourished in the north in spite of several serious accidents—including that one fatal incident—but this official attitude must have discouraged its spread.

Then, on 6 April 1926, the SMMT forbade its members to take

part in future competitions of any description, making only very few exceptions. At the time, the weight of opinion in this august, but blinkered, body held that competition served no useful purpose. The only two sprints permissible were Saltburn (which hardly counts, as it was cancelled in 1926 because of the General Strike, did not recur for many years, and was then revived on a very small scale), and the 'open' Shelsley Walsh meeting ('open' because the Midland AC had instituted an additional 'amateur' climb there for the benefit of sports-starved clubmen in 1926). This ban did not stop some firms entering unapproved sprints but, together with a general falling-off of interest, it reduced their numbers grievously. At this late date it is not a practicable proposition to identify all trade, as opposed to private entries, but one can say positively that at least twenty representatives of just over forty makes gaining successes in the 1924 season were from the trade. In the 1926–30 seasons, the figure falls to a yearly average of half-a-dozen, among twenty to thirty makes represented.

The shortage of courses that could be closed was an ancient problem, as we have already seen. Led by the RAC, the clubs hunted feverishly for new ones, with the lack of success reflected in the figures quoted.

'Closable' speed trial courses being far easier to find than similar hillclimb sites, the proportion of speed trials increased: from rather over 40 per cent in the last pre-1925 seasons to between two-thirds and three-quarters of the total in the years up to 1938. The sport as a whole suffered, because speed trials were much less interesting to take part in and to watch. Events in general were repetitive, for what few were left were being run on even fewer courses. In 1930, twelve speed trials were shared between only five courses. Six of the twelve were on Southport Sands, and three of the remainder on the Race Hill at Lewes.

This situation was fairly typical of this period of sad decline. Many of the courses which existed were desperately bleak and circumscribed, and unopened lengths of by-pass road, unfinished building estate service ways and the miniature test tracks of motor factories or driving schools became popular—or rather, indispensable. Of the promenade courses, classic Blackpool survived until 1928, and Colwyn Bay until 1927, but Herne Bay was not used after 1925, and so they, too, had faded from the scene.

If anything, hillclimbs suffered an even more horrid fate. In 1929, five were recorded. One was the Oxford University CC meeting on

Ewelme Down, offering excellent sport to a few sportsmen, and two were 'freaks'. Leaving aside Alms Hill and Rosedale Abbey Bank, both being insufficiently steep public road courses, and therefore the most dubious of ancestors, the freak hillclimb first appeared in its true, hideous form in 1926, as a direct result of the ban.

It was some northern clubs' idea of a safe hillclimb: on private ground so that the spectators could be controlled and a permit granted, and so steep and rough that high speeds were impossible and any forward motion at all a cause for congratulation. The surface was necessarily bad, for no road would be found climbing the face of a cliff, and it might deliberately be made worse in the interests of 'sport'.

The Leeds AC used Post Hill (worst gradient 1-in-1½); the Huddersfield & District Motor Sports Club used Dalton Bank (1-in-1½, average 1-in-3, loose and sandy, 185 yd); while the Bradford MC & LCC disported themselves on Hepolite Scar (likewise 1-in-1½—anything less was obviously thought sissy—broken stones, 409 yd). Cars which failed were salvaged with the aid of ropes, hooks and chocks, and it was not unusual for every one of the starters in an event to need rescue in this way. So desperate were Britain's motor sportsmen for some sport, any sport, that drivers of the stature of Frazer-Nash might enter from time to time. Yet even this meagre fare was denied to the south: only the northern clubs took it up at first and then, when 'freaks' died out in the north, at the beginning of the 1930s, they reappeared in much less savage form in the south, notably at Rushmere and Knatt's Valley.

One and two from five leaves two; and they were both Shelsley Walsh. Shelsley was synonymous with truly 'open' serious hillclimbing in Britain until the 1930s. Until the war, it retained absolute supremacy over all other courses, to a degree unknown before 1925, and in 1930 and 1931 it was one of the courses used for the European Hill Climbing Championship.

If there was much appeal left in British sprints after the massacre of the courses, it departed, for this author, with the advent of the 'special' car in its extreme form. Basil Davenport's GN, nicknamed 'Spider', which we have already watched building up its reputation, made fourth fastest time of the day in the last 'singleton' Shelsley in 1925. It then made fastest time of the day at the open meeting of 1926, and at that same moment, the Shelsley Special, as well as 'Spider', had arrived.

Given the overwhelming predominance of Shelsley in the sport, it is probable that a narrowly-specialised type of car, designed mainly if not entirely to suit the characteristics of that course, would have evolved without Davenport or 'Spider'. But once Davenport's car proved its ability to beat the best the country could offer on Shelsley, the particular basic form of the Shelsley Special was determined, the more decisively because 'Spider' was temptingly easy to imitate, if not to emulate. The GN chain-driven chassis and motor-cycle engine or engines were simple, cheap and strong, and thus the Shelsley Special was born, and was to multiply. As more brains were applied to it, it took on an endless variety of forms, all designed according to the individual constructor's theory of what would match or surpass 'Spider' and the other leading specials. Some people favoured cheap, sturdy, proprietary engines with more cylinders: Austin 'Seven', Morris 'Eight', Ford large and small. A few specials, such as Mays's Vauxhall-Villiers (later Villiers Supercharge) were extremely complex and expensive beasts, but these were exceptions.

Most specials might be built mainly for Shelsley, but with different gearing they could be adapted to other courses, those of speed trials included. Few people wanted to compete at Shelsley only. Their cars were found to be just as formidable when pitted elsewhere against more conventional machinery. 'Spider' was extremely successful on the sands at Southport, for example, while Raymond Mays's Vauxhall-Villiers, R. G. J. Nash's succession of highly-modified Frazer Nashes beginning with 'The Terror', and John Bolster's awe-inspiring permutations on 'Bloody Mary' were as much feared at Lewes as elsewhere.

Sports and racing cars in fair variety still greatly predominated in numbers over the specials—class divisions saw to that. Also, not everyone wanted, or could afford, a second, so specialised vehicle. However, their multiplication had aroused comment by 1929. In the 1930's, because they were so prominent and spectacular, they became the 'image' of the sprint car; and remained so even when, with the advent of ERA and Maserati, absolute fastest times began to elude them.

Different theories and different courses imposed some variety on the form of the special. As reflections of the extremes of human ingenuity they were interesting, but to the present writer most were aesthetically unattractive. They were bastardised mechanically and usually monstrous in shape. While preference for a car that can also be used on the road or the track is no doubt proof of a lamentably *dilettante* attitude, there is something more satisfying about *le pur sang* in a Bugatti, Morris Cowley or Austin 'Seven'. The 'special's' domination of sprinting was also out of character, for these, too, were traditionally the home of the basically touring or sports car as sold to the public. Even the pure-bred racing car had not really belonged here; its gearing found it out. Some specials were technically unpleasing as well, for the theories of the amateur engineer could well produce little more than a four-wheeled nightmare.

Trials assumed more prominence, and then the horrors of motor-car dirt-track and grass-track racing burst upon the land in 1928. The rally in the modern sense, including timed long-distance road sections, driving tests and *concours d'élégance*, was encouraged by the popularity of the revived Monte Carlo Rally (first won by a British team in 1926), arrived in 1928, and was given its liberty by the abolition of the universal 20 mph speed limit in 1930.

Although specials became more popular and ingenious as the thirties wore on, the prospect for sprinting began to look up. More and better courses were found, and interest revived, if not on the scale of the early 1920s. This interest grew more among amateurs than in the trade, and it was a very slow, gradual revival which could hardly be so termed with any confidence until 1935 in terms of numbers of new, good-quality courses, and 1938 so far as hillclimbs were concerned. In 1938 and 1939 the number of hillclimbs held more than doubled the 1937 figure, and accounted for nearly half the sprints run. Only about thirty were held in each of these two years, but they were of good quality: the 1911–14 situation repeated, in fact.

Speed trials were held on the Race Hill at Lewes three or four times a year from 1925 to 1939, at the instance of the Brighton & Hove MC, the Kent & Sussex LCC, the Bugatti Owners' Club and the Vintage Sports Car Club, so its use hardly counts as a symptom of the revival. Shelsley and Southport, of course, never died, even if the latter faded a bit. Chalfont St Peter's hillclimbs (on an incomplete building estate) flourished in the hands of the Bugatti OC, but only between 1931 and 1935.

However, Dancer's End became a classic hillclimb course during its lifetime from 1930 to the war, in the hands of the Berkhamsted & District MC. Regular meetings were held here from 1933 onwards. The Brighton Speed Trials were revived on the grand scale in 1932, and at the instance of the Scottish Sporting Car Club, cars first raced up Bo'ness in 1934. In 1934 or 1935, Wetherby (the Yorkshire Sporting Car Club's speed trial course) and—in 1935—Backwell (the

Bristol MC and LCC's hillclimb) were inaugurated. Speed trials at Saltburn were run for the first time since 1924 (though they were on a much smaller scale and did not survive after 1938), and Syston Park was brought back into use for the Cambridge University AC's speed trials.

In 1936 the Poole speed trials of the West Hampshire & Dorset Car Club were launched and the Southsea speed trials resuscitated. The year 1938 saw the first Prescott meetings, which were to be run by the Bugatti OC and the Vintage Sports Car Club. In 1939 Great Auclum and Trengwainton were brought into use for hillclimbs, but these were only the better-known courses: many others, less important and more ephemeral, were utilised. Several were used more than once a year and none except Chalfont St Peter and Saltburn dropped out. (Incidentally, the revivals among them were not necessarily run on the same ground as the originals.)

Especially fine cars and good sport were also to be seen at university sprints. Their organisers introduced timing by photo-electric cell (Ewelme Down, 1931). The most enterprising clubs not only had the finest cars, but were also the most progressive: the Brighton & Hove MC pioneered 'traffic light' starting in their speed trials of 1932, for example. As a matter of interest, though the fact is hardly relevant to the history of serious sprints, the Veteran Car Club were able to revive the Tilburstowe climb between 1934 and 1939; even though it was run on a public road and the speeds set up were often not very much more than a walking pace.

But the revival of interest in motor sport was general, and included road and circuit racing, with Donington coming into use in 1933, and the course at Crystal Palace and the artificial Campbell Circuit at Brooklands in 1937. Motor sport, in this form, was firmly entrenched when once more war in Europe, and eventually throughout the globe, engulfed us all.

* * *

The war put a stop to this revival, but it picked up again as soon as any form of motor sport was possible. At first, circuit racing for the 'small' man was difficult because of lack of petrol, suitable new cars, and courses; so sprints and other events such as trials flourished for a time. When these shortages were alleviated, and road rallies in addition became so popular, sprinting began to fade into the background. More recently, when circuit racing came to lose a lot of its appeal—perhaps because over-commercialism appeared to be submerging the sport—and rally organisers, emulating their 'sprint' predecessors, tended to over-reach themselves and encountered bitter public and police opposition, sprinting—the oldest form of the sport—started to revive. Currently, although both racing and rallies have taken on new life, hillclimbing flourishes, particularly as a proving-ground for four-wheel drive machines; though conventional speed trials have been put in the shade by the American importation of drag racing.

Acknowledgments

All of the figures and most of the facts in this book came from the principal surviving source of such information, the motoring press: *The Autocar*, *The Automotor & Horseless Vehicle Journal*, *The Motor*, *The Light Car & Cyclecar*, *The Automobile Club Journal*, *Motor Sport* and (for Ireland) *The Motor News*. However, these magazines (especially before 1914) provided little more than tables of results. The background—the layman's-eye-view—was ably provided by the reporters of the lay press. Borne away by the excitement of the new locomotion, they sometimes also contributed valuable topographical data. They wrote for *The Sussex Daily News*, *The Western Mail*, *The Southend Observer*, *The Portsmouth Times*, *The Saltburn Times*, *The Skegness Herald*, *The Blackpool Times*, *The Bexhill-on-Sea Observer*, *The Southport Guardian* and *The Brighton Gazette*.

The other sort of background, the personal memories of competitors, came partly from books (*The Cars in My Life* and *W.O.* by W. O. Bentley, *The Lure of Speed* by H. O. D. Segrave, *My Thirty Years of Speed* by Malcolm Campbell, *Split Seconds* by Raymond Mays, *The Brabazon Story* by Lord Brabazon of Tara), but mainly, over the last few years, from the men themselves, living or now dead. The author is greatly indebted to Lord Brabazon of Tara, Mr H. W. Cook, Mr A. Frazer-Nash, Mr H. R. Godfrey, Mr R. R. Jackson, Mr P. C. Kidner, Captain D. M. K. Marendaz, Mr J. A Malins, Mr St John C. Nixon, and Mr R. S. Witchell for their kindness in providing personal reminiscences and impressions of cars, courses and personalities. The late Mr Godfrey also related some interesting stories told to him by Sir Algernon Lee Guinness.

The following secondary works were useful as sources of information on events and technical data: *The Motoring Annual and Motorists' Year Book, 1903–1908*; *A Record of Motor Racing* by Gerald Rose;

Motoring Entente by Ian Nickols and Kent Karslake; *Aston Martin: The Story of a Sports Car* by Dudley Coram and others; *The History of Brooklands Motor Course* by William Boddy; an article on sprints 1919–25 in *Motor Sport* for April 1955, by William Boddy; and an article on 25 hp Talbots in the Vintage Sports Car Club Bulletin for Autumn 1961, by B. M. Clarke.

For help and advice of many other kinds, the author is deeply obliged to the following: the Library of the Royal Automobile Club, the Library of Temple Press Ltd, the Veteran Car Club of Great Britain, Mr R. Barry, Mr William Boddy, The Director of Brighton Public Libraries, the Chief Librarian of Atkinson Central Library, Southport and, particularly, Mr Michael Sedgwick. The author's thanks for permission to use illustrations go to *The Autocar*, the Montagu Motor Museum (for pictures in the Brunell Collection), Mr Cyril Posthumus, Mr R. S. Witchell, and to Mr R. R. Jackson.

APPENDIX

Sprints in Ireland and the Isle of Man: 1903-1925

(ST = speed trials; all others hillclimbs. FTD = fastest time of the day. s/s = standing start; f/s = flying start)

1903	ACGBI 'Irish Fortnight'
4 July	Phoenix Park, Dublin. ST. 1 mile s/s and 1 km f/s. Touring car events (price classes): Henry Sturmey, 10 hp Duryea; J. T. Overton, 24 hp Georges-Richard (mile 1m 31s, km 45·8s); J. W. Cross, 20 hp Humber (mile 1m 24·6s, km 41·6s) beat E. Manville, 22 hp Daimler: Douglas B. Hall, 30 hp Wolseley (mile 1m 28·6s, km 45s) beat C. S. Rolls, 20 hp Panhard. Racing car events: 650 kg: Théry, Decauville (mile + km consecutively 1m 53·2s) beat A. Rawlinson, 30 hp Darracq (2m 10s). 1,000 kg: J. E. Hutton, 60 hp Mercedes (mile 1m 0·2s, km 28·4s) beat Baron de Forest, 70 hp Paris-Madrid Mors (mile 1m 3·2s, km 26·4s) and C. S. Rolls, 80 hp Panhard. *Daily Mail* Challenge Cup (1 km, 1,000 kg): Baron de Forest, 27·2s beat C. S. Rolls, 28s. *Autocar* Challenge Cup (1 km): Baron de Forest, 26·6s, beat Gabriel, 80 hp Mors, 26·8s.
July	Ballybannon Hill, Castlewellan. Distance uncertain; possibly about 600 yd, except where specified. Touring Car Events (price classes): Henry Edmunds Trophy: H. Sturmey, 10 hp Duryea (walkover), 1m 2·4s, E. M. C. Instone, 22 hp Daimler, 55·8s.

Graphic Trophy (handicap, about $2\frac{1}{2}$ miles): J. W. Scott, 20 hp Humber (scratch), 3m 20s, beat Hon J. Scott-Montagu, 22 hp Daimler, 3m 33·2s.
Racing car events:
650 kg: A. Rawlinson, 30 hp Darracq, 56·4s.
1,000 kg: E. Campbell Muir, 60 hp Mercedes, 32·4s, beat C. S. Rolls, 70 hp Mors, 33·8s.

15 July Killorglin Hill, between Killarney and Tralee. 1,200 yd. Handicap. Result in final: C. S. Rolls, 80 hp Mors, 1m 0·8s, beat P. G. Garrard, 22 hp Daimler, 2m 13s.

1 Oct Irish AC, Glendhu Hill. $\frac{3}{4}$ mile, av 1-in-12·2, sharp turns. FTD: W. G. D. Goff, 12 hp Napier, 5m 1s. 2nd, W. Sexton, 10 hp Siddeley, 5m 11s.

1904 ACGBI Gordon Bennett Eliminating Trials

11 May Port Vuillen. Isle of Man. $\frac{1}{2}$ mile. FTD: S. F. Edge, 80 hp Napier, 38·4s (47 mph). 2nd, Clifford Earp, 55 hp Napier, 42·8s (42·1 mph). 3rd, Girling, 72 hp Wolseley, 43·6s (41·4 mph).

12 May Douglas Promenade, Isle of Man. ST. 1 km, f/s. FTD: S. F. Edge, 80 hp Napier, 39s (57·3 mph). 2nd, Clifford Earp, 55 hp Napier, 42s (53·2 mph). 3rd, Girling, 72 hp Wolseley, 43s (52 mph).

Other hillclimbs and speed trials held during these and the 1905 Gordon Bennett Eliminating Trials in the Isle of Man were not sprints, but were timed during non-stop circuits of the island.

6–7 Sept Irish AC, 'The Velvet Strand', Portmarnock, near Dublin. ST. 1 mile, s/s.
Touring car events (price classes):
Henry Sturmey, 10 hp Duryea, 1m 53·8s; F. Churchill, 14/18 hp Hallamshire, 1m 57·6s; A. Huntley Walker, 15 hp Darracq, 1m 58·2s, beat A. Rawlinson's ditto; Percy Martin, 28 hp Daimler, 1m 31·2s; Algernon Lee-Guinness, 60 hp Mercedes, 1m 19·4s, beat A. Rawlinson, 40 hp Darracq. T. L. Plunkett, 28 hp Daimler, won two handicaps, one in 1m 37·4s.
Racing car events:
'Light Racers': A. Rawlinson, Gordon Bennett British Darracq, beat 45 hp Darracq by 30 yd.
1,000 kg: McDonald, 6-cylinder Napier, beat C. S. Rolls, 100 hp Mors.

Informal races (1 km, f/s):
A. Rawlinson, 28·8s (77·62 mph); Algernon Lee-Guinness, Gordon Bennett British Darracq, 30s; C. S. Rolls, 100 hp Mors, 32·8s.

This event lost £170. A number of motor-cycle race meetings were subsequently held here, but none for cars.

October Irish AC, Glendhu Hill. 1st in classes: Mrs Mecredy, 6 hp De Dion, 4m 37s; F. V. Westby, 16/20 hp Argyll, 3m 22s; W. G. D. Goff, 20 hp Clément, 3m 15s.

1905

13 May Irish AC, Glendhu Hill. Now $\frac{7}{8}$ mile, av 1-in-11, max 1-in-8. 1st in classes: Dr Colohan, 6 hp Wolseley, 3m 17s; J. O'Connor, 12 hp Darracq, 3m 8·2s; T. Henshaw, 28/36 hp Daimler, 2m 11s.

29 July Irish AC, Glenmacnass. 1st in classes: R. J. Mecredy, 8 hp Rover, 3m 48·2s; J. H. Peard, 12 hp Wolseley, 3m 56s; S. T. Robinson, 12/16 hp Talbot, 2m 47·2s; S. H. Cochrane, 60 hp Mercedes, 1m 35s.

26 Aug Irish AC, Callow Hill. 1st in classes: H. Green, 8 hp Rover, 2m 1s; J. R. A. Colley, 10 hp Argyll, 2m 15·8s; S. T. Robinson, 12/16 hp Talbot, 1m 51s; T. Henshaw, 28 hp Daimler, 1m 35s; S. H. Cochrane, 60 hp Mercedes, 1m 8s.

1906

7 April Motor Cycle Union (Ulster Centre), Knock. 1st in car class (handicap): T. H. Dunlop, 5 hp Peugeot.

21 April Motor Cycle Union (Ulster Centre), Bangor. 1st in car class (handicap): S. P. Corry, 10/12 hp Humber.

Irish AC Reliability Trials

16 June Callow Hill. 1st in classes: 8 hp Chambers, 5m 52·6s; 8/9 hp Talbot, 4m 11·6s; 12 hp New Orleans, 3m 47·6s; 22 hp Minerva, 2m 21·8s; 28 hp Daimler, 2m 24s; 40 hp Ariel, 3m 12·4s.

4 Aug Irish AC, Ballinaslaughter. Open. 2,522 yd, max 1-in-8·1. 1st in classes: F. Wilkinson, 8 hp Stanley steamer; F. Wilkinson, 10 hp Stanley; F. Wilkinson, 20 hp Stanley. 2nd, A. Rawlinson, 20/35 hp Darracq by 40·8s; Straker and McConnell, 40 hp Bianchi; F. A. Bolton, Daimler.

Bolton walked over, but took FTD from Wilkinson's 20 hp Stanley by 5·8s.

11 Aug Motor Cycle Union (Ulster Centre), Ballycastle. 1st in car class (handicap): R. Dunlop, 10/12 hp Humber.

25 Aug Motor Cycle Union (Ulster Centre), Ballybannon Hill, Castlewellan. 1st in car class (handicap): J. N. McCammond, 15 hp Darracq.

22 Sept Motor Cycle Union (Ulster Centre), Knock. 1st in car class (handicap): T. H. Dunlop, 5 hp Peugeot.

Sept ACGBI, *Graphic* Trophy, Isle of Man. ST. 4¼ miles. FTD: C. A. Glentworth, 50 hp Napier, 4m 39·8s. 2nd, G. S. Barwick, 30/40 hp Daimler, 5m 3s.

1907

6 April Motor Cycle Union (Ulster Centre), Bangor. FTD (car class): A. F. Craig, 28 hp Daimler.

25 April Limerick MC, Adare Manor. FTD: M. Shaw, 14 hp Whitlock–Aster.

18 May Motor Cycle Union (Ulster Centre), Ballybannon Hill, Castlewellan. 765 yd. FTD (car class): J. S. Garrett, 10/12 hp Humber, 1m 55·4s.

25 May Limerick MC, Delmege's Glen. 1st on formula: J. P. Goodbody, 10/12 hp Peugeot.

Irish AC Reliability Trials

May Magilligan Strand, near Coleraine. ST. 3 miles. 1st in classes: A. W. Inglis, 9 hp Adams-Hewitt, 5m 13·2s; J. H. Chambers, 10 hp Chambers, 6m 14·6s; G. W. Hands, 16/20 hp Calthorpe, 4m 11·2s; S. T. Robinson, 15 hp Talbot, 4m 10·4s; 20 hp Talbot (works), 4m 2·4s, beat Sidney Straker, Straker-Squire, 4m 7·2s; E. Herington, 30/40 hp Ariel, 3m 19s; Thos Shaw, 35/40 hp Ariel, 3m 19·2s.

May Hollywood Hill. 1 mile 71 yd, av 1-in-14·8. 1st in classes: R. Burns, 10/12 hp Swift, 4m 16·8s; J. H. Chambers, 10 hp Chambers, 6m 21·4s; G. W. Hands, 16/20 hp Calthorpe, 3m 13s; S. T. Robinson, 15 hp Talbot, 3m 5·6s; W. Sexton, 20/24 hp Talbot, 3m 13·4s; T. Henshaw, 35 hp Daimler, 2m 3·6s.

May Graiguenamanagh Hill. 1,718 yd. 1st in classes: R. Burns, 10/12 hp Swift, 4m 16·4s; J. H. Chambers, 10 hp Chambers,

6m 4·8s; G. W. Hands, 16/20 hp Calthorpe, 3m 11·6s; S. T. Robinson, 15 hp Talbot, 2m 28·4s; T. C. Pullinger, 30 hp Humber, 2m 29·8s; T. Henshaw, 35 hp Daimler, 1m 49·6s.

27 July Irish AC, Altidore. 1,284 yd, max 1-in-5·3. 1st in classes: P. L. D. Perry, 15 hp Ford, 3m 15·2s; 16/20 hp Calthorpe (works), 3m 4·8s; T. C. Pullinger, 16/20 hp Humber, 2m 47·4s; T. M. Greer, 24 hp Minerva, 3m 8·2s; T. Henshaw, 35 hp Daimler, 1m 51·2s.

27 July Irish AC, Ballinaslaughter. 1 mile 755 yd, max 1-in-6·8. 1st in classes: P. L. D. Perry, 15 hp Ford, 4m 16·2s; 16/20 hp Calthorpe (works), 4m 10·8s; T. C. Pullinger, 16/20 hp Humber, 3m 37·4s; W. Sexton, 20/24 hp Talbot, 4m 9s; T. Henshaw, 35 hp Daimler, 2m 28·4s.

1908

23 May Motor Cycle Union (Ulster Centre), Ballycastle. FTD and 1st on handicap: I. G. Davidson, 15 hp Ford, 7m 45·2s.

May Motor Cycle Union (Ulster Centre), Carnmoney. FTD: H. G. Ferguson, 14/16 hp Argyll, 1m 10s.

Irish AC Reliability Trials

May Rosbeigh Strand. ST. 1 mile 70 yd. Mean of 2 runs in opposite directions. 1st in classes: H. A. Bates, 15 hp Ford, 32·53 mph; E. A. Anthony, 15 hp Ford, 34·79 mph; T. Woods, 14/16 hp Belsize, 33·91 mph; G. W. Hands, 16/20 hp Calthorpe, 39·35 mph; 15 hp Talbot (either J. Hedge or S. T. Robinson), 45·84 mph; G. Day, 25 hp Talbot, 46·39 mph; T. Henshaw, 48 hp Daimler, 51·42 mph; F. G. Cundy, 60 hp Napier, 62·92 mph.

May Hollywood Hill. 1st in classes: H. A. Bates, 15 hp Ford, 3m 37s; E. A. Anthony, 15 hp Ford, 3m 31·2s; G. Phillips, 10/12 hp Humber, 3m 41·4s; G. W. Hands, 16/20 hp Calthorpe, 2m 55·4s; S. T. Robinson, 15 hp Talbot and J. Hedge, 15 hp Talbot tied 2m 30·4s; G. Day, 25 hp Talbot, 2m 7s; T. Henshaw, 48 hp Daimler, 1m 52·2s; F. G. Cundy, 60 hp Napier, 1m 46·8s.

May Ballinaslaughter. 1st in classes: 15 hp Ford, 4m 58s; 10/12 hp Swift, 6m 10s; P. Hallinan, 12/18 hp Riley, 5m 17·4s; G. W. Hands, 16/20 hp Calthorpe, 4m 9s; 15 hp Talbot, 3m 11s; G. Day, 25 hp Talbot, 2m 53·8s; T. Henshaw,

48 hp Daimler, 2m 30·4s; F. G. Cundy, 60 hp Napier, 2m 38s.

July — Motor Yacht Club of Ireland, Garvagh Hill, Enniskillen. $\frac{3}{4}$ mile. 1st in classes: B. L. Winslow, 18/20 hp Reo, 2m 28·8s; J. B. Dunlop, 16/20 hp Calthorpe, 1m 39·2s; S. Pringle, 15 hp Talbot, 1m 27·2s; T. Henshaw, 48 hp Daimler, 1m 3·2s.

21 Aug — Irish AC, Ballinaslaughter. $1\frac{7}{8}$ miles. 1st in open classes: H. S. Huet, 10 hp Royal Starling, 7m 5·4s; 10/12 hp Chambers, 4m 41s; T. Woods, 14/16 hp Belsize, 5m 58·8s; J. B. Dunlop, 16/20 hp Calthorpe, 4m 12s. The following open classes were all walkovers. S. T. Robinson, 15 hp Talbot, 2m 53·4s; P. Robinson, 28 hp Minerva, 2m 36s; T. Henshaw, 48 hp Daimler, 2m 24s; S. F. Edge, 60 hp Napier, 2m 7·6s. 1st in amateur classes: 12/18 hp Riley, 15 hp Talbot, 48 hp Daimler. J. B. Dunlop's Calthorpe also won an amateur handicap.

1909

April — Motor Cycle Union (Ulster Centre), Bangor. FTD: S. P. Corry, 10 hp Stanley, 45·2s.

May (early) — Motor Cycle Union (Ulster Centre), Ballycastle. FTD (car class): C. B. Hurst, 12/16 hp Chambers. 1st on handicap: J. Holden, 6 hp Rover.

Irish AC Reliability Trials

May–June — Magilligan Strand. ST. 1·2 miles. 1st in classes: 15/18 hp Bedford, 1m 58·8s; 15/18 hp Bedford, 1m 51·2s; 12 hp Riley, 2m 8s; 12/14 hp Chambers, 1m 47·2s; 16 hp Humber, 1m 29s; 15 hp Talbot, 1m 32·6s; 24 hp Vauxhall, 1m 24s.

May–June — Greenan Hill (Speenogue). 1,363 yd, max 1-in-5. 1st in classes: 15/18 hp Bedford, 3m 19·4s; 12 hp Little Briton, 3m 10·8s; 12 hp Riley, 3m 32·4s; 12 hp Star, 3m 55s; 16 hp Humber, 2m 11·8s; 20 hp Vauxhall, 2m 11·4s; 25 hp Talbot, 1m 57·4s.

May–June — Farmer's Bridge. $1\frac{1}{2}$ miles. 1st in classes: 15/18 hp Bedford, 3m 53·8s; 12 hp Adler, 4m 1·8s; 12 hp Riley, 4m 0·6s; 12 hp Star, 3m 58·2s; 16 hp Humber, 2m 23s; 20 hp Vauxhall, 2m 39·6s; 25 hp Talbot, 2m 11·6s.

August — Motor Cycle Union (Ulster Centre), Magheramorne, near Lorne. FTD: E. Graham, 20 hp Vauxhall, 1m 11s.

1910

April — Royal North of Ireland Yacht Club, Cultra, Belfast Lough. FTD: J. W. Scott, 20 hp Standard, 50·6s. This club had already run hillclimbs here, but they had involved the dropping of potatoes in buckets by lady passengers. . . .

April — Motor Cycle Union (Ulster Centre), Magheramorne. FTD (car class): E. Graham, 12 hp Talbot, 59s.

14 May — Motor Cycle Union (Ulster Centre), Magheramorne. FTD (car class): E. Graham, 12 hp Talbot, 1m 3·6s.

1911

May — Royal North of Ireland Yacht Club, Cultra. FTD: C. Hurst, 20/30 hp RMC, 52·4s. 1st on formula: W. Hume, 16/20 hp Calthorpe. 'The only sporting motoring fixture now held in Ireland' (*The Motor News*)

1913

24 May — Society of Motor Manufacturers and Traders, Irish Section, Craigantlet. $1\frac{1}{8}$ miles. 1st (private class): J. Coote, 25 hp Talbot, 2m 17·4s. 1st (trade class): Harry Ferguson, 25 hp Vauxhall, 1m 43s. 1st (open): R. C. Robb, 12/16 hp Sunbeam, 2m 1·2s. The first climb on this course; a great success.

5–6 Sept — Irish AC, Rosslare Strand. ST. 4 miles s/s, 1 mile f/s.

4-mile open races (2-mile straightaway; cars stopped, turned, re-started):

S. T. Robinson, 25 hp Talbot, 73·47 mph, beat 58 hp Daimler, 56·78 mph; S. T. Robinson, 15 hp Talbot, 64·29 mph, beat Edward Lisle, 14 hp Briton, 51·48 mph; S. T. Robinson, 12 hp Talbot, 61·22 mph, beat W. G. Tuck, 14 hp Humber, 57·51 mph; S. T. Robinson, 25 hp Talbot, 80·18 mph, beat a 15 hp Talbot also entered by himself, 66·54 mph. This 25 hp Talbot, a racing car, was timed at 107 mph.

4-mile race for private owners:

T. T. Power, 24 hp Lancia; C. P. Kirk, 16 hp Darracq, beat E. W. Eyre, 15·9 hp Hispano-Suiza (a handicap); J. A. Carvill, 12 hp Talbot (a handicap).

1-mile open race:
Spence & Johnston, 15 hp Straker-Squire, beat S. T. Robinson, 25 hp Talbot (handicap).

1914

Irish AC Light Car Trial

27 May Glendhu. 1st in classes: J. T. Wood, GWK, 2m 33s; Jules Nardini, 10/15 hp Nardini, 2m 5s.

28 May Ballinascorney Gap. 1st in classes: J. T. Wood, GWK, 3m 4s; Roberts, Singer, 2m 19s.

1924

July Motor Trade Association, Ulster Division, Red Brae Hill. FTD: 12/50 hp Alvis, 1m 31·4s. 2nd, 30/98 hp Vauxhall, 1m 38s. 1st on handicap in classes: W. Noble, Star; Windsor (OD Cars Ltd), 2 classes; Harry Ferguson, 20 hp Austin.

The Irish AC had planned a hillclimb on Ligoniel Hill, Belfast, for June 1914. It was abandoned for lack of entries. Another Irish AC climb, on Ballinaslaughter, was to take place on 14 September after the Rosslare speed trials, but, naturally, nothing came of either. After the war and up to the end of the period covered in this book, 'The Troubles' virtually put an end to motor sport. In Northern Ireland public roads could be closed by Act of Parliament for sprints as well as races, and were, long after the ban stopping other public-road sprints came into force.

Indexes

1. COURSES, DATES AND ORGANISING CLUBS

2. PERSONALITIES

3. CARS